# THE INTERCORPOREAL SELF

A VOLUME IN THE SUNY SERIES IN CONTEMPORARY FRENCH THOUGHT

David Pettigrew and Francois Raffoul, editors

# THE INTERCORPOREAL SELF

## Merleau-Ponty on Subjectivity

SCOTT L. MARRATTO

STATE UNIVERSITY OF NEW YORK PRESS

Published by
STATE UNIVERSITY OF NEW YORK PRESS, ALBANY

© 2012 State University of New York

All rights reserved

Printed in the United States of America

No part of this book may be used or reproduced in any manner whatsoever without written permission. No part of this book may be stored in a retrieval system or transmitted in any form or by any means including electronic, electrostatic, magnetic tape, mechanical, photocopying, recording, or otherwise without the prior permission in writing of the publisher.

For information, contact
State University of New York Press, Albany, NY
www.sunypress.edu

Production, Kelli W. LeRoux
Marketing, Anne M. Valentine

**Library of Congress Cataloging-in-Publication Data**

Marratto, Scott L. (Scott Louis), 1968–
The intercorporeal self : Merleau-Ponty on subjectivity / Scott L. Marratto.
    p. cm.
Includes bibliographical references (p. ) and index.
ISBN 978-1-4384-4231-0 (hardcover : alk. paper)
ISBN 978-1-4384-4232-7 (pbk. : alk. paper)
1. Merleau-Ponty, Maurice, 1908–1961.   2. Subjectivity.   I. Title.

B2430.M3764M373 2012
194—dc23                                                    2011027049

10 9 8 7 6 5 4 3 2 1

*In memory of my mother, Melody McLoughlin*

# CONTENTS

# ACKNOWLEDGMENTS

In *Phenomenology of Perception*, Maurice Merleau-Ponty remarks on the strange manner in which we discover, in a kind of unending process, the patterns of our own thinking only by letting it find its expression in the context of our relations with others. He writes, "There is . . . a taking up of others' thought through speech, a reflection in others, an ability to think *according to others* which enriches our own thoughts" (*PhP*, 179/208). The process of writing a book, which is inevitably a reflection of many conversations, collaborations, helpful comments, criticisms, and suggestions, is particularly exemplary of this philosophical insight.

There are a great many people to whom acknowledgment is due, and any list is sure to be incomplete. I would like to express my particular gratitude to John Russon, who has been an inspiring and challenging teacher, mentor, and friend to me. His comments and reflections on this manuscript have been crucial to its development. I am grateful for John's work as a gifted philosopher and teacher, and also for his efforts in organizing an ongoing philosophical conversation among a group of scholars who have been meeting, for a number of years now, a few days each summer, in Toronto. It has been my privilege to participate in a number of these 'Toronto Seminars' to discuss the works of Merleau-Ponty, Derrida, Hegel, Heidegger, Plato, and Fichte. The list of participants in these conversations over the years includes Ömer Aygün, Don Beith, Noah Moss Brender, Susan Bredlau, David Ciavatta, Peter Costello, Bruce Gilbert, Jill Gilbert, Shannon Hoff, Kirsten Jacobson, Kym Maclaren, David Morris, Alexandra Morrison, Gregory Recco, and Maria Talero. These conversations have shaped my own approach to the practice of philosophy as well as my interpretation of Merleau-Ponty, and I am grateful to all of them.

My exploration of the relationship between Merleau-Ponty's phenomenology and Derrida's 'deconstruction,' reflected in chapters 4 and 5 of this book, began with a paper that I presented at the Collegium Phaenomenologicum in Città di Castello, Italy, in 2006. I am grateful to the coordinator of that year's Collegium, Michael Naas, and to those participants and faculty who have shared insights and helpful comments in the course of an ongoing philosophical conversation. I am thinking, in particular, of Bryan Bannon,

Maxime Doyon, Donald Landes, and François Raffoul. My exploration of the relations between Merleau-Ponty's philosophy, cognitive science, and naturalism, reflected in chapters 1 and 3 of this book, began in conversations with Andrew Bailey. His thoughtful approach to my questions and ideas stands, for me, as a model of open-minded philosophical dialogue.

Several people have offered detailed suggestions and comments on versions of the manuscript as a whole. Kirsten Jacobson's very insightful and helpful suggestions motivated and guided my attempts to clarify some key passages. I would also like to express my appreciation for the way in which her work effectively demonstrates the pertinence of Merleau-Ponty's analyses of embodiment and spatiality to a number of issues and debates in contemporary empirical research on child development, gender, mental health, and politics. I am grateful to Leonard Lawlor for his comments and encouragement as well as for his many excellent books and articles on Merleau-Ponty, Husserl, Derrida, and contemporary French philosophy. His work as an interpreter of the continental tradition and as a philosopher has made a deep impression on me, and I can only hope that this is reflected in the pages of this book. I am grateful to Kym Maclaren for her comments, questions, and suggestions on an earlier version of the manuscript as well as for her work as a phenomenologist and scholar of Merleau-Ponty. Her insights on expression, intersubjectivity, self-consciousness, and development have significantly informed my work on these issues. Thanks also to Jeff Mitscherling for his helpful comments on an earlier version of the manuscript.

I would also like to thank Jay Lampert and Graeme Nicholson for their work as extraordinarily gifted teachers and philosophers, as well as for their friendship and encouragement. Lawrence E. Schmidt and Bernard Hammond are two mentors and long-time friends whose approaches to the vocation of teacher and scholar give powerful expression to their abiding concerns for justice and the Good. I am deeply grateful for both of them.

I want to gratefully acknowledge the support of my family, especially my sisters, Laura Ogden and Tracy Fleet.

I acknowledge the Social Sciences and Humanities Research Council of Canada, the Department of Philosophy at the University of Guelph, and the University of King's College in Halifax with gratitude for their support of my research. I would also like to thank Andrew Kenyon and Kelli Williams-LeRoux at SUNY Press for guiding the process of bringing this work to publication.

Lastly, I would like to thank Alexandra Morrison. I am grateful for the joy of her companionship, her support and assistance and, most especially, for a rich philosophical conversation whose various strands weave their way through our daily life together.

# LIST OF ABBREVIATIONS

VI      *The Visible and the Invisible*. Translated by Alphonso Lingis. Evan-
        ston, IL: Northwestern University Press, 1968. (*Le visible et l'invisible*.
        Paris: Gallimard, 1964.)

The citations used in this book refer first to the English translation, then
to the French edition.

# INTRODUCTION

In fact I cannot totally grasp all that I am. Thus the mind is not large enough to contain itself: but where can that part be which it does not contain? Is it outside itself and not within? How can it not contain itself?

—Augustine, *Confessions*

*"Who Comes After the Subject?"*: this title of a 1991 collection of essays edited by Eduardo Cadava, Peter Connor, and Jean-Luc Nancy reflects a certain anxiety felt by many contemporary thinkers concerning the status of the modern subject (in the ontological, epistemological, and ethico-political senses). The modern concept of the 'subject,' as it is developed, for example, in the philosophies of Descartes, Locke, and Kant, has informed liberal accounts of the self, of ethical and political autonomy and responsibility, of universal human rights. This concept, which, to be sure, is by no means univocal, is subjected to a radical questioning in the twentieth century. This interrogation has occurred, perhaps most famously, in the context of so-called 'continental' thought (in which, for example, the modern metaphysics of subjectivity has been subjected to a 'deconstructive' appraisal), but arguably no less so in the 'Anglo-American,' or 'analytic,' tradition, as well as in the fields of cognitive neuroscience and psychology. In any case, it is not clear that the subjects of the cogito, of rational, voluntary, action, of political rights and freedoms, and of ethical normativity, have survived this interrogation intact. It is undoubtedly, at least in part, because of the ethical and political implications of this development that the question 'who comes after the subject?' is asked with a certain sense of urgency.

In this book, I argue that Merleau-Ponty's philosophy offers profound resources for thinking about the nature of subjectivity. It is well known that Merleau-Ponty criticizes a certain Cartesian inheritance in the modern philosophical tradition, while at the same time criticizing the naturalistic reductionism evident in certain contemporary approaches to the philosophy of mind. That is to say, he claims, at once, that the thinking subject is necessarily an incarnate subject *and* that the body (and bodily behavior) is not simply characterized by biological, or mechanistic, processes, but is, rather,

1

the very matrix of intelligence and meaning. In this sense, Merleau-Ponty's philosophy makes an assertion concerning the primacy of the relation between a perceiving body and its surrounding world. But all of this must be understood in the context of Merleau-Ponty's wider claims concerning the ontology of the living body and its worldly situation. To see this we need to direct our attention to Merleau-Ponty's analysis of expressive movement, for it is only on the basis of this analysis that we can come to understand what he is really saying about the *being* of incarnate subjectivity. I argue that Merleau-Ponty's philosophy pointedly aims to avoid any kind of reification of the subject, either as a mind *or* as a body, and instead seeks to understand subjectivity as a dynamic and open-ended process of emergence. Subjectivity emerges with the emergence of meaning in the world on the basis of the self-articulating character of living movement. What Merleau-Ponty calls 'perceptual meaning' thus arises on the basis of a dynamic that is, as it were, older than subjective *consciousness*. As a reflectively self-conscious subject, then, I am always haunted by a pre-history that both is and is not mine. To be a subject is to be *responsive* to the manifestation of being—not because the subject is passively receptive to sensations, but because the subject only ever inherits, takes up, and transforms meanings that are generated in living movement, meanings of which it is not itself the ultimate source or ground, and which are thus never absolutely transparent to it. Before we are able to clarify this thesis further, it will be necessary to say a little more about the question of subjectivity.

What we are here calling 'modern subjectivity' is, in very general terms, characterized by a certain sense of *interiority*. This is reflected in the essential epistemological concern of both empiricist and rationalist philosophy, beginning in the early modern period: if the subject encounters an external world only by means of *inner* representations of that world, how then can it ever be assured of possessing the kind of genuine knowledge necessary to realize the goals of an enlightened science and politics? A key concept in this line of questioning is 'representation.' If the world of my experience is merely an *appearance*, of which I come to be in possession evidently by means of sensations, then I can never be assured of knowing how it is in itself. According to Descartes and the rationalist tradition, rather than leaving us in the grip of an irremediable scepticism, the conception of the subject as interiority (that of a *res cogitans* that can be essentially distinguished from the *extended* things making up the external world) provides us with the only means of ever truly overcoming scepticism. While it is true, according to the rationalists, that experience provides me merely with a representation of the world, this does not mean that I am simply passively dependent upon sensations, subject to the vagaries of passing affections. Rather, my representation of the world is characterized by a kind of

lawfulness and coherence whose grounds I can discover, by means of reflection, in pure thought, in those 'clear and distinct ideas' the deployment of
which is my sole means of making sense of the world. It is, then, for this
tradition, in subjectivity itself that the grounds of universality, necessity,
truth, objectivity, and ethical normativity, are to be sought. In the notion of
the subject as a subject of representations, the tradition that Merleau-Ponty
calls "intellectualism" locates the grounds of a norm of self-responsibility, of
rational self-consistency and dedication to universal truth, precisely *in* the
experience of interiority. What is essential to this concept of the subject is
its difference from anything worldly, a difference of which it assures itself
by means of philosophical reflection. This absolute difference between the
'I' and the world is reflected in a series of conceptual oppositions (flowing
from the opposition of pure thought to sensation) that seem to govern
modern thought: autonomy and heteronomy, understanding and intuition,
activity and passivity, mind and body, self and other, the 'for itself' and the
'in itself.' It is this series of oppositions that has become questionable for
contemporary thinking.

To say that this determination of the essence of modern subjectivity (according to the categories of interiority, autonomy, reason) has been
particularly destabilized in the twentieth century is, in one sense, arguably
misleading—it has, perhaps, never ceased to be unstable. But there is a particular way in which, in the twentieth century, this concept of subjectivity
has been confronted with the problem of language. Jacques Derrida (whom
we will consider in chapter 4), for example, argues that the notion of the
self-presence of the thinking subject (which, he says, is implied in the very
concept of 'consciousness') is a metaphysical determination that is contested
from within by a dependence of thinking on language. According to Derrida,
if the essence of subjectivity is determined as consciousness, the presence
of the self to itself in the interiority of pure thought, then it must also be
admitted that the experience of self-presence presupposes an experience of
language. Ideality, for Derrida, is subtended by language, which is to say
that it is dependent on signs whose meaning is never stable because the
meaning of signs is a function of their difference from other signs within an
existing system of language. On the one hand, ideality is made possible by
signification, but, on other hand, since ideality implies the trans-temporal
identity of a meaning, this very dependence undermines ideality as such.
This would mean that the self-identity of the subject, of the 'I think,' is
precisely also a dependence on difference. And the sense of the interiority
of the subject, its difference from anything worldly, masks its dependence
on historical languages, and, in connection with this, intersubjectivity, culture, and so forth. Since all meaning is dependent on language, there is,
according to Derrida, no identity that is not also traversed by what he calls

"*différance*." He writes, "This movement of *différance* is not something that happens to a transcendental subject; it produces a subject."[1]

There is a superficial (but, in my view, not insignificant) resemblance between this claim and those of Daniel Dennett, who says that selves are to be understood as "centres of narrative gravity." The 'conscious' self is, in his view, a *function*, rather than the *source*, of the things we *say* about the nature of self and consciousness: "Our tales are spun, but for the most part we don't spin them; they spin us. Our human consciousness, and our narrative selfhood, is their product, not their source."[2] There are profound differences between the philosophies of Dennett and Derrida, but they share the view that what is called consciousness, the sense of subjective self-presence, is subtended by language, and that this recognition must profoundly alter the way in which we conceive of subjectivity.

This challenge of language dovetails with other challenges to the modern subject, having to do with temporality, embodiment, and intersubjectivity. For example, Husserl's analyses of 'time-consciousness' show that there is no punctual 'now' in experience, that experience thus takes the form of a temporal unfolding in which the very presence of objects, including ideal objects, is dependent upon a non-presence with which the phenomenal *present* is necessarily compounded. Thus, at least according to some of Husserl's readers, the very idea of *consciousness*, as a presence of the self to itself, is put into question by the temporally dispersed and open-ended character of phenomenal presence. Similarly, if, as Merleau-Ponty and others have said, mental life is fundamentally rooted in *bodily* life and behavior, if meaning is rooted in the dynamic structures of behavior by which I make sense of my surrounding world precisely in responding to its complex demands, then we must also say that 'mind' has its origins, as it were, outside of itself; mind is something that emerges in the relation between body and world and can no longer be understood simply in terms of interiority. Lastly, it has been widely recognized that the sense of one's own subjectivity is constitutively bound up with the experience of others and the experience of being regarded by others. This dimension of subjectivity, already brought out in Hegel's famous analyses of the struggle to the death and its resolution in "mutual recognition," is developed, in the twentieth century, in Husserl's analyses of our experience of other selves in *Cartesian Meditations*, in Heidegger's concept of *Mitsein* (being-with) as a constitutive structure of existence, and in Sartre's accounts of the often fraught terrain of our relations with others. Paraphrasing Husserl, we could say that there is no *subjectivity* that is not also an *intersubjectivity*. The so-called 'problem of other minds,' which has vexed many modern philosophers, is therefore merely a reflection of a certain Cartesian inheritance in modern thought. It is, in a sense, only a problem for a philosophy that begins with the presupposition that the subject is an essentially solitary, and disembodied, mind. We can sum up these various challenges with the observation that the subject, for many twentieth century thinkers, is necessarily a *situated* subject. As Heidegger says, using a phrase that Merleau-Ponty also uses, the subject is fundamentally a being-*in*-the-world.

The various spheres that we have just cursorily marked out—language, temporality, embodiment, intersubjectivity—and in which the modern concept of the subject has been challenged, constitute the central concerns for Merleau-Ponty's philosophy, and we will be addressing each of them in the chapters that follow. As I have indicated, according to Merleau-Ponty, the subject must first of all be understood as an *embodied* subject. As he writes in *Phenomenology of Perception*, "If the subject *is* in a situation, even if he is no more than the possibility of situations, this is because he forces his ipseity into reality by actually being a body, and by entering the world through that body" (*PhP*, 408/467). The profound phenomenological descriptions supporting the claim that the subject is necessarily embodied, that mental life is ultimately rooted in bodily behavior, and that intersubjectivity and language are themselves constitutive features of the life of the perceiving body, are among the singular achievements of *Phenomenology of Perception*. In chapter 1, I will offer an account of Merleau-Ponty's argument for his claim that cognitive life is necessarily situated and embodied, and I will do so with particular reference to his discussions of spatiality and sensation. According to Merleau-Ponty, it is only in thinking of the subject as a situated body that we can overcome the impasses confronting traditional approaches to these problems.

Let us note, however, that some of Merleau-Ponty's readers do not think he went far enough in developing the implications of his phenomenological descriptions. According to these critics, Merleau-Ponty's philosophy (at least in *Phenomenology of Perception*) does not go far enough in overcoming the modern notion of subjectivity; the evidence of this shortcoming, they claim, is in his continued deployment of the category of 'consciousness.' According to Renaud Barbaras, whose 1991 *De l'être du phénomène* [*The Being of the Phenomenon*] perhaps best exemplifies this type of interpretation, Merleau-Ponty's *Phenomenology of Perception*, for all its cogent criticisms of modern epistemology, still retains the sense of a fundamental opposition between subjective 'consciousness' and objective 'nature.' This opposition, Barbaras argues, affects and constrains the analyses of perception, intersubjectivity, and language in that work.[3] Such interpreters of *Phenomenology of Perception* often suggest that it is only in Merleau-Ponty's later works, with the emergence of the concepts of "chiasm (*chiasme*)," "the invisible (*l'invisible*)," "flesh (*chair*)," and "institution (*institution, Stiftung*)," that we come to see an *ontological* explication of the results of *Phenomenology of*

*Perception.* Thus, according to these interpreters, it is only in the later works that Merleau-Ponty realizes the aim of overcoming the modern concept of the subject. It is common to identify an increasing concern with expression and language as a crucial step in this development from the earlier, to the later, Merleau-Ponty.

Nevertheless, in this book I am particularly concerned with the implications of the analyses in *Phenomenology of Perception* with regard to subjectivity. I have three reasons for this. First, I am not particularly concerned here to engage in debates concerning the chronological development of Merleau-Ponty's philosophy; rather, it is my principal aim to enquire into his challenge to traditional accounts of the subject, and to see how his analyses of perception and expression lead us to a new sense of subjectivity. Second, I believe that the analyses of perception in *Phenomenology of Perception*, with regard to sensation and spatiality, in particular, are among the richest and most detailed that we find in all of Merleau-Ponty's work. Even if Merleau-Ponty later develops a new conceptual vocabulary and further develops his interpretations of the phenomena, we do not find any more detailed accounts of the phenomena of spatiality and sensation than those we find in *Phenomenology of Perception*. Third, I do not share the view that Merleau-Ponty was inattentive to ontological concerns in his early work. In fact, I interpret *Phenomenology of Perception* as a profound realization of what Merleau-Ponty, in a later essay, calls "an ontological rehabilitation of the sensible" (*S*, 167/271). This rehabilitation is effected in the recognition that perception is fundamentally a matter of movement. According to Merleau-Ponty, sensible being only ever reveals itself by means of expressive movement, and so the sensible is precisely neither an in-itself, nor an immanent datum that a consciousness would need to synthesize with other data by means of its own connecting activity. As a sentient motor subject, the *conscious* subject, in Merleau-Ponty's sense, is always already responding to being's manifestation. The sensible, as Merleau-Ponty remarks at the end of the "*Sentir*" chapter of *Phenomenology of Perception*, is, for the conscious subject, "a past which has never been a present" (*PhP*, 242/280). The sensible is, then, for the subject, an element of alterity that ceaselessly haunts its conscious life; it never appears to a consciousness but as an absent origin, or a call to which it is always already answering. As Merleau-Ponty says, of sensation, "its origin is anterior to myself" (*PhP*, 215–6/249–50). In a sense then, as a sentient subject, I ceaselessly take up and develop a responsive activity that is older than my consciousness. And because the movement whereby the sensible reveals itself is, according to Merleau-Ponty, fundamentally *expressive* movement, the manifestation of the sensible is at the same time the opening-up of the sphere of language. The subject, then, lives out its life in a responsive activity that is at once both sentience and speech.

In chapter 1 ("Situation and the Embodied Mind"), as I have indicated, I will explore Merleau-Ponty's accounts of sensation and space. In my interpretation of these accounts, I will develop the framework for the interpretation of subjectivity that I have outlined above. But I will also read Merleau-Ponty's accounts of these dimensions alongside two more recent accounts of what I will call 'situated cognition': the 'sensorimotor' approach to perception, developed by Kevin O'Regan and Alva Noë, and the ecological psychology of J.J. Gibson. All three approaches to the study of perception aim to overcome the epistemology of representation that is the hallmark of modern accounts of the epistemological subject.

In chapter 2 ("Making Space"), I will draw out the implications of Merleau-Ponty's account of perception-as-movement with respect to the problems of sensation and space. This will lead us into a discussion of the unity of the sentient body. Merleau-Ponty's claims that the origin of sensation is 'older than [one]self' and that each sensation calls for its own 'total space' mean that the unity of the body can only be a dynamic unity, a unity only ever incompletely accomplished in movement that stylizes. Movement responds to what I will call the 'singularity of the sensible,' but in doing so, it incorporates that singularity into the generality of a style and it is this that subtends the unity of the body. If the subject is haunted by the anteriority of the sensible, it is also haunted by the contingency of its own unity. This very contingency is also, I will argue, what motivates learning. The mode of being of the subject is a responsivity to what it cannot anticipate, and thus its identity is achieved only through a constant process of self-transformation, of the formation of new habits.

In chapter 3 ("Subjectivity and the 'Style' of the World"), I will reconsider the sensorimotor and ecological accounts of perception that we study in chapter 1. Both aim to offer broadly naturalistic, non-representationalist accounts of cognition, and, in fact, the advocates of the sensorimotor account have suggested that their approach may offer a way to 'naturalize phenomenology.' I will argue that these kinds of naturalistic approaches end up appealing to a notion of psycho-physical law that is precisely the kind of thing that Merleau-Ponty overcomes with his concept of 'style.' The notion of law, I will argue, ends up appealing to what Merleau-Ponty calls a "ready-made" world, and therefore misses the ontological originality of the phenomena of perception. Most importantly, for our purposes, these naturalistic approaches seem to avoid the fundamental problems of subjectivity.

In chapter 4 ("Auto-affection and Alterity"), I will examine Merleau-Ponty's account of time as auto-affection. I will argue that this notion of auto-affection must be understood as a claim concerning the temporalizing character of living movement. I will also offer a response to those who consider Merleau-Ponty's identification of time and subjectivity to be evidence of a commitment to a 'metaphysics of presence.' Merleau-Ponty's own analyses lead us to understand that subjectivity depends upon what he calls a 'dehiscence' of time, and this, I will argue, is a function of the self-articulating and self-temporalizing character of living movement. In this chapter I will also examine Derrida's interpretation of the phenomenological notions of consciousness and auto-affection, particularly with respect to the concept of the lived, or 'own,' body (*Leib, le corps propre*). Derrida is critical of Merleau-Ponty's notion of the lived body and the related notion of intercorporeity. According to Derrida's interpretation, Merleau-Ponty's notion of intercorporeity occludes the alterity of the other precisely insofar as it also occludes the dimensions of alterity and difference that subtend and, at the same time, threaten the sense of 'one's own body.' I will argue that Derrida does not sufficiently recognize the sense of alterity that is a constitutive feature of what Merleau-Ponty understands by *le corps propre*, and, further, I will argue that Merleau-Ponty's account of the intercorporeal body anticipates Derrida's own concerns.

Finally, in chapter 5 ("Ipseity and Language"), I will respond to the view held by some interpreters that Merleau-Ponty (in *Phenomenology of Perception*) privileges perception over language. While I acknowledge that Merleau-Ponty's account of language undergoes significant development in the period after the writing of the *Phenomenology of Perception*, our interpretations of the notions of sensation and expressive movement in that work will have already given us the means to understand how it is that language, like the sensible, manifests itself in living movement. The movements of our bodies are a response to a call of the sensible, and, by the same token, a response to the demands of language. Our gestures are expressive and generative of meaning insofar as they articulate and differentiate themselves according to the same kinds of diacritical structures that govern the relations between signs in any conventional language. The body is thus an incarnate logos, and subjective movement must be understood as an inscription of subjectivity in the open-ended system of language, an inscription that is also the transformation and renewal of that system.

Central to Merleau-Ponty's account of subjectivity is his notion of 'intercorporeity.' In this book, I aim, in part, to demonstrate that the import of this concept, which is not explicitly invoked in Merleau-Ponty's writings until the 1950s, but which is, in my view, implicit throughout his 1945 *Phenomenology of Perception*, has not been sufficiently recognized by some of Merleau-Ponty's most influential interpreters. With the notion of intercorporeity, it seems to me, Merleau-Ponty deepens the phenomenological insights, already brilliantly elaborated by Husserl, concerning the fundamentally intersubjective character of self-consciousness. There is, according to Merleau-Ponty, beneath my explicit self-consciousness, a fecund layer of anonymous life; it is this dimension of anonymity characterizing my bodily experience that Merleau-Ponty designates with the term 'intercorporeity.' The presence of sensible reality in our conscious experience is a kind of mysterious contact, a communion with otherness, but this communion also always involves a certain threat of dispossession. The sense of anonymity persists throughout our experience insofar as our bodies are sentient bodies, bodies open to and pervaded by a reality that does not wait for us to set the terms of its appearance and thus whose appearance always holds for us a sense of our own vulnerability and exposure. The appearance of the foreign in my experience, the undeniable presence of sensible being, is subtended by this anonymity of my own sentient flesh; in this mass that is my sentient body it is never immediately clear where the 'other' ends and the 'I' begins. Thus, the sense of anonymity is also the mark of a certain primitive kinship between my body and the bodies of other selves. 'Intercorporeity' names at once this mysterious familiarity of my body with things and with the bodies of others and, at the same time, a no-less-mysterious sense of the strangeness of 'my own' body. An appreciation of both of these dimensions, the familiarity and the irreducible strangeness characterizing my bodily life, is crucial for any adequate account of subjectivity and self-consciousness.

According to Merleau-Ponty, a primitive involvement with others is indeed attested to in our most intimate bodily lives: in the manner of our walking; in the way our bodies respond to music; in the solitary, restless, nocturnal hours in which we strive to entrust ourselves to the embrace of sleep; in the way we hold a wineglass delicately in our fingers even when alone; in the way our eyes are drawn, as though by a kind of magnetism, to the human physiognomy of a figure in a painting; in the visceral responses of our bodies to the unexpected touch of another living body. We are intercorporeal selves insofar as our involvement with otherness constitutes for us a kind of archaeological pre-history subtending our present experience: older than any consciousness, but present at every moment, 'in the flesh.' As conscious selves we inherit, so to speak, the memory of an originary contact with otherness. We are, as Merleau-Ponty sometimes says, *haunted* by others.

In this book I argue that no account of cognition and self-consciousness, or of language, can be sufficient without an appreciation of the intercorporeal character of subjectivity such as it is elaborated by Merleau-Ponty. Merleau-Ponty's insight into the intercorporeal constitution of the subject affirms a kind of an-archic dimension in our conscious experience that makes it resistant to any form of reductionist explanation. The field of experience that we share with others is not reducible either to any fixed a priori structures located within the consciousness of an intellectualist subjectivity, nor to the objective 'parts and processes' that, according to naturalistic accounts of cognition, putatively subtend our conscious experiences or constitute the fixed natural setting of our cognitive lives. Rather, between my body and those of others, from a dimension that precedes both the differences between us and the differences between our own bodies and the worlds they inhabit, there is always already emerging a self-articulating structure, a "wildflowering world and mind" (S 181/294). Phenomenology attempts to do justice to this emergence insofar as it attempts a rigorous description of the constitutive relations between a mind and its world, but a philosophy distorts the character of self-consciousness insofar as it allows this originary *relation* to be reduced to one of its terms, to something other than the relation itself. What I believe Merleau-Ponty's philosophy is uniquely equipped to help us see is that, in order to do justice to the phenomena of experience, we must remain faithful in our descriptions to the very event of the emergence of meaning, as it unfolds. This emergence occurs in the expressive movement of intercorporeal bodies, bodies always already intertwined with, and, so to speak, committed to, otherness. Only in grasping the originary character of this emergence can we make real progress with the many important philosophical problems concerning subjectivity and self-consciousness. And it is only on the basis of such an understanding of the dependence of subjectivity on the event of the emergence of meaning that we can understand the compelling character of the demands to which, as intercorporeal selves, we find ourselves beholden in our lives with others: the norms of objectivity in our sciences, the idea of universality informing our concepts of law and right, and in that ethical comportment for which Kant used the term 'respect' (*Achtung*) and which would seem to presuppose a primitive sense of my answerability to and for the other person.

ONE

# SITUATION AND THE EMBODIED MIND

If the subject *is* in a situation, even if he is no more than the possibility of situations, this is because he forces his ipseity into reality only by actually being a body, and entering the world through that body.

—Merleau-Ponty

## I. MIND, SELF, WORLD

Merleau-Ponty's phenomenology has been influential in a number of recent attempts to rethink the nature of cognition. Against a prevalent tendency in cognitive science and neuroscience to model cognition after computational processes, some have insisted that cognition must be understood as necessarily embodied and as situated within an ecological milieu. They argue that cognitive life is rooted in bodily movement and, in particular, in what is sometimes called 'coping' behavior.[1] This means that cognition is rooted in the temporal *dynamics* of perception and motility rather than internal maps, or representations, of the external world. Some of these contemporary challenges to representationalist epistemology are not only influenced by Merleau-Ponty's phenomenology, but reflect explicit attempts to give phenomenology a 'naturalistic' foundation.[2] Advocates of this research program seek to develop phenomenological approaches to cognition alongside empirical scientific approaches being pursued in psychology, cognitive science, neuroscience, artificial intelligence, and so on. In this chapter I will examine some of Merleau-Ponty's claims about the situated character of cognition in his 1945 *Phenomenology of Perception*, and I will consider these claims alongside theoretical proposals made by advocates of two contemporary, broadly 'naturalistic,' approaches to the study of cognition: the sensorimotor approach, developed by Kevin O'Regan and Alva Noë, and the ecological psychology developed by J.J. Gibson.

11

I do this for two reasons: First, these empirical scientific approaches utilize relatively recent experimental data that both support and help to clarify some of Merleau-Ponty's phenomenological claims with respect to the situated character of cognition. Furthermore, the sensorimotor approach in particular effectively deploys some of these findings against recent versions of neurophysiological reductionism, and considering this approach can help us to grasp the radical challenge that the argument for situatedness represents with respect to what remains a dominant paradigm in the study of cognition. My second reason for considering Merleau-Ponty's claims alongside these other approaches to situated cognition will become evident in chapter 3, but it will be helpful to briefly note it here. While these naturalistic approaches can teach us much about the mutual implication of cognition and behavior, they fall short of the radical challenge implied in Merleau-Ponty's thought with respect to the nature of situated subjectivity. This shortcoming, I will argue, is a function of the limits of a too narrowly epistemological approach to the nature of 'situation': Merleau-Ponty's philosophy makes clear that any adequate understanding of the situatedness of subjectivity must also involve a critique of the implicit *ontology* of modern science. Considering Merleau-Ponty's phenomenology of perception alongside these other approaches can help us to understand why such a critique is necessary, why a challenge to representationalism must also be a critique of the metaphysics that has supported it.

In this chapter I will show that Merleau-Ponty's account of the situatedness of the subject turns on the phenomenological concept of 'motivation,' which Merleau-Ponty pairs with his own concept of 'decision' (a term that is sometimes modified to suggest a process that is not explicit, or conscious, as in 'tacit decision,' or 'secret decision'). The subject of perception is first and foremost a self-moving subjectivity. Self-movement is a 'tacit decision' which lets features of environments appear *as* meaningful for a sentient body, but this means that movement always involves the enactment of a tacit decision concerning what will count as a 'motivation' for the self-moving body. As we shall see, Merleau-Ponty's use of the concepts of motivation and decision enables him to overcome a whole set of traditional oppositions—between sensation and understanding, stimulus and response, cause and effect, matter and form, information and processing, passivity and activity—that have traditionally determined epistemological accounts of subjectivity. The subject is situated insofar as, on the one hand, its behavior is directly responsive to 'information' about the conditions and features of its environment and, on the other hand, its behavior is a decision concerning the meaning and value of that 'information.'

*Representation*

According to the mainstream of modern epistemology, human cognition consists of operations inwardly performed on tokens of the external world. The mind, in this view, is a zone of interiority, or immanence, within which the world is more or less faithfully mapped or 'represented.' The processes by which the world is internally represented have been modeled by various thinkers in various ways, but, according to a presently well-established view, they are at bottom, and without remainder, *physically* instantiated in the brain. In other words, for each detail of the world, insofar as it appears in perception, memory, or imagination—that is, insofar as it is available to be thought about or acted upon—there is some set of activated neurons serving as a stand-in. Cognition and behavior, on this account, are dependent on symbol-processing operations that proceed according to computational rules. Dorothea Olkowski describes this approach:

> This is the model of an isolated body that causally affects the mind, both of which are situated in a physical universe of purely mechanical relations. In such a universe, the interior or mental world organizes itself in the image of the external, physical world, a second reality added to the first, but always with the proviso that it can be reduced to the physiochemical world of pure material causation.[3]

This account of cognition promises a scientific rendering of the workings of the mind that would be expressible entirely in terms of physical processes characterized by relations of cause and effect.

If such a promise could be realized, it would offer an account of the mind in third-person terms. It would demonstrate that cognition is not a 'spiritual' operation performed by some mysterious and ineffable 'I'; rather, a natural science of the mind would allow us to see that a mundane (if remarkably complex) organ, the brain, carries out the functions of thinking, imagining, remembering, and acting in the manner of a very sophisticated machine.[4] However, among a number of problems encountered by such theories of the mind is the fact that they seem to leave out what is perhaps the most remarkable and pervasive feature of mental life: subjectivity. As David Chalmers has observed: "It still seems utterly mysterious that the causation of behavior should be accompanied by a subjective inner life. . . . How could a physical system such as a brain also be an *experiencer?*"[5] In short, there persists what many have termed an 'explanatory gap' between accounts of cognition in terms of third-person processes and what we could call the first-personal character of experience.[6]

There have been attempts to address this problem within the framework of representationalist accounts of the mind. For example, Albert Newen and Kai Vogeley have recently proposed a model for understanding the 'first-person perspective' on the basis of various types of 'self-representation,' which, in their view, are concurrent with other cognitive processes. They offer a précis of experimental data that apparently indicates a consistent ('hard-wired') pattern of neural activation associated with this 'self-representation.' Thus, they claim, it is possible to identify a "neural signature of self-consciousness."[7] But even if neural correlates of self-representation could be identified, the explanatory gap between a pattern of neural activation and the first-personal character of *experience* would undoubtedly persist.

Indeed, one glaring problem concerns the assumed identification of the 'first-person perspective' with a 'self-representation.' It is difficult to be precise about what we mean by the 'first-person perspective' because it is not really some*thing* we experience; rather it can be said to constitute the very *form* of our experience. Perhaps the most obvious sense of the first-person perspective consists in the fact that we always perceive the world from a spatial 'here.' My perceptual experience of the world is not a view from nowhere but is always a view from the place where I am standing or sitting or walking. My view-point is embodied. But in noticing that it is embodied we also notice another feature of the first-personal, spatial view-point: it is, in fact, not a mere *point.* When I perceive my own hands busily typing at the keyboard, I see them as extensions of my own self. I am living through the seeing of them *and* I am living through their activity, the sensation of their motion and their pressure upon the keys. I am at once 'here' (in the seeing) and 'there' (where my hands tap at the keys): in fact my hands belong to the 'here' of my spatial viewpoint no less than the eyes that are seeing them. There seems to be a kind of two-sidedness to the experience of perceiving my own body—it is a *thing* I can see, but it is also *me.* We have been compelled to use the phrase 'living through' in order to account for the unity of the experience of seeing my hand and of feeling its activity, its active and sentient contact with the world, but this term also expresses a more general two-sidedness manifested in our experiences of ourselves. When I recall events from my recent past, I recall them *as* lived through by me, but I am also living through the memory of them. There is a kind of spatial and temporal thickness to what we are calling the first-person perspective. And, in fact, even as I try to reflect on my experience in the present—if I, for example, try to investigate the first-personal character of the experience of looking at the lamp on my desk—I find that both the act of looking and the act of reflecting are *my* experiences. What holds these experiences together (the seeing and the reflecting on my seeing) is what we are calling the 'lived through' character of our various experiences. This is what, according to thinkers in the phenomenological tradition, is designated by the term 'first-person perspective.'[8]

Our examples thus far have concerned acts of reflection or self-observation. Of course, before we actually reflect, we are not explicitly conscious of the 'first-person perspective' as such. Nevertheless, considering the two-sidedness of our experience on occasions when we are engaged in acts of reflection or self-observation draws our attention to a form of self-awareness that was implicitly already there before we began to reflect. Dan Zahavi puts it this way:

> If I am engaged in some conscious activity, such as the reading of a story, my attention is neither on myself nor on my activity of reading, but on the story. If my reading is interrupted by someone asking me what I am doing, I immediately reply that I am (and have been for some time) reading; the self-consciousness on the basis of which I answer the question is not something acquired at just that moment, but a consciousness of myself that has been present all along.[9]

Merleau-Ponty makes a similar observation in the preface to *Phenomenology of Perception*, where he writes the following:

> When I begin to reflect my reflection bears upon an unreflective experience; moreover my reflection cannot be unaware of itself as an event, and so it appears to itself in the light of a truly creative act [*une véritable création*], of a changed structure of consciousness, and yet it has to recognize, as having priority over its own operations, the world which is given to the subject because the subject is given to himself. (*PhP*, x/iv)

The 'first-person perspective' thus concerns the way in which "the subject is [unreflectively] given to himself" even while he is occupied with other things. Considered in these terms, it poses a serious problem for representationalist accounts of cognition not just because it is, in general, famously impossible to establish convincingly the identify of neuronal activity with a cognitive process (though this is a serious and related problem), but first of all because it is not possible to say *what* a representation of the first-person perspective would actually represent.

*Behavior*

Beginning with his 1942 *The Structure of Behavior*, Merleau-Ponty offers a decisive challenge to the representationalist account of mind and self-consciousness. In his view, the problem of subjectivity is not merely a regional problem in modern science—as though self-consciousness were simply one particularly intractable difficulty in the scientific explanation of cognition and behavior. Rather, the inability of modern science to do justice to what we are calling the first-person perspective is, for Merleau-Ponty, an indication of a deeper and more general problem involving the fundamental ontological commitments of that science. "The object of science," Merleau-Ponty observes, "is defined by the mutual exteriority of parts and processes" (SB, 9/8). This means that modern science is committed to understanding the world as a totality of discrete material elements whose relationships to each other are governed by fundamental laws, laws which can be formalized in abstraction from those elements whose interactions they putatively govern. The world of modern science is a totality of discrete objectivities. Science thus understands its task in reductionist terms: it must demonstrate that all appearances of intelligence, significance, and value in the world (the province of 'mind') are somehow reducible to mutually exterior 'parts and processes' or admit that it has failed to explain reality.[10] It is often conceded that the problems of subjectivity and mind pose special difficulties for such an enterprise, but it is equally often maintained that with improvements in technology, and with greater insight into the workings of the brain, these problems can in principle be overcome. And yet, to frame the problem of subjectivity in these narrow terms is to overlook a more unsettling and inescapable truth: explanations of phenomena (including phenomena pertaining to cognition) in terms of underlying 'parts and processes' are in every case dependent upon manifestations of the world *for* someone.[11] The third-personal objective world of the sciences owes its very appearance to a first-personal perspective. This truth, which in Merleau-Ponty's view was not grasped with sufficient radicality by the thinkers of the Enlightenment, implies a serious challenge to the assumptions of modern science, a challenge that is effectively neutralized when the problem of subjectivity is relegated to a region of psychological research. This is why, according to Merleau-Ponty, the question concerning subjectivity cannot be answered in the terms of a science whose object is "defined by the mutual exteriority of parts and processes."[12]

According to Merleau-Ponty this fundamental problem, which, at least until the twentieth century, is generally ignored in the modern natural sciences, is inescapable for biology and psychology when it is a question of explaining, in empirical-scientific terms, the observed behavior of living things. In *The Structure of Behavior*, Merleau-Ponty argues that experimental observations of the complex behavior of organisms remain inexplicable as long as we try to construe behavior as a set of predictable reflex responses to stimuli (that is, insofar as we try to explain behavior in terms of interactions governed by fundamental natural laws). Rather, he insists, as we shall see, that behavior only becomes intelligible when we understand it as the enactment of a nexus of *meanings* linking an organism to its 'environment' (what the biologist Jakob von Uexküll calls the organism's *Umwelt*[13]). Merleau-Ponty claims (on the basis of his interpretations of findings from early twentieth century psychological research, especially in the field of Gestalt psychology) that the *behavior* of organisms in fact determines the *value* or *significance* of stimuli. Thus the relation of stimulus and response is neither statically law-governed nor unidirectional; what appears to be a manifestation of reflex responses to stimuli should rather be understood as manifesting a kind of responsive activity on the part of an organism. Merleau-Ponty writes,

> One cannot discern in animal behavior something like a first layer of reactions which would correspond to the physical and chemical properties of the world and to which an acquired significance would subsequently be attached by the transference of reflexogenic powers. In an organism, experience is not the recording and fixation of certain actually accomplished movements: it builds up aptitudes, that is, the general power of responding to situations of a certain type by means of varied reactions which have nothing in common but the meaning [*sens*]. Reactions are not therefore a sequence of events; they carry within themselves an immanent intelligibility. (SB, 130/140)[14]

This view poses a challenge to the epistemology of representation. That is to say, it challenges the presuppositions (1) that the external world must be somehow stably represented in a brain or a consciousness (via causal processes that would carry information through the nervous system to the brain) in order to supply the material for cognition and (2) that behaviors must somehow be represented in the brain (in the form of motor programs or goal-directed plans) prior to their execution. It challenges these notions by affirming the fundamental role of 'meaning' (*sens*) in any explanation of behavior.[15] The hypothesis of internal representations, even if it could be shown to be warranted by certain forms of cognition and action, does not in fact promise a solution to the problems raised by the study of behavior, for to explain the function of representations in behavior we would still have to explain how a representation could become a matter of significance for an organism:

> In recognizing that behavior has a meaning [*sens*] and depends upon the vital significance of situations, biological science is prohibited

from conceiving of it as a thing in-itself (*en soi*) which would exist, *partes extra partes*, in the nervous system or *in* the body; rather it sees in behavior an embodied dialectic [*dialectiques incarnées*] which radiates over a milieu immanent to it. (*SB*, 161/174)

With this in mind, we may say that, for Merleau-Ponty, organisms must be understood as beings that are in some sense *selves*.[16] And this must be taken seriously by science. The features of the organism's environment provide explanations for the organism's behavior only to the extent that those features become significant *for* the organism. Organisms are situated bodily in a world with which they are actively engaged and their activity thereby constitutes in and around themselves a milieu of "living significance" (*PhP*, 209/243).

We must notice that the constitution of an organism's horizon of living significance is, for Merleau-Ponty, a *dynamic* process. Scientific objectivity (involving the separation and reification of parts and processes) is characterized by a peculiarly static view of the organism and its surrounding world—one in which events and developments in the lives of organisms are understood as reducible to more basic elements and laws. The process of coming to understand an organism, in the perspective of modern science, involves *analysis*—a taking-apart. This taking-apart of living things in order to understand them happens not merely in the literal sense, as dissection or vivisection, or as the removal of organisms from environments in order to study them under laboratory conditions, but also occurs in the form of an analysis of developmental and cognitive processes into discrete levels and stages. Merleau-Ponty's notion of an 'embodied dialectic' asserts that cognition is a living *process*. He thus contests not only the assumption that cognition can be analyzed into discrete elements and causal connections but also the related assumption that structures of behavior are built up in discrete strata proceeding from a chemical basis to a biological level upon which are then grafted distinct behavioral and cognitive levels.[17] As he writes, "The advent of higher orders, to the extent that they are accomplished, eliminate the autonomy of the lower orders and give a new signification to the steps which constitute them" (*SB*, 180/195). This is why, in *The Structure of Behavior*, Merleau-Ponty's challenge to a certain philosophy of mind is situated within a general critique of science; to properly understand mind (and subjectivity) we must develop a more adequate view of nature, one in which it will be possible to see how these 'higher orders' reveal what is already implicit in the 'lower' ones. He writes, "Mind is not a specific difference which would be added to vital or psychological being in order to constitute a man. Man is not a rational animal. The appearance of reason and mind does not leave intact a sphere of self-enclosed instincts in man"

(SB, 181/196). To be a self, in the sense I am proposing here (on the basis of Merleau-Ponty's claims in *The Structure of Behavior*), is to embody an immanent logos of development in terms of which higher forms of consciousness emerge only as articulations or restructurations of more fundamental dynamics of life.[18]

According to Merleau-Ponty, the self is thus not merely another fact or complex of facts to be discovered in the world (or in the brain); instead, it concerns the very form of the world's appearance in the domain marked out by the responsive activity (life) of a living being.[19] A self is a paradoxical being, at once situated within, and thus dependent upon, the world of whose appearance it is also the condition. As we shall see, this account of the self is crucial for understanding Merleau-Ponty's account of developed forms of mind and self-consciousness.

*Situated Cognition*

Recently, a number of researchers in the fields of cognitive science, psychology, artificial intelligence, and neuroscience, some of them directly inspired by Merleau-Ponty's challenge to recognize the 'embodied dialectic' underlying mental life, have begun to advocate alternative accounts of cognition as, variously, "embedded," "enactive," "embodied," "situated," "sensorimotor," "existential," or "ecological."[20] I will use the term 'situated cognition' when I am speaking of these approaches (in terms of what they have in common) because whether the emphasis is placed on embodiment, on the environment construed as a meaningful ecology, or on intersubjectivity, all of these approaches hold that cognition necessarily occurs in some kind of meaningful 'situation.' Thus one of the things that these challengers share is a conviction that representationalist (computational) cognitivism has too narrowly construed the locus of cognition.[21] Without a proper understanding of the 'situatedness' of cognition, there is little to be learned from 'neural signatures.' As with Merleau-Ponty, the emphasis for these critics of traditional epistemology is on the intrinsic meaningfulness of *behavioral dynamics* rather than on representational content. The advocates of this approach are primarily concerned with the way in which an organism's 'phenomenal environment' is articulated with reference to the organism, and thus with reference to the skills, habits, and dispositions relevant to and constitutive of its mode of life.[22] The cognitive lives of organisms are, for advocates of situated cognition, deeply rooted in the structures of meaningful behaviors and the ways in which these in turn actively structure the organism's phenomenal environment. It follows that, in order to understand human cognition, we must first of all recognize that the human being is a living organism, an embodied agent 'situated' in a (human) environment. In short, mind is something that occurs *between* a living body and its world. As Evan Thompson writes, "the human mind is embodied in our entire organism and embedded in the world, and hence not reducible to structures inside the head."[23]

For the advocates of situated cognition, this insight is crucial for understanding the nature of subjectivity. The subject is first of all, as Merleau-Ponty says, an "incarnate subject" (*PhP*, 52/64). Advocates of situated cognition note that even our most sophisticated cognitive achievements, having to do with concept-formation and language, reflect a fundamental concern with the milieu of our bodies.[24] They also note that while we human beings are evidently deeply absorbed in our bodily situation, and are only very occasionally concerned with our own mental states and processes, this does not mean that our experience lacks a sense of subjectivity. The point is that a self *is*, first of all, a being-in-a-situation.[25] As Merleau-Ponty says, following Husserl, subjectivity is not first and foremost revealed as an "I think [*je pense que*]" but rather as an embodied "I can [*je peux*]" (*PhP*, 137/160).[26]

The challenge of situated cognition has thus been aimed in two directions at once. On the one hand, against the reductionist approach that we have just briefly touched on, the challengers have insisted that the sense of self is indeed a real problem, that the first-person perspective, the lived-through character of experience, is not simply an illusion. But they have, on the other hand, also challenged the notion that the primary object of inquiry into the problem of subjectivity is the self as it appears in acts of explicit reflection—e.g., the Cartesian *res cogitans*.[27] The two positions to which the thesis of situated cognition opposes itself are clearly not unrelated: they both hold that the subject is, or is reducible to, some kind of entity that can be made an object of scientific or reflective inquiry (either to be elucidated or to be explained away), whereas the challengers insist that subjectivity reveals itself first and foremost in the 'manners of givenness' whereby a world appears to an engaged, outwardly-directed, living being.

This challenge has provoked a number of worries. Galen Strawson expresses a common concern when he writes:

> Many psychologists and anthropologists are quite rightly concerned to stress the embedded, embodied, ecological or 'EEE' aspects of our experiential predicament as social and organic beings located in a physical environment; but they risk losing sight of the respect in which Self-experience—the experience of oneself as a specifically mental something—is nonetheless, the central or fundamental way (although it is obviously not the only way) in which human beings experience themselves.[28]

Strawson worries that advocates of situated (what he calls 'EEE') cognition are simply ignoring the real problem of the self and self-consciousness. As we have already indicated, it is certainly the case that what Strawson calls the 'Self'—a 'specifically mental something'—is largely absent from the *immediate* concerns of the advocates of situated cognition.[29] To take a couple of clear examples: summing up the results of their own investigation of the problem of the self and self-awareness in their 1991 *The Embodied Mind*, Varela, Thompson, and Rosch concede (in terms reminiscent of Hume) that, having "entered the very storm of experience, we . . . could discern there no self, no 'I.'"[30] In fact, in their view, there is nothing necessary or universal about the belief in a "truly existing self"; it is not merely the case that Strawson's sort of "self-experience" is not the fundamental form of self-awareness, but, on the basis of their encounter with Buddhist philosophy, they are prepared to diagnose this "habitual belief" as a kind of pathology supported by a long-standing (largely occidental) cultural prejudice.[31] Andy Clark, unlike Varela et al., seems a little reticent about parting ways with the 'mental something' when he expresses the worry that "the putative spread of mental and cognitive processes into the world [implies] some correlative (and surely unsettling) leakage of the self into the local surroundings."[32] Though some of them may find it 'unsettling,' those in sympathy with its challenge to traditional cognitivism generally acknowledge that, with the thesis of situated cognition, for good or ill, "the bounds of the self . . . threaten to push out into the world."[33]

Over the rest of this chapter, I will explore some of the arguments, made by Merleau-Ponty and the proponents of situated cognition, for the claim that the bounds of the self are indeed 'pushed out into the world.' Coming to terms with the meaning of this claim is among the central concerns of Merleau-Ponty's philosophy. In *Phenomenology of Perception*, he formulates the problem as follows:

> Whether we are concerned with my body, the natural world, the past, birth or death, the question is always how I can be open to phenomena which transcend me, and which nevertheless exist only to the extent that I take them up and live them; *how the presence to myself (Urpräsenz) which establishes my own limits and conditions every alien presence is at the same time depresentation (Entgegenwärtingung) and throws me outside of myself.* (PhP, 363/417)

Before we proceed, let us recall again here that the argument for the situatedness of the self can be understood in at least two different ways: 1) It can be understood in an *epistemological* sense, as a claim concerning the nature of *cognition*. In this case, the claim would entail that cognitive processes are directly grounded in behavior, in the intrinsic meaningfulness of dynamic sensorimotor structures, and thus do not presuppose an internal mapping of the external world. The environment, or 'world,' would be of interest to such an epistemology only insofar as it is perceived—that is, insofar as its features correlate with sensorimotor structures. 2) It can also be understood as an *ontological* claim. In this case there would be no sense in which the category of 'external world' would be left unaffected by the claim that 'the bounds of self are pushed out into the world.' The study of cognition would not merely be a study of the way in which a perceptual system makes selective use of information about the objective world (thereby constituting for itself an environmental setting) but rather an investigation of the manner in which a world *is*. It would thus be concerned with cognition insofar as it reveals the ontological dynamics underlying the co-belonging and the difference between subjectivity and its 'objects.' These two positions will not be clearly differentiated in this chapter (we will establish the necessity of distinguishing them in chapters 2 and 3); rather, in the next section, as we have indicated, we will explore the epistemological dimensions of the claim. But we will be doing so with a view to eventually demonstrating that the epistemological claim is insufficient even in its own terms. That is, we will be arguing in subsequent chapters that the accounts of perception that we touch upon here can only be properly developed in the context of an ontology.

## II. PERCEPTION

*Sensation*

Empiricist epistemology takes for its starting point the impressional datum conceived as 'sensation': "the experience of an undifferentiated, instantaneous, dotlike impact [*d'un 'choc' indifférencié, instantané et ponctuel*]" (*PhP*, 3/9). In fact, as Merleau-Ponty points out, this idea of sensation corresponds to nothing in our ordinary perceptual experience, which is typically the experience of things in situations: we see 'green' *as* the green *of* leaves *on* the maple tree; we feel 'smoothness' *as* the smoothness *of* the granite countertop. But even if we try to conjure a perceptual setting in which we are confronted with a seemingly simple datum such as a colored patch, we shall find (as Gestalt psychologists have shown) that in fact we cannot avoid seeing the patch as a certain shape against some kind of background. The datum thus appears as bounded, with the background seeming to pass under the colored patch. The putatively simple datum thus appears in the context of a system of relations. Indeed, Merleau-Ponty observes that the most basic elements of perception always already appear as "charged with a *meaning* [*sens*]" (*PhP*, 4/9). In the terms of Husserlian phenomenology this finding can be grasped as an 'eidetic' necessity: it is *only* in terms of its *meaningfulness* within a context that any datum can appear in perception. As Merleau-Ponty writes,

> When Gestalt theory informs us that a figure on a background is the simplest sense-given available to us, we reply that this is not a contingent characteristic of factual perception, which leaves us free in an ideal analysis, to bring in the notion of impressions. It is the very definition of the phenomenon of perception, that without which a phenomenon cannot be said to be perception at all. The perceptual 'something' is always in the middle of something else, it always forms part of a 'field.' (*PhP*, 4/10)

If the figure-ground structure is the most basic conceivable unit of perception, this would not only make the question of the emergence of 'significance' (*sens*) central to the study of perception, but would render the traditional empiricist problematic of impressions, and the association of discrete impressional contents in conscious experience, otiose. Let us consider this implication.

Empiricist epistemology has traditionally asserted a distinction between 'primary' and 'secondary' qualities. According to this thinking, objects are, *in themselves*, characterized by their primary qualities (shape, extension, solidity); secondary qualities are understood to be those powers, vested in objects by virtue of their primary qualities, of producing *in us* the sensations of, say, colour, or taste. Whatever the metaphysical or scientific objections to which this Lockean picture is subject, it remains the case that the primary-secondary quality distinction is implied in the very idea of sensibility as a passive receptivity to impressions. If we perceive things by way of impressions, then it must be possible to distinguish (even if only abstractly) that in the object which is capable of so affecting our sensibility from that which more generally characterizes the being of the object in itself. Secondary qualities are the powers of objects enabling them to appear to a receptive subject. The primary-secondary quality distinction thus implies a further distinction, within the subject, between sensibility (as receptivity to impressions) and the power of understanding. The most persistent epistemological problems have stemmed from this assumed distinction: the subject is a subject of *appearance* insofar as it is passive; it is a subject of *knowledge* insofar as it is active. But the study of perception does not appear to support this distinction. Merleau-Ponty writes:

One can discern, at the rudimentary stage of sensibility, a working together on the part of the partial stimuli and a collaboration of the sensory with the motor system which, in a variable physiological constellation, keeps sensation constant and rules out any definition of the nervous process as the simple transmission of a given message. (*PhP*, 9/14)

Perception thus does not begin with the passive reception of secondary qualities. "In fact," Merleau-Ponty observes, "each of the alleged qualities—red, blue, colour, sound—is inserted into a certain form of behaviour" (*PhP*, 208–9/241–2). He cites the results of experiments carried out by Kurt Goldstein and Otto Rosenthal involving patients with damage to the cerebellum or the frontal cortex in which marked changes in patterns of movements are observed in the presence of different colors. For example, red and yellow are noted to produce smooth movements whereas blue and green produce jerky ones. These results, according to Merleau-Ponty, indicate a more general correlation of sensibility and motility. That is to say, these results "show what effect sensory excitations would have on muscular tonicity, if they were not integrated into a comprehensive situation, and if tonicity were not, in the normal person, adjusted to certain special tasks" (*PhP*, 209/242).[34] The experiments show that different colors motivate different behaviors in more or less predictable ways. "In these various experiments each colour always acts with the same tendency, with the result that a definite motor significance [*valeur motrice définie*] can be assigned to it" (*PhP*, 209/242). It is the concept of 'motor significance,' rather than that of simple 'sensation,' that, in Merleau-Ponty's view, enables us to understand what is really going on in perception. "Sensations, 'sensible qualities' are then far from being reducible to a certain indescribable state or *quale*; they present themselves with a motor physiognomy, and are enveloped in a living significance [*signification vitale*]" (*PhP*, 209/242–3). What must be understood is the nature of the relationship between the appearance and the 'motor physiognomy' to which it is apparently correlated.

Recently, Kevin O'Regan and Alva Noë have proposed a model for understanding the relationship between sensation and motility with respect to vision in particular, and they offer a wide-ranging survey of experimental data on visual perception, which, as they convincingly demonstrate, appears to support their approach. They propose that vision be understood as "a mode of exploration of the world that is mediated by knowledge of what we call sensorimotor contingencies."[35] 'Sensorimotor contingencies' refer to the structural invariants between patterns of sensory information (co-determined by the structure of the perceiving body, the sensory organs in particular, and the relevant objective features of the environment) and possible motor actions. The visual perception of a three dimensional object, for example, happens, by their account, only when the sensorimotor contingencies associated with possible visual exploration of the object become known. The visual quality of shape, O'Regan and Noë propose, "is *precisely* the set of all potential distortions that the shape undergoes when it is moved relative to us, or when we move relative to it. Although this is an infinite set, the brain can abstract from this set a series of laws, and it is this set of laws that codes shape."[36] In other words, perception of the object is *mediated* by the knowledge of how the sensory information would (predictably, lawfully) change if or when a particular path of exploratory movement is pursued. Notice that such knowledge does not depend on the actual execution of the exploratory movement; rather, it involves a tacit sense of the structures of 'if/then' co-variants inhering between an open-ended range of possible motor actions and the correlative range of possible changes in sensory information. This, O'Regan and Noë stress, is "a practical, not a propositional form of knowledge."[37] Perception, by this account, is a kind of sensorimotor know-how.

It is important to note that O'Regan and Noë's account of vision is meant to address the problem of visual *experience*. Their theory is intended as a challenge to theories that would explain "the subjective impression of seeing" by appealing to some putatively unique character of visual *representations* (having to do, for example, with the fact that such representations depend on cortical maps wherein information from the retina seems to be organized and stored).[38] Theories concerning the origin of visual representations, or concerning differences in the neural coding of representations, do not provide satisfying answers to questions about what differentiates *experiences*—what it is like to see rather than smell, or what it is like to see the color pink rather than red.[39] For O'Regan and Noë, the crucial fact about vision is that it is a form of *exploratory activity* rather than of *passive receptivity*. According to their proposal, visual experience is differentiated by the unique "*structure of the rules* governing the sensory changes produced by . . . visual explorations."[40] They claim that there are in fact two relevant sets of laws. The first set pertains to the structure of the eye: "These laws are determined by the fact that the exploration is being done with the visual apparatus." For example, because of the spherical shape of the retina, as the eye ranges over a straight black line inscribed on a white page, the projection of the line onto the retina will be more or less curved, like an image in a distorting mirror.[41] The structures of these changes are lawful, and it is the knowledge of just such structural invariants that constitutes the perceptual experience of seeing a line. A second set of laws pertains to visual attributes. For example, visible objects are always seen perspectivally, entailing that certain types of movements are required in order to see different profiles of a three dimensional object, and the perspectival appearance of such objects is affected by variations in ambient and reflected light. To understand the specific character of visual experience, according to O'Regan and Noë, we need to understand how these two sets of laws determine the structures of sensorimotor changes associated with seeing. The two sets of laws cannot be neatly distinguished (laws governing perceived variations in light are obviously also related to the structure of the visual apparatus) but separating them helps us to catalogue the features distinguishing the structures of changes corresponding to visual experience from, say, those corresponding to tactual experience: e.g., the latter are not affected by changes in ambient light.

Let us consider this proposal with respect to the perception of a putatively simple datum: a patch of color. It is not, at first, obvious that perceiver motility would be relevant to our understanding of perception in this case. Indeed, the example of a simple colored patch recommends itself precisely because it seems to involve a pure seeing, where we do not need to *do* anything aside from simply directing our eyes toward the spectacle. But a great deal of research on visual perception has been devoted to observing the effects of small eye movements that occur even when the subject's vision is fixed on a well-defined mark (these include involuntary rapid 'saccadic' movements lasting only about 20 to 30 milliseconds, with an intervening 'saccadic latency period' of about 150 milliseconds).[42] Not only do these movements not interfere with normal perception of a fixed object (and the experience of it *as* fixed), but experiments involving the use of various devices designed to stabilize the retinal image—that is, in such a way as to neutralize the effects of eye movements on visual perception—show that, when images are more or less completely stabilized relative to the moving eye, they appear to the subjects to "fade out."[43] The implication here is that visual perception actually *requires* these small eye movements. O'Regan and Noë contend that this fact is significant for our understanding of color perception.

They note that the retina is nonhomogeneous with respect to its capacity for processing color. There are three classes of photoreceptor cones that permit color discrimination, and the density of these cones decreases significantly in the peripheral area of the retina (drastically affecting color receptivity in peripheral vision). Further, they note that even the central region of the eye is affected by the macular pigment, a yellowish jelly covering the macula that absorbs fifty percent of the light in the short wavelength range. These nonhomogeneities *should* have a drastic effect on color sensitivity. Nevertheless, O'Regan and Noë observe that, in spite of these features of the structure of the eye, our subjective experience of color does not in fact seem to be adversely affected. Now, they concede that it might be possible to explain this surprising fact by appealing to some kind of filling-in mechanism—where, *ex hypothesi*, the brain would have to correct the gaps and discrepancies in its representations by making use of data from other internal representations. In this case we would be able to retain the idea that representations are formed on the basis of sensation, and we would have to add to the picture a further mechanism for correcting errors in the representations. But O'Regan and Noë claim that their model renders such extravagant hypotheses otiose. "Under the present view of what seeing is, the visual experience of a red color patch depends on the *structure of the changes* in sensory input that occur when you move your eyes around relative to the patch, or when you move the patch around relative to yourself."[44] The nonhomogeneities in the structure of the eye would thus in fact *enable* color discrimination because movements of the eye would be able to produce the characteristic changes in the sensory information corresponding to the experience of, say, the color red. The perception of a uniformly colored patch thus relies on the structures of nonhomogeneous information as discerned by a sensorimotor perceptual system.

Thus, according to O'Regan and Noë, the correlation discovered by psychologists and highlighted by Merleau-Ponty between stimuli and motility is constitutive of perception itself. And this is also what Merleau-Ponty maintains:

> Thus, before becoming an objective spectacle, quality is revealed by a type of behaviour which is directed toward it in its essence, and this is why my body has no sooner adopted the attitude of blue than I am vouchsafed a quasi-presence of blue . . . We must be understood as meaning that red, by its texture as followed and adhered to by our gaze, is already the amplification of our motor being. (*PhP*, 211/245)

But as with O'Regan and Noë's account, Merleau-Ponty's idea that perception is an exploratory activity carried out by a sensorimotor subject means that we cannot isolate the perception of the 'simple' datum from the horizonal context within which it confronts a perceiver:

> To see red, is to see red actively in existence. . . . The very quality itself, in its specific texture, is the suggestion of a certain way of existing put to us, and responded to by us, in so far as we have sensory fields . . . [and] the perception of colour, endowed with a definite structure (in the way of surface or area of colour), at a place or distance away either definite or vague, presupposes our opening on to a reality or a world. (*PhP*, 374–5/429)

Sensibility, for Merleau-Ponty, is always already an opening onto a world; the distinction between passive receptivity and the activity of the understanding is thus overcome in Merleau-Ponty's philosophy.

*Spatiality*

Already in considering sensation we have broached the problem of space. That is, we have noticed that colors and textures cannot show themselves otherwise than to a body capable of exploratory *movements*. The structure of the phenomenon of the patch of color includes, among its various meanings, being available for exploration—being in a 'place,' a 'certain distance away.' It is thus because my body is in a certain 'situation' with respect to the perceived that there can be perception at all. This inescapable situatedness of our bodies implies a sense of spatiality that is at odds with our inclination to think of space as a container within which objects are arrayed—each at a certain fixed and measurable distance from all of the others. Rather, our experience of space is first and foremost as the dimensionality of a world in which things are up, or down, above our heads, or on the ground beneath us, to the right, to the left, reachable, or out of reach, in front of us, or behind our backs.

But, in noticing all of this, we must take particular notice of the uniqueness of *depth* as a dimension of space. The things in our environment do not appear to us as simply arrayed alongside each other in a flat two-dimensional plain. The being-alongside-each-other of objects in two-dimensional space seems to subtend our judgment that each thing is numerically distinct; but it is only in appreciating the special character of depth that we can understand how things also appear as somehow enveloped within one world (*PhP*, 265/306–7). This is in fact what we typically mean when we say that things are in space: they appear as having a certain volume, a depth, and they appear as near or far—that is, again, at a certain depth. The world is, for us, a universal milieu in which different objects can appear together, in meaningful relations to each other, because it is a world-in-depth. For Merleau-Ponty, then, depth is what Husserl would have called a phenomenological 'clue' leading us to the consideration of deep philosophical problems. He writes,

> More directly than the other dimensions of space, depth forces us to reject the preconceived notion of the world and rediscover the primordial experience from which it springs: it is, so to speak, the most 'existential' of all dimensions [*de toutes les dimensions, la plus 'existentielle'*], because . . . it is not impressed upon the object itself, it quite clearly belongs to the perspective and not to things. (*PhP*, 256/296)

The problem of depth directly concerns the problem of the 'first-person perspective,' the situatedness of subjectivity. However, as Merleau-Ponty points out, traditional epistemologies overlook this important clue because they presume that depth is not really visible (*PhP*, 254/294). That is to say, the *appearance* of depth is taken to be explicable only as a derivation from a retinal image that would in fact be two-dimensional. On this view, there is no real distinction to be made between the depth 'information' that is available to us when we look through an open door into the visible distance, and the 'information' that is available to us when we look at an image of the same scene in a photograph. (In fact, it is true that we often do not fail to perceive things in depth when they are effectively represented in a two-dimensional image, but we ought not to presuppose for that reason that the perception of the scene viewed through the door is picture-like; rather, it may be that the picture is able to reveal beings in depth only because it is somehow relevantly scene-like.[45]) As Merleau-Ponty puts it, depth, on this account, is "tacitly equated with *breadth seen from the side*" (*PhP*, 255/295).[46] For these traditional epistemologies, then, the problem of depth is assumed to be a matter of accounting for our (or our brain's) ability to produce an *experience* of depth on the basis of two-dimensional information.

In fact, we need not make this assumption; we may assume, as Descartes does, that the information on the basis of which we experience depth is not actually two-dimensional either. It may be that the sensory information is not determined by the structure of a retinal image at all. Whichever of these two hypotheses we choose to adopt, the problem of depth remains essentially the same: it must be explained how it is that we (or our brains) are able to infer three-dimensional space on the basis of non-three-dimensional data. David Morris labels such approaches to the problem of depth as "inferential accounts."[47] This type of approach continues to be reflected in attempts made by researchers in artificial intelligence to model spatial cognition as some form of computational—symbol-processing—system. However, as Morris points out, these attempts have in fact been notoriously unsuccessful:

> In machines that take two-dimensional input as premises for inferences about a three-dimensional world, it turns out that the input radically underdetermines what there is in the world. The machine needs to assume quite an elaborate model of the world. Putting aside the question of where all those assumptions come from (could the machine *learn* them?), and whether we, as opposed to machines, really need an elaborate model of the world to see it in depth, building machines upon assumptions makes them extremely limited and inflexible. Put them in a different sort of environment and they fail. In contrast, our living vision . . . is quite plastic and resilient.[48]

Inferential accounts attempt to understand how a perceiver *would* perceive beings in depth if she had only non-three-dimensional data to begin with; but such models prove inadequate to account for the actual experience of depth.

Inferential accounts remove the living subject from the context of perception—this is why they end up equating depth with breadth seen from the side. In theorizing that depth can somehow be derived from two-dimensional or non-spatial representational data they presume, as Merleau-Ponty says, a god-like standpoint: "for God, who is everywhere, breadth is immediately equivalent to depth" (*PhP*, 255/295–6). As we shall see, the key to understanding the 'plasticity' and 'resilience' of our own perception lies in noticing the fact that it occurs from 'somewhere' rather than from 'everywhere.' But let us continue our consideration of traditional approaches to the problem.

Inferential accounts have traditionally relied on a number of mechanisms to explain how it is that representational data (derived in some form from the retinal image) can come to possess the appropriate 'cues' for triggering a three dimensional spatial representation.[49] These include the so-called oculomotor cues, i.e., information about adjustments of the eye muscles which cause the lens to become more convex in order to maintain a precise focus when a perceived object is close to the perceiver. This mechanism is called 'accommodation.' A second mechanism is 'binocular convergence,' which, as the name suggests, involves movements of the eyes inward toward the nose as objects are moved closer in order to sustain fixation on a single image. Other traditionally recognized cues include the perception of the sizes of objects in relation to visual-angle information; 'aerial perspective,' which relies on moisture or pollutants in the atmosphere to discern the distance of objects; and 'stereopsis,' which involves making use of the disparity between the monocular images of nearby objects when we fixate on objects that are farther away. Of course, it is understood that these cues must all be contributing to the constitution of an experience of a relatively continuous space, so much of the research is dedicated to understanding the rules for the integration of all these different types of information. But it is also generally recognized that not all information is equally relevant, or indeed even relevant at all, for the perception of depth at different distances. Further, it is clear that motion, whether the motion of the perceiver, the object, or both, will affect the relative importance of the different cues. In short, the problem of depth is not solved by cataloguing the possible sources of depth-information, for we would still need an account of how the information is integrated and of how the relevance and relative value of 'cues' are determined under the conditions of actual perception. Psychologists James E. Cutting and Peter M. Vishton write that,

Whereas an understanding of the rules of information integration in visual perception is important, it is surely less interesting than an understanding of the *weights*. That is, what we and everyone else really want to ask are the following questions: which sources of information are most important? When are they important? And Why? How much does relative size contribute to impressions of layout, say, as compared with stereopsis? How important is accommodation compared with aerial perspective? And so forth. These are the questions about *weights* for various sources of information.[50]

Cutting and Vishton understand this research to be aimed at the development of a model for what they call "a situation-sensitive dominance hierarchy of information sources."[51]

The questions that Cutting and Vishton are asking here address a problem that Merleau-Ponty raises with respect to traditional accounts of depth-perception. Merleau-Ponty argues that the information, or 'cues,' available from various sources can only offer a scientific explanation of depth perception for the scientist who begins "by placing them in the context of objective relations which explain them" (*PhP*, 257/297). The scientist takes the 'known' objective spatial relationships as a given and then asks how the brain could, say, 'infer' these relationships on the basis of (often unconsciously registered) cues embedded in the data. But in actually perceiving space, the brain would not have the advantage of this 'knowledge': it could not 'know' what it is aiming at. This is, again, why inferential models instantiated in computers and robots end up producing an underdetermined and inflexible spatial world. I must somehow know myself to be situated in the world in order to make use of any information, or any combination of information. And this sense of my own situatedness is thus a crucial feature of the sense of space. For example, in order for the information from binocular convergence (by which the brain would somehow 'know' that the eyes have moved closer together in fixating the object) to be relevant to the perception of depth, the brain would have to already 'know' that the body is 'situated' in space along with the perceived objects. Only on this basis could the relative weights of the various 'cues' be determined. Merleau-Ponty thus draws a distinction between the spatiality of 'position,' space as a nexus of abstractly calculable 'objective relations,' and the spatiality of 'situation,' the space within which I am situated as a living being capable of moving and touching and grasping (*PhP*, 100/116; 244/282). Cutting and Vishton's requirement for a 'situation-sensitive' hierarchy of information sources makes explicit that the real problem of depth concerns the meaning of 'situation.'[52]

Merleau-Ponty's approach to the problem of depth thus involves a change of starting points. We have already noticed, in our brief consideration of the problem of sensation, that perceptual experience is not built up out of discrete meaningless contents (as is supposed by traditional epistemologies); rather, it initially concerns the significance of sensations with respect to the motor powers of a perceiver. We perceive things as eliciting the movements of our bodies; every putative stimulus is, for us, "potential movement [*mouvement virtuel*]" (*PhP*, 109/126). The hypothesized information sources, or 'cues,' putatively triggering the representation of spatial depth, are reconceived by Merleau-Ponty as 'motives':

> Convergence and apparent size are neither signs nor causes of depth: they are present in the experience of depth in the way that a *motive* [*motif*], even when it is not articulate and separately posited, is present in a decision. . . . The motive is an antecedent which acts only through significance [*sens*], and it must be added that it is the decision which affirms the validity of this significance [*ce sens*] and gives it its force and efficacy. (*PhP*, 258–9/299)[53]

Thus, in order to answer Cutting and Vishton's questions concerning the relative 'weights' of the various 'cues' triggering the experience of space, we need to put the perceiving subject back into her context of 'living significance.' We must think of the relative values of these cues as determined by what we could call, adapting Merleau-Ponty's terms, a 'motivated decision' (a decision that contains, or envelops, its motivation) on the part of a perceiving body. As Merleau-Ponty writes, "Everything throws us back on to the organic relations between subject and space, to that gearing of the subject onto his world which is the origin of space [*à cette prise du sujet sur son monde qui est l'origine de l'espace*]" (*PhP*, 251/291).

J.J. Gibson's ecological psychology is a sort of answer to the demand to attend to the situatedness of a sensorimotor body. One of Gibson's important contributions to the study of perception within psychology is his notion that what we perceive are not first and foremost discrete objects but 'affordances.' The appearance of an affordance is a function of the relations between an organism and its environment.[54] Gibson writes: "The *affordances* of the environment are what it *offers* the animal, what it *provides* or *furnishes*, either for good or ill."[55] To see affordances is simply to see one's environment (that is, in particular, its various surfaces) in terms of what it allows one to do—in seeing the surfaces of one's environment one in fact sees what is edible, what is climb-up-able, what is graspable, what is safely traversable, and so forth. And of course, what constitutes an affordance for, say, a bird is going to depend entirely on the kinds of things that birds do. The geneticist Richard Lewontin nicely captures this idea in reflecting on the meaning of 'environment':

Are the stones and the grass in my garden part of the environment of a bird? The grass is certainly part of the environment of a phoebe that gathers dry grass to make a nest. But the stone around which the grass is growing means nothing to the phoebe. On the other hand, the stone is part of the environment of a thrush that may come along with a garden snail and break the shell of the snail against a stone. Neither the grass nor the stone are part of the environment of a woodpecker that is living in a hole in a tree. That is, bits and pieces of the world outside of these organisms are made relevant to them by their own life activities.[56]

In fact, the phoebe, by Gibson's account, would not ever just see 'bits and pieces of the world'; rather it would see the grass *as* an affordance for nest building. The environment of an animal is a texture of affordances, and its constitution is thus determined by the 'relevance' of its features to some animal or other. The important thing to note here is that, as with O'Regan and Noë, the perception of the environment is accomplished by a moving body and not merely a sense organ: "One sees the environment not with the eyes but with the eyes-in-the-head-on-the-body-resting-on-the-ground."[57]

So how does the ecological approach help us to deal with the problem of depth? Gibson's view is that we should stop talking about the problem of 'depth' as such. That is, we should not understand the problem of spatiality in terms of "abstract depth perception but [in terms of] affordance perception."[58] He invokes, in this connection, a contrast that is similar to Merleau-Ponty's contrast between the spatiality of position and the spatiality of situation. Gibson writes, "Whereas abstract space consists of points, ecological space consists of places—locations or positions."[59] Note that Gibson, unlike Merleau-Ponty, here uses 'position' to designate location with respect to the capabilities of the organism. So Gibson's 'abstract space' is analogous to Merleau-Ponty's 'spatiality of position'; the former's 'ecological space' is analogous to the latter's 'spatiality of situation.'[60] For Gibson, the perceiver initially (that is, directly) 'sees' the correlation between her body (as a self-moving body) and the 'places' in her milieu.[61] So, as with Merleau-Ponty, the problem of depth, for ecological psychology, is not that of how we infer a three-dimensional space from two-dimensional data—with its attendant problem of placing *ourselves* into that inferred spatial grid. In fact, perception *is* the perception of our relations to things in terms of their availability for our actions.

Let us consider this in a little more detail. In order to pick out affordances I must pick out "invariant" structures within the "sequential transformations" of what Gibson calls "the optical array."[62] Unlike the supposed retinal image, then, the optical array is an intrinsically dynamic perceptual field. As with O'Regan and Noë's sensorimotor approach, I see invariant structures because my perception anticipates possibilities attaching to my own powers of self-movement. The optical array is a moving field, but not everything in it moves in the same way. Some movements are produced only by virtue of the movements of my own body. The power of movement that is my own body is also the power of disclosing what is invariant in the environment. The large rock in the fast moving water of the river I am trying to get across appears as a possible foothold precisely by the way in which it, in contrast to the rushing water, directly answers to my power of moving toward it—it is an affordance for stepping. I perceive invariants, as Gibson says, directly—I do not need to infer or construct them. "The moving self and the unmoving world are reciprocal aspects of the same perception."[63] I do not need to possess an internal map with spatial coordinates in order to see things in depth; rather, what I directly perceive are the structural invariants emerging in the dynamic correlation between my powers of moving-toward (or moving-away, or grasping, touching, pushing, stepping, jumping, climbing, etc.) and the affordances available to me. The important thing, again, is to recall that human perceivers are situated in relation to the ground. To perceive affordances is thus to perceive things directly in terms of a spatial 'layout.' Gibson explains that "by layout, I mean the relations of surfaces to the ground and to one another, their arrangement. The layout includes both places and objects, together with other features. The [ecological] theory asserts that the perception of surface layout is direct." This approach thus eliminates the need for the hypothetical cues that would be needed to explain the perception of depth in traditional accounts: "I . . . say that there is information in ambient light for the perception of the layout of surfaces but not that there are cues or clues for the perception of depth."[64] Earlier I said that, according to Gibson, we initially perceive the surfaces of our environment in terms of what those surfaces afford. But this is just to say that, in perceiving those surfaces, we do not *merely* perceive the surfaces: we perceive the reachability of affordances, their graspability and their heft; we perceive the partial occlusion of affordances by other affordances; and we perceive the power of moving, reaching and grasping that is vested in our own bodies.

## III. SITUATED SUBJECTIVITY

Gibson's explanation of depth perception thus relies on a sense of self, on a sense of oneself as situated in the environment. But the claim that the perceiver is situated in the environment by means of self-specifying information made available in perception has recently been challenged by some phenomenologists. It has been argued that this kind of 'co-perception' of the self *presupposes* a fundamental sense of self and does not in fact explain it. We will consider this challenge in some detail in chapter 3, but already in considering the criticisms of traditional approaches to the phenomena of sensation and depth-perception—put forward by Merleau-Ponty as well as by the advocates of the sensorimotor and ecological accounts—we have been able to see a demand that must be met by a theory of situated subjectivity.

This demand can perhaps be clarified by considering Cutting and Vishton's observation that an explanation of depth-perception must do more than simply list the 'cues' that putatively allow us to discern spatial depth on the basis of a retinal image. Rather, according to them, it must explain how perception can generate and employ a 'situation sensitive dominance hierarchy of information sources.' Such a dominance hierarchy would explain how a perceiver actively evaluates sensory 'information.' But the dominance hierarchy must not be merely a static framework or logarithm for processing 'information'; rather it must itself be 'situation sensitive.' In these terms, then, we can say that cognition is situated only insofar as its way of being open to things and situations is also a constitutive openness to the *sense* of situations. Its way of determining its environment must also be a way of being determined. This is what is implied in Merleau-Ponty's claim, in *The Structure of Behavior*, that higher orders of biological and cognitive development do not leave the lower orders intact but rather "give a new signification to the steps which constitute them" (SB, 180/195). Learning about, or adapting to, an environment is not merely a matter of an organism's (or a species') having new facts or information at its disposal; it is also a matter of learning (or, at the species level, evolving) new ways of making sense of that information. (We will consider this problem more directly with respect to learning in chapter 2.) This is also what is entailed by the concepts of motivation and decision that Merleau-Ponty invokes in the context of his analysis of depth perception.

As we have seen, according to Merleau-Ponty, the hypothesis that 'convergence' and 'apparent size' function as 'cues' for the perception of depth is inadequate because, in implying a sort of causal, mechanistic relationship, such a hypothesis cannot account for the plasticity of living perception. Rather, he says, these so-called cues are present in perception in the way that a motive is present in a decision. We have already indicated that the concept of motivation is a fundamental concept in Merleau-Ponty's philosophy, one that he employs repeatedly in *Phenomenology of Perception*. But we should also emphasize the corresponding concept of 'decision.' Merleau-Ponty is speaking of a more fundamental sense of 'decision' than the one we ordinary have in mind. In ordinary usage, the word typically designates an explicit choice made after some kind of conscious deliberation

on motives or reasons. But as Merleau-Ponty writes, in the chapter on freedom in *Phenomenology of Perception*, in the case of deliberative choice, "the
deliberation follows the decision, and it is my secret decision which brings
the motives to light, for it would be difficult to conceive what the force
of a motive might be in the absence of a decision which it confirms or to
which it runs counter" (*PhP*, 435/498). In other words, a deliberative process
considers the relative weights of values that have already been made relevant
by 'secret decisions,' or what Merleau-Ponty also describes as "the tacit
decisions whereby we have marked out [*articulé*] round ourselves the field
of possibility." (*PhP*, 438/500–1). This more fundamental sense of decision,
the 'tacit decision,' is the one that Merleau-Ponty has in mind when he says
that in depth-perception the motives are *present* in the decision—the 'decisions' of our moving bodies *articulate* the perceptual field. What motivates
the tacit decision only appears *in* what it motivates. And what it motivates
is a certain sensorimotor know-how, a *form* of responsive movement. This is
why we are, of course, not explicitly conscious of the 'decisions' we make
concerning our perception of beings in depth. But, again, this does not mean
that the concept of decision is only employed metaphorically here—the
important insight in Merleau-Ponty's thinking about depth is that nothing
external to behavior *causes* the perception of spatial depth. As we shall see
in coming chapters, the 'situation sensitive' character of depth-perception
opens it to developmental and historical variations. In a very important
sense, space is a matter of decision, or, as Merleau-Ponty says in some of
his later works, 'institution.'

   *What* motivates the decision only appears *in* the decision. This exemplifies a phenomenological principle, a fundamental logic of manifestation,
which, according to Merleau-Ponty, is evident in Husserl's philosophy in
the concept of *Fundierung*, or 'foundation.' *Fundierung*, according to Merleau-Ponty, designates a 'two-way relationship' in which:

> the founding term, or originator . . . is primary in the sense that
> the originated is presented as a determinate or explicit form of the
> originator, which prevents the latter from reabsorbing the former
> [*ce qui lui interdit de le résorber jamais*], and yet the originator is not
> primary in the empiricist sense and the originated is not simply
> derived from it [*le fondé n'en est pas simplement dérivé*], since it is
> through the originated that the originator is made manifest. (*PhP*,
> 394/451)

Thus, if perception is to be thought of as dynamic sensorimotor perception,
then what motivates the movements of our bodies is only made manifest
in the movement. Subjective movement, the movement of a living body,
is thus the condition of phenomena.[65] But it functions as such because, so

to speak, it makes *sense*; which means that it appears *as* founded upon a more original relation or orientation—subjective movement manifests itself as a subject's response to, or aim toward, the world (including itself as a being in the world). As Merleau-Ponty says, "We say that events have a meaning when they appear as the achievement or the expression of a single aim" (*PhP*, 428/490). Movement 'anticipates' the world, 'projects toward' it; Merleau-Ponty says that movement refers to things in the sense that it 'haunts' them (*PhP*, 138/161). In fact, as we shall see, subjective movement has a way of not manifesting itself as such, but rather of effacing itself in favor of the world that it makes appear. The very *distinction* between the *subjectivity* of movement and the *world* that subjective movement makes appear is itself made possible by the tacit or secret character of the decisions that are enacted in, or, rather, *as* subjective movement:

> I move external objects with the aid of my body, which takes hold of them in one place and shifts them to another. But my body itself I move directly, I do not find it at one point of objective space and transfer it to another, I have no need to look for it, it is already with me—I do not need to lead it towards the movement's completion, it is in contact with it from the start [*il y touche dès le début*] and propels itself towards that end. The relationships between my decision and my body are, in movement, magic ones. (*PhP*, 94/110)

If subjectivity is what makes a world appear, then it is by interrogating the 'magic' relationships between decision and subjective movement that we will move toward an understanding of subjectivity. By way of anticipating the development of our theme over the course of subsequent chapters, let us point out that this way of approaching the problem of subjectivity means that the identity of the embodied subject is precisely what is questionable. If subjective movement is a decision, in the sense that we have just described, it is not clear that it is the decision *of* a subject, even that of a subject-body understood as a "natural self [*un moi naturel*]" and "the subject of perception" (*PhP*, 206/239). That is to say (by way of setting forth a hypothesis to be defended in subsequent chapters) that the 'decision' of subjective movement is also a decision *of* what motivates it. As Merleau-Ponty writes, for example, about vision, in *Eye and Mind*: "The eye is an instrument that moves itself [*qui se meut lui-même*], a means which invents its own ends; it is *that which* has been moved [*ce qui a été ému*] by some impact of the world." (*EM*, 165/26). The eye is, at once, that which moves itself, and that which has been moved.

If subjective movement reveals the relation between a subject and its world, it is because subjective movement manifests a subject *in* a situation (that is, an embodied subject), but it accomplishes this only by occluding '*itself*' as the subjectivity *of* situations.[66] The sense of movement *as* the meaning of subjectivity will become clearer in the next chapter wherein we consider the phenomenon that Merleau-Ponty understands as fundamental to his critique of traditional metaphysical determinations of the subject: the phenomenon of learning.

TWO

# MAKING SPACE

We have the experience of an *I* not in the sense of an absolute subjectivity, but indivisibly demolished and remade [*défait et refait*] by the course of time.

—Merleau-Ponty

## I. SUBJECTIVITY, SENSATION, AND DEPTH

We concluded chapter 1 by drawing attention to the continuity between Merleau-Ponty's accounts of sensation and spatiality. The claim that sensations are intrinsically spatial is, as we have seen, crucial to Merleau-Ponty's argument against the empiricist notion of atomic sense data:

> Every sensation is spatial; we have adopted this thesis, not because the quality as an object cannot be thought otherwise than in space, but because the primordial contact with being, as the assumption by a sentient subject of a form of existence to which the sensible points, and as the co-existence of sentient and sensible, is itself constitutive of a setting for co-existence, in other words, of a space. (*PhP*, 221/255–6)

Thus, when Merleau-Ponty says that the most basic elements of perception always already appear as "charged with a meaning," we are to understand this intrinsic meaningfulness as having a fundamentally spatial character: the perceived appears as a foreground set off against a certain background (*PhP*, 4/9). As we have seen, the sensible qualities of things are inserted into forms of behavior and it is insofar as behavior (subjective movement) articulates the sense of a spatial surround that it lets the sensible appear as a quality within the meaningful form of a surrounding world.

39

What Merleau-Ponty's phenomenology thus shares with the sensorimotor and ecological accounts of perception (which we examined in chapter
1) is a critique of the traditional concept of 'sensation.' In particular, as
we have seen, all three approaches criticize accounts of space that would
begin by reducing the phenomenon of depth to non-three-dimensional
sense-data on the basis of which depth would then have to be inferred.
For all three approaches, then, depth is an original feature of perceptual
experience because perception begins in behavior (in the movements of
reaching, grasping, traversing, etc.), not in passive receptivity to simple
impressions. The claim that perception begins as behavior entails that the
perceptual world always already has a certain form or structure determined
by our aims and projects. It is insofar as behavior is structured, or, insofar as
it conforms to a structure of sensorimotor invariants, that it lets something
appear. The advocates of the sensorimotor and ecological accounts of perception thus maintain that no raw sensory datum ever appears in perception.
The assertion that perception begins as behavior is thus a claim concerning the priority of form over the contents of experience. On this view, the
traditional concept of 'sensation' betrays an abstract way of thinking about
perception; it arises from a misguided attempt to understand how the *forms*
of the perceived world arise from the *contents* of sensory experience, whereas,
in fact, isolated contents are only ever posited by abstraction from an already
structured perceptual field.

But while Merleau-Ponty shares this critique of sense-data empiricism,
he does not simply deny the legitimacy of the concept of sensation. Instead,
he seeks to uncover the phenomenological grounds of the traditional
distinction between sensation and understanding *within* perceptual
experience. He asks: "how can we distinguish sensible consciousness from
intellectual consciousness?" And he answers:

Every perception takes place in an atmosphere of generality and is
presented to us anonymously. I cannot say that *I* see the blue of the
sky in the sense in which I understand a book or again in which
I decide to devote my life to mathematics. My perception, even
when seen from the inside, expresses a given situation: I can see
blue because I am *sensitive* to colours, wheras personal acts create
a situation: I am a mathematician because I have decided to be
one. So, if I wanted to render precisely the perceptual experience,
I ought to say that *one* perceives in me (*je devrais dire qu'on perçoit
en moi*), and not that I perceive. Every sensation carries within it
the germ of a dream or depersonalization such as we experience in
that quasi-stupor to which we are reduced when we really try to
live at the level of sensation. (*PhP*, 215/249)

Perceptual experience contains *within itself* a stratum of sensation. In other words, we could say that our behavior, as subjective *activity* manifesting a certain perceptual sense (*sens*), also involves a certain *passivity* or dependence which is attested to in our experience. Taken by itself, Merleau-Ponty says, "apart from the probing of my eye or my hand . . . the sensible is nothing but a vague beckoning [*sollicitation vague*]" (*PhP*, 214/248). But this vague beckoning of the sensible has a distinctive mode of appearance within perception. The 'appearance' of the sensible within perceptual experience is a kind of instability of the spatio-temporal form of the perceptual field— it is a residue of non-sense within perceptual sense. Merleau-Ponty says that "a sensible datum which is on the point of being felt sets a kind of muddled problem for my body to solve. I must find the attitude which *will* provide it with the means of becoming determinate, of showing up as blue; I must find the reply to a question which is obscurely expressed" (*PhP*, 214/248). As phenomenologists, we must say that perceptual experience is rooted in the sentience of our bodies not because we assume that perceptual appearance is an effect that must have a cause external to itself, but because perceptual experience has the phenomenal character of being a response to 'a question which is obscurely expressed.' We are open to the possibility of being surprised by the world, open to the possibility that things are not as they initially appear. There is an element of contingency in our perceptual experience which prevents us from asserting the absolute priority of form, or structure, over content. Insofar as we are sensori*motor* subjects, our environment always has a certain spatio-temporal form; but insofar as we are sentient, the stability of this form is always contested from within. Our perceptual surround portends its own possible transformation. Thus, while we want to affirm, with the sensorimotor and ecological accounts, that perception is an activity, a form of active engagement that lets a world appear, we do not want to overlook the way in which perception announces its own dependence or openness to a reality that is neither simply given nor simply produced by a subject.

In this chapter I will argue that Merleau-Ponty's analysis of sensation entails a certain understanding of the temporal structure of our experience. We have seen that Merleau-Ponty shares with the ecological and sensorimotor accounts of perception the thesis that perception is always temporally spread out. According to all three approaches, we perceive an *environment* insofar as we anticipate possibilities for engaging with things in the environment and because we retain, in the perceptual present, the presence of those background features of the environment that we have already encountered. But, according to Merleau-Ponty, we must say that the subject is *sentient* because our present experience also refers to a more original past. He writes, "Between my sensation and myself there stands always the thickness of some *primal acquisition* [*acquis originaire*] which prevents my experience from being clear for itself [*qui empêche mon expérience d'être claire pour elle-même*]" (*PhP*, 216/250—translation slightly modified). Our present experience refers to an original stratum, upon which it depends, and that has no determinate place within the present. In chapter 3, I will argue that the sensorimotor and ecological accounts of perception overlook this original stratum because they assume that the forms of perceptual experience reflect underlying sensorimotor or ecological 'laws' or structures of 'invariants' which, they also assume, reflect physical structures of organic bodies and environmental surfaces. They thus do not directly address the question of the original *emergence* of structure in behavior, and, I will argue, they consequently overlook a central problem concerning situated subjectivity. To grasp the logic of this emergence we must begin from within perceptual experience and see how *it* reveals the history of its own unfolding. In this chapter, then, I want to show that Merleau-Ponty is precisely concerned with the emergence of structure within behaviour, and that his account of sensation is crucial for understanding what he is saying about the character of this emergence. Subjective movement makes sense insofar as it is an activity that is also a certain receptivity. Let me offer a brief outline of this position before we turn to a more detailed interpretation of Merleau-Ponty's text.

The sense (*sens*) of subjective movement, upon which depends the senses of everything perceived, consists, first of all, in its being *oriented* ("as the achievement or the expression of a single aim" [*PhP*, 428/490]). But if sensation is always already spatial (it is always already, as Merleau-Ponty says, "making space" [*PhP*, 221/256]), it is because the 'primordial contact with being' is, in a sense, always already in the past of experience as the solicitation toward a future in which some determinacy can appear. That is to say, movement makes something appear in the present only insofar as it has already begun to respond to the 'vague beckoning' of the sensible, the call for a motor articulation of the space in which some determinate thing or quality might be able to appear. Movement alone lets the perceived appear but this also ensures that the perceived can never appear *immediately*, on its own terms, in the plenitude of sensible presence. The 'contact' of sentient and sensible is only ever manifested in its effects, and thus the sense (meaning, orientation) of movement never quite overcomes a residue of contingency, the contingency of *creative* acts, of those 'tacit decisions whereby we have marked out round ourselves the field of possibility.' If we are going to remain faithful to Merleau-Ponty's express intention to overcome the alternatives of empiricism and intellectualism, then we must say that the sensible, as such, does not appear in the immediate givenness of a punctual sensation *and* that no a priori law determines, once and for all, the structure of the space in which something can appear. As Merleau-Ponty says, "The *a priori* is the fact understood, made explicit, and followed through into all the consequences of its latent logic [*logique tacite*]; the *a posteriori* is the isolated and implicit fact" (*PhP*, 221/256). With regard to the problems of spatiality and sensation, this means that, while the world of perception always has a spatial structure, this spatial structure has the character of being a response to the 'obscure' question, or 'vague beckoning,' of the sensible, and is thus never completely stable.

A constitutive instability of space is, for Merleau-Ponty, a crucial phenomenological feature of depth. There is thus an important connection between what Merleau-Ponty says about sensation and what he says about the character of depth, and this connection will be of particular concern to us in this chapter. In chapter 1 we showed how the phenomenon of space, and, in particular, depth, must be understood in terms of the bodily 'I can,' as the arena of an organism's possibilities for acting: the space of affordances. Thus Merleau-Ponty distinguishes between a spatiality of position, the 'objective' space of geometry and classical physics, and the spatiality of situation— space as it is rooted in the spatiality of one's own situated body. But in an article on the concept of depth, Anthony Steinbock has argued that, in Merleau-Ponty's later writings (especially in the working notes to *The Visible and the Invisible*), it is possible to make a further distinction between two concepts of depth (as a characteristic of the spatiality of situation). In what Steinbock calls the 'mundane sense' of depth, Merleau-Ponty equates depth with horizonality, with the relation of foreground and background, or prominence and latency, in the perceptual field. But, Steinbock contends, "The more profound sense occurs when he uses it *as the condition of there being prominence and latency*, tension-holding non-coincidence."[1] In this chapter I will argue that this sense of depth as 'tension-holding non-coincidence' is already implicit in the analysis of sensation in *Phenomenology of Perception*. The profound sense of depth, the *condition* of there being prominence and latency, is the non-presence, *within* the present, of the event of sensation. This non-presence, like presence itself, is double-sided. If 'presence' is the presence of an object to a self-present subject, then this non-presence is both a non-presence of sentient subjectivity and the non-presence of an objective correlate (a sensible). A pure 'sensation' would be a coinciding of a sentient with a sensible reality; but this coincidence cannot happen in the field of presence whose sensorimotor articulation it motivates. This is because, as we have seen, the sensible only ever appears within the spatial horizon of a sensorimotor subjectivity. We speak of sensation as an immediate contact or coincidence between sentient body and sensible being because the perception (movement) implicitly refers back to this contact as to its originating term. The non-presence of the sensation, then, is not *merely* an absence. It is what Merleau-Ponty, in the later essay "Eye and Mind," calls "a certain constitutive emptiness [*un certain vide constituant*]—an emptiness which . . . upholds the pretended positivity of things" (EM, 184/76). The 'more profound sense' of depth reflects the irremediable haunting of the field of the present by what Merleau-Ponty, at the very end of the "*Sentir*" chapter, calls an "original past, a past which has never been a present [*un passé qui n'a jamais été présent*]" (PhP, 242/280). In this chapter I shall show that this doctrine of an original past is entailed by the claim that sense first emerges in movement itself.

Intellectualism discerns a sense in living movement insofar as it can construe it as an act intended by a subject; empiricism believes it has explained living movement insofar as it can locate its causal basis in reflex, or as a response to a stimulus. But when Merleau-Ponty compares perception (which, as we have seen, is a matter of movement) to a 'decision' which must first of all affirm the value of *its own* motivation, he is insisting that we cannot ground the sense of behavior in anything outside the behavior itself. The movement must itself be the enactment of *its own* sense. But a movement that must be the enactment of *its own* sense cannot be said to *begin* as meaningful—rather, the *sense* of movement must appear as that which cuts across, and unifies, the phases of a whole movement. David Morris illustrates the consequences of this thought:

> In a peculiar way, to become a beginning, the beginning of a movement has to wait for the whole of the movement. When I wander out the front door, my steps are not really the beginning of a walk until I wind up at home after having taken the walk; at a given moment I could decide to dance or go to a café, in which case my initial steps would not have been the beginning of a walk . . . [Similarly] the beginning of a gesture is not really the beginning of a gesture until it unfurls in gestural expression. Even though a movement is a continuous whole, or precisely because it can only be a whole, there is a peculiar *discontinuity* between the moments of movement and the movement as a whole.[2]

This means that for a living movement to *make* sense it must be able to retroactively absorb the facticity of its own beginnings and its own discontinuity into the order of sense that it inaugurates.[3] That which comes to function as the proper motivation for a living movement that would make sense (e.g., an intentional object, a stimulus, a desideratum, a 'thought' that a subject would 'express') is able to do so only insofar as the movement, in inaugurating an order of sense, sublimates the 'non-sense' of its own beginning. Again, this *other* past, the beginning of the movement, cannot itself appear within the order of sense that the movement inaugurates. I will argue that the very non-presence (non-sense) of the 'original past' is a function of this (necessarily) retroactive determination of each of the phases of a movement according to the order of sense that the whole movement announces. The empiricist notion of a punctual 'sensation' is thus not simply a mistake; instead, it reflects the dissimulation of the 'original past' of living movement, a dissimulation that is a function of *Sinngenesis*-in-movement. The absence of the sensation is at once the condition of the present (as the demand for an articulation of the field of presence) *and*, for this reason, is also a persistent element of instability, a 'tension-holding non-coincidence,' *within* the field of presence. Movement, as *sens*, must at once absorb the facticity of its beginnings *and* it must preserve that facticity in order that it might let something *other* than itself appear *as* its proper motivation (the latter may then be understood either as a stimulus or as a telos). If what motivates the movement is to be something other than itself, then movement lets this otherness appear only insofar as movement remains open to its own transformation. Movement makes sense (i.e, orients itself in relation to a ground, a cause, or a destination) insofar as it preserves, within itself, an element of non-sense. Thus movement can be the opening of a *self* to something *other* than the self only to the extent that movement remains open to the possibility of its own transformation.[4]

In the concluding section of this chapter, I will argue that this paradoxical demand, implied by the presence/non-presence of the original past in our experience, is what motivates *learning*. Perception is behavior that generates sense. It generates sense, as we have seen, by announcing, or conforming to, some form of sensorimotor know-how; but in order to do this it must remain responsive to what can never appear in any punctual intuition. So, in order to make sense, it must articulate the meaning of an *immemorial* event, a sentient subject's coincidence with sensible being. Learning is a transformation of behavior that is motivated by the striving of behavior to be an adequate response to what cannot be made to appear within any *present forms* of behavior. Behavior articulates a situation, the situation of a subject within its world. But it can only remain open to a 'reality' beyond itself (a real situation) by remaining open to the contingencies that would motivate its own further transformations. It is thus the task of an account of the subjectivity of situations to explain how a subjective movement can give rise to an identity only by ceaselessly undergoing its own transformation.

I have indicated that there are two senses of depth in *Phenomenology of Perception*: the sense of depth as horizon—as the relation of foreground and background, prominence and latency—and Steinbock's 'more profound' sense of depth. Let us begin by differentiating these more clearly.

*Affordance Depth*

Let us first of all recall the philosophical significance of the problem of depth for Merleau-Ponty. In *Phenomenology of Perception*, he writes, concerning depth:

> It announces a certain indissoluble link between things and myself by which I am placed in front of them, whereas breadth can, at first sight, pass for a relationship between things themselves, in which the perceiving subject is not implied. By discovering the vision of depth, that is to say, of a depth which is not yet objectified and made up of mutually external points, we shall once more outrun the traditional alternatives and elucidate the relation between subject and object. (*PhP*, 256/296)

The 'traditional alternatives' referred to here are of course those of empiricism and 'intellectualism,' each of which, in its own way, equates depth with 'breadth seen from the side.' Because they equate depth with breadth, they persist in conceiving the subject and the object as mutually exterior, whereas Merleau-Ponty wants to show that the phenomenon of depth points to a more original mutual implication of subjectivity and world. For Merleau-Ponty, the irreducibility of depth to breadth means that the phenomenon of space eludes any realist interpretation; it is only explicable with reference to a subject and, in particular, to a subject whose situation has both a spatial and a temporal character, or, rather, a subject that has a spatial structure *because* it is temporal. He writes,

> When I say that I see an object at a distance, I mean that I already hold it, or that I still hold it, it is in the future or in the past as well as being in space. It will perhaps be said that this is so only for me; in itself the lamp which I perceive exists at the same time I do, that distance is between simultaneous objects, and that this simultaneity is contained in the very meaning [*sens*] of perception. No doubt. But co-existence, which in fact defines space, is not alien to time, but is the fact of two phenomena belonging to the same temporal wave. . . . Perception provides me with a 'field of presence' in the broad sense, extending in two dimensions: the here-there dimension and the past-present-future dimension. The second elucidates the first. (*PhP*, 265/306–7)

This determination of space according to the structure of a 'field of presence' is what Steinbock has in mind when he refers to the 'mundane sense' of depth, where depth is thought of in terms of the relation between fore-ground and background. The principle of the unity and structure of the field of presence is 'one's own body' (le corps propre). As Merleau-Ponty says, "The presence and absence of external objects are only variations within a field of primordial presence, a perceptual domain over which my body exercises power [d'un domaine perceptif sur lesquels mon corps a puissance]" (PhP, 92/108). The structural relation of foreground and background is, as we showed in chapter 1, presided over by the body as an 'I can' because the latter's powers of self-motion, its sensorimotor know-how, serve as the original index of near and far.

Our experience of space is unified and obviously extends beyond the field of the immediate present—that is, beyond the domain of what is immediately within our grasp, or within the horizon of our present perception.[5] But the hold that the 'I can' has upon its immediate domain lays down the 'essential structures' in terms of which the world beyond our present field of perception can be anticipated:

In so far as I know that a tree on the horizon remains what it is for closer perception, and retains its real shape and size, it is simply that this horizon is the horizon of my immediate environment [mon entourage immédiat], and that the gradual perceptual possession of the things which it contains is guaranteed to me. In other words, perceptual experiences hang together, are mutually motivating and implicatory; the perception of the world is simply an expansion of my field of presence [la perception du monde n'est qu'une dilation de mon champ de présence] without any outrunning of the latter's essential structures, and the body remains in it but at no time becomes an object in it. (PhP, 304/350–1)

As we saw in considering the sensorimotor approach to cognition, the logic governing the relation of the foreground to the background, or horizon, is that of an implicit understanding, a know-how. As Husserl says, in explaining the meaning of the phenomenological concept of 'horizon,' there is, in the present of consciousness, a foreshadowing or 'predelineation' of the ways in which the indeterminate can be made determinate: "The predelineation itself, to be sure, is at all times imperfect; yet, with its indeterminateness, it has a determinate structure."[6] To the extent that indeterminateness appears in terms of a 'determinate structure,' it is, according to Merleau-Ponty, thanks to the tacit reflexivity of the body; there is a "logic of the world to which my body in its entirety conforms," and thus "we carry with us," in virtue of our embodiment, "the basic structures" according to which beings will show themselves (PhP, 326/377). Thus depth, in this sense, is a function of the spatiality of affordances. It is a spatial dimension that is determined in reference to the *here* of my body. It is thus also a function of self-consciousness; insofar as 'the logic of the world' is something 'we carry with us,' my body 'knows' the world to the exact extent that it 'knows' itself.

Now I want to show that this sense of depth, what we could call 'affordance depth,' presupposes a more radical sense of depth in Merleau-Ponty. There is a sense in which space manifests itself as an arena that is subject to the powers of my body, as the field of my 'I can'; but there is also a sense in which the experience of space includes a sense of the limits of the powers of my body. Indeed we could say that these limits are the sole means by which a world-in-depth is able to show itself. And in terms of the temporal structure of space to which we alluded above (the past-present-future dimension corresponding to the here-there dimension) we could say that this second sense of depth corresponds to the original past, the past that has never been a present.

*Spectral Depth*

The present, which encompasses within itself the futural possibilities for determining the horizonal aspects of our perceptual field, is, of course, not a punctual 'now.' It is not determined by an act that would encompass the spatio-temporal depth of the perceptual field within an immediate present, according to a determinate sense, or, in other words, an *idea*. This is just another way of asserting the difference between the spatiality of situation, or lived space, and the spatiality of positon, or objective space. It is because early modern thinkers like Descartes conflated space as it is lived in experience with the *idea* of space (the spatiality of position) that they mistakenly identified depth with 'breadth seen from the side.' Let us again contrast this intellectualist conception of space with what Merleau-Ponty says:

> This being simultaneously present in experiences which are *nevertheless mutually exclusive* [*qui pourtant s'excluent*], this implication of one in the other, this contraction into one perceptual act of a whole possible process, constitute the originality of depth. It is the dimension in which things or elements of things envelop each other, whereas breadth and height are the dimensions in which they are juxtaposed. (*PhP*, 264–5/306; my italics)

Notice that the descriptions of the phenomenon of depth, in *Phenomenology of Perception*, are pointedly ambiguous. What Merleau-Ponty calls the 'originality of depth' is, *at the same time*, the necessity that it be thought in relation to a subject—that is, in relation to a self-consciousness which 'contracts' the elements of a field into a 'whole possible process'—*and* the necessity that we recognize as irreducible the mutual exclusivity of the elements 'contracted' in the 'perceptual act.' The act must accomplish a unity precisely by not completely accomplishing it.

The sense of incompleteness here cannot simply be the incompleteness of an *actual* consciousness in relation to a horizon of *predelineated* possibilities. That is, it cannot merely be a *possible* determinacy in the Husserlian sense (an indeterminacy with a determinate structure), for precisely to the extent that we subordinate indeterminacy to a determinate structure we cede the ground to intellectualism—in the end we would have to think of depth as actively constituted by a subject whose powers of anticipation would always already have exhausted (in thinking) the possibilities suggested to it by its spatio-temporal surround. We would thus not be far from a (Cartesian) inferential account of depth, and we have already seen that such an account is not adequate to the sense of depth as we live it. We avoid this mistake to the extent that we are able to affirm in our description a constitutive *structural* indeterminacy at the heart of space. This element of structural indeterminacy (which appears as conflict and the mutual exclusion of elements within the field) brought out in Merleau-Ponty's account of depth is the more profound sense of depth indicated by Anthony Steinbock. He writes:

> Depth is a relation of antagonism: it holds things together while ensuring their integrity, their difference, without however resolving the openness and contingency of the antagonistic relationships. Depth allows the emphasis on one thing to be perpetually threatened with eclipse by another, even to portend such eclipsing while it conceals; it is the tension of presence and absence, the strive [sic] of the unity and plurality, the interplay of sameness and otherness, what Merleau-Ponty has called a dynamic identity, an identity-in-difference.[7]

Thus, depth, in this sense, designates that instability in the structure of the horizon that "*announces both its possible disjunction and its possible replacement by another perception*" (*PhP*, 344/396). But just as the stability, or structural determinacy, of the field of presence and its horizons is ensured by the fact that 'my body exercises power' over it, we must say that the subjective correlate of this structural *in*determinacy is a certain powerlessness and disunity of the subject. I want here to observe some of the ways in which this second sense of depth is manifested in forms of experience that are highlighted by Merleau-Ponty. I will note four points at which, in *Phenomenology of Perception*, Merleau-Ponty highlights experiences of what I am calling structural indeterminacy in the spatiality of perception. These are in connection with: 1) dreams, myths, and psychopathology; 2) exhaustion or illness; 3) monocular images; 4) intermodal encroachment, or the momentary tension between sensations in different sensory modes. Notice that in the first three of these cases, Merleau-Ponty invokes the figure of the ghost, indicating a haunting of the spatial field of presence by that which has no proper spatio-temporal location within it.

1) Merleau-Ponty says that dreaming constitutes its own spatiality, which is not that of 'physical space.' It constitutes a kind of 'existential space,' and the things appearing in the dream appear not according to given spatial coordinates but in reference to the "direction [*sens*] of our existence":

> The bird which hovers, falls and becomes a handful of ash, does not hover and fall in physical space; it rises and falls with the existential tide running through it, . . . it is the pulse of my existence, its systole and diastole. The level of this tide at each moment conditions a space peopled with *phantasms* [*un espace des fantasmes*], just as, in waking life, our dealings with the world which is offered to us conditioned a space peopled with realities. (*PhP*, 285/330; my italics)

Merleau-Ponty adds that 'primitive peoples' who live in a world of myth do not venture forth from this 'existential space' and thus do not distinguish between the spatiality of a dream-world and a spatiality of the perceived world. Rather, they dwell in a "mythical space in which directions and positions are determined by the residence in it of great affective entities" (*PhP*, 285/330). Lastly, Merleau-Ponty notes that schizophrenics often report finding themselves in a world characterized not by "geographical space," but by a "landscape space [*l'espace de paysage*]" which, in being cut off from "the common property world," appears to the patient to be "amazing, absurd or unreal" (*PhP*, 287/332). Merleau-Ponty refers to this as a "murky space," a "second space," a "*phantom* [*fantôme*]" (*PhP*, 288/334; my italics).

2) The whole point of the discussion of dreams, myths, and psychopathology is to show that these spectral phenomena are not foreign to the world of ordinary perception. In other words, we may find, in these forms of experience, possibilities of being spatial that are no less rooted in our prereflective encounter with the world than the objective geographical and mathematical space of the scientist. Merleau-Ponty offers a description of an occasion in which our 'normal' experience of space might partially dissolve so as to intimate these other possibilities:

At those times when we allow ourselves simply to be in the world
without actively assuming it, or in cases of illness favouring this
passive attitude, different planes are no longer distinguishable, and
colours are no longer condensed into surface colours, but are diffused
round about objects and become atmospheric colours. For example,
the patient who writes on a sheet of paper has to penetrate a certain
thickness of whiteness with his pen before reaching the paper. This
voluminosity varies with the colour in question, and is, as it were,
the expression of its qualitative essence. There is, then, a depth
which does not yet operate between objects . . . and which is simply
the opening of perception upon some ghost thing [fantôme de chose]
as yet scarcely qualified. (PhP, 266/308; my italics)

Thus, the difference between depth and breadth is fundamental. The
perception of being in depth is not merely the function of a third dimension,
but reflects a constitutive instability of space, a voluminosity which seems
to precede the predicable relations between objects or objective features of
the environment.

3) In the "Sentir" chapter Merleau-Ponty argues, as we have indicated,
that sensations must always already open onto a spatial world. This is because
sensation must be the sensation of something, of specific qualities, and this
can only happen insofar as that which sensation reveals can be put into
some spatial perspective. He then adds:

And, by the same necessity, they must all open on the same
space, otherwise the sensory beings with which they bring us into
communication would exist only for the relevant sense—like ghosts
which appear only in the night [comme les fantômes ne se manifestent
que la nuit]—they would lack fullness of being and we could not
be truly conscious of them, that is to say, posit them as true beings.
(PhP, 217/251; my italics)

We can glimpse this necessity, he says later, by considering the monocular
image, which confronts us, again, with some ghosts: "Monocular images float
vaguely in front of things, having no real place in the world [elles n'avaient
pas de place dans le monde]; then suddenly they fall back towards a certain
location in the world and are swallowed up in it, as ghosts [(comme les
fantômes); my italics], at daybreak, repair to the rift in the earth which let
them forth" (PhP, 233/269).

4) We cannot simply say that the unity of the senses, and the unity
of the space that is apparently manifested by means of their operations,

is vouchsafed by the *fact* that they are functions of the organs of one perceiving body. For this would be to conflate the body as it is lived with the body as an object. Neither can we simply say that the unity is a priori, for to do so would be to deny the element of contingency in perception, a contingency attested to by all of the aforementioned ghosts or phantasms appearing within the range of human experience. As Merleau-Ponty says, "The unity of the senses, which was regarded as an *a priori* truth, is no longer anything but the formal expression of a fundamental contingency" (*PhP*, 221/255). This sense of contingency also arises in the experience of a certain mutual encroachment of sensory modes. Merleau-Ponty describes this kind of encroachment in connection with the 'spatiality' of a concert hall during a musical performance:

> When, in the concert hall, I open my eyes, visible space seems to me cramped compared to that other space through which, a moment ago, the music was being unfolded, and even if I keep my eyes open while the piece is being played, I have the impression that the music is not really contained within this circumscribed and unimpressive space. It brings a new dimension stealing through the visible space, and in this it surges forward, just as, in victims of hallucinations, the clear space of things perceived is mysteriously duplicated by a 'dark space [*espace noir*]' in which other presences are possible. (*PhP*, 222/256–7)

Sensation opens up the spatiality of the perceptual world and at the same time installs itself, as an element of facticity, in our perceptual experience, a facticity that is manifested in the openness of our experience to conflict and instability. Merleau-Ponty says that "the spatial realm of each sense is an unknowable absolute [*un inconnaisable absolu*] for all the others, and to that extent limits their spatiality" (*PhP*, 222/257). The sound of the music is in its own space, one that "besieges, undermines and displaces" the visible space of the concert hall. But, Merleau-Ponty says, the sense of encroachment here does not *just* imply conflict—the very thing that makes their conflict inevitable is also an immanent demand within experience for their resolution into a common space: "The two spaces are distinguishable only against the background of a common world, and can compete with each other only because they both lay claim to a total being. They are united at the very instant in which they clash [*Ils s'unissent dans le moment même où ils s'opposent*]" (*PhP*, 225/260). We should note, however, that though 'they are united at the very instant in which they clash,' Merleau-Ponty's description of the experience in the concert hall is meant to show that the clashing is itself also preserved in the present of experience.

This double-necessity of a clashing among and a unification of the 'spaces' of the different sensory modes, is the very formula for the 'more profound' sense of depth that, according to Steinbock, is made explicit only in Merleau-Ponty's later works. Why do I associate these experiences of structural indeterminacy, all of which concern space in general, with depth in particular? Recall that, for Merleau-Ponty, depth is not simply another spatial dimension alongside height and breadth. What distinguishes depth phenomenologically (as opposed to its determination according to Euclidian geometry), is the fact that, in depth, things are experienced as enveloped in one space. What particularly characterizes the dimensions of height and breadth, by contrast, is that they manifest the being-alongside each other of things, their numerical distinctness. The problem of the *unity* of our spatial world, whose problematic character is demonstrated in each of the examples that we have just considered, is, in a special way, the problem of depth. In each of these cases there is a sense of a tension that underlies and occasionally pokes through into our ordinary experience of a more or less coherent and continuous space. It is not by chance that, in these examples, Merleau-Ponty repeatedly speaks of 'ghosts' and 'phantoms.' There is a sense in which depth designates a dimension in which space, in its very structure, is 'haunted' by other possibilities for being spatial, by a 'dark' space, a phantom space. For this reason I will use the term *spectral depth* to designate what Steinbock rightly calls the more profound sense of depth. In doing so I want to make clear that this does not designate another (a fourth) dimension. But it is necessary to distinguish terminologically between the 'profound' sense of depth—which I take to be related to what David Morris has called the "lability" of depth—and the other important phenomenological sense of depth, the horizonal field of an 'I can.'[8] That field is, as we have said, unified by the 'power' of the body with its accretions of skills and habits, and these constitute, for us, the first and fundamental reliable index of near and far, of the voluminousness of things and places. But, as I indicated earlier, I want to argue that the lability of depth points to a certain constitutive *disability* of the 'I can'—to an 'I cannot' that expresses a dependence of the subject, a constitutive openness to its own transformation.[9] I call this a *constitutive* disability because it is not *merely* a negation, something *opposed* to consciousness (as the tacit reflexivity of the 'I can'), but a condition of the space in which one can be 'able.' The spatio-temporal determination of the field of presence, the arena of the 'I can,' is a matter of a 'decision' (in the sense of the 'tacit' or 'secret' decision that we discussed in chapter 1), but this decision also preserves a sense of its own contingency, and thus the spatio-temporal present remains labile. This constitutive disability of the 'I can' is entailed by the argument of the "*Sentir*" chapter as well as by the phenomenon of learning with which Merleau-Ponty confronts empiricism and intellectualism.[10] But before we turn to these, I want to highlight a particular theme from the chapter on space that will help us to appreciate the sense of the lability of space in Merleau-Ponty's phenomenology.

## Spatial 'Levels'

Merleau-Ponty comments on an experiment conducted by Max Wertheimer, in which, by means of a mirror, a subject is made to see a room in which he is situated at a 45° angle to the vertical. Merleau-Ponty reports the subject's impressions:

> A man walking about in it seems to lean to one side as he goes. A piece of cardboard falling down the door-frame looks to be falling obliquely. The general effect is 'queer.' After a few minutes a sudden change occurs: the walls, the man walking about the room, and the line in which the cardboard falls become vertical. (*PhP*, 248/287)

Merleau-Ponty interprets these results as follows:

> Let us say that perception before the experiment recognizes a certain *spatial level* [*niveau spatial*], in relation to which the spectacle provided in the experiment first of all appears oblique, and that during the experiment this spectacle induces another level in relation to which the whole of the visual field can once more seem straight. (*PhP*, 248–9/287)

This possible transformation of space, the emergence, from within one level, of another level, points to the fact that the body is not *in* space in the manner of an object. Rather, the body is spatial because it is constitutively situated in relation to a milieu of vital significance—"My body is wherever there is something to be done" (*PhP*, 250/289). But it is situated in such a manner that the field can induce structural changes in the body's spatiality. (The body's spatiality *is* a spatiality of 'situation.') That is, the body can encounter, in its environment, motivations to transform its very manner of determining its spatiality and that of its surround. In the case under consideration, this is clearly not a simple adjustment. It must involve a profound transformation of the way the body 'interprets' the sensorimotor 'information' pertaining to the distribution of its own weight, its powers of movement, the data of visual sensation, and so forth. And because the body 'interprets' its spatial orientation in relation to all of these other 'interpretations,' we must say that the body has undergone a radical transformation in the process of 'adjusting' to the transformation of its visible field.[11]

But we need to be careful here with the manner in which we interpret this transformation. We can neither interpret Wertheimer's experiment as the provocation by artifice of a subjective illusion—where the subject's adjustment would be understood to have been made against the background of an absolute space, a *normal*, or correct, orientation to which the subject subsequently returns—nor as an indication of a complete malleability of the spatiality of situations. The body seeks *an* orientation, a level. In this connection, Merleau-Ponty makes use of the different meanings of the French word *sens*: as we have seen, it can be translated as 'sense,' 'significance,' 'meaning,' or 'direction.' A situation makes sense insofar as it establishes an orientation—"we cannot dissociate being from oriented being" (*PhP*, 253/293). We also said, in chapter 1, that the movements of our bodies make sense insofar as they manifest themselves in relation to some determinacy. That is, the sense of movement emerges as it articulates, across its discontinuous phases, some kind of relation to a motivation; this relation necessarily involves some kind of direction or spatial orientation—in short, a level. Thus each new crystallization of bodily spatiality, each new spatial level, occurs *as* a *re*constitution against the background of a given space. As Merleau-Ponty writes:

> The primordial level is on the horizon of all of our perceptions, but it is a horizon which cannot in principle ever be reached and thematized in our express perception. Each of the levels in which we successively live makes its appearance when we cast anchor in some 'setting' which is offered to us. This setting itself is spatially particularized [*spatialement défini*] only for a previous given level. Thus each of the whole succession of our experiences, including the first, passes on an already acquired spatiality. The condition of our first perception's being spatial is that it should have referred to some orientation which preceded it. (*PhP*, 254/293)

To be a subject of experience is to be embodied in a spatial situation, and the space in which the subject finds herself situated is always 'older' than the present of experience. That is to say, the subject's situation is always spatial because it is, on the one hand, always open to transformations from within and, on the other hand, always experienced as something *given*.[12]

*Time, Space, and Sensation*

The concept of spatial levels manifests a tension that will be of concern to us in chapter 3 and especially in chapter 4. This tension concerns the relations of continuity and discontinuity between the various spatial levels as well as between the spatial domains of the senses. Let us highlight the two poles of this tension here. 1) Merleau-Ponty says that a 'primordial level is on the horizon of all of our perceptions.' Horizon, as we have said, is understood as the background of the field of presence—what is *in* the background is indeterminate, but its possible determinations are anticipated by the *form* of presence, by the 'essential structures' of the field of presence, the know-how of the 'I can.' The field of presence is not merely a 'now,' but includes what is immediately anticipated, and immediately retained, throughout our explorations and practical engagements in the present. This temporal thickness of the present would entail that no determination of the 'field of presence' is radically discontinuous in relation to a previous determination—rather, our past is woven together with our present by the continuous overlapping of retentions of retentions (to use the terms that Merleau-Ponty borrows from Husserl). Similarly, our futural possibilities are 'predelineated' in terms of the 'essential structures' of the field of presence. The time of our experience, so to speak, is always present. Thus when Merleau-Ponty raises the concern, in the chapter on space, that his analyses of the various forms of what we have called 'spectral depth' might imply a radical *dis*continuity between diverse cultural-anthropological and psychological determinations of space, he responds to the concern by affirming a "natural and non-human space" as the common background to all of these possible determinations (*PhP*, 293/339). And this 'natural' basis motivates what he (following Husserl) calls a "teleology of consciousness." That is, rather than an 'objective' space *external* to consciousness, this 'natural and non-human space,' which *is* only insofar as it is always implicitly in the background of our conscious life, acts as the motivation toward a 'true' universal determination of objects and the totality of objective realities, but one that is in principle never reachable. He writes:

> Natural and primordial space is not geometrical space, nor, correspondingly, is the unity of experience guaranteed by any universal thinker arraying its contents before me and ensuring that I possess complete knowledge of, and exercise complete power over it. It is merely foreshadowed by the horizons of possible objectification [*Elle n'est qu'indiquée par les horizons d'objectivication possible*], and it frees me from every particular setting only because it ties me to the world of nature or the *in-itself*, which includes all of them. We must contrive to understand how, at a stroke, existence projects around itself worlds which hide objectivity from me [*qui me masquent l'objectivité*], at the same time fastening upon it as the aim of the teleology of consciousness [*et l'assigne comme but à la téléologie de la conscience*], by picking out these 'worlds' against the background of one single natural world. (*PhP*, 294/340)

Again, this teleology is not an aiming-toward an objective realm that would exist outside of consciousness. Rather, it is the claim that experience, *under the form of a flowing unity of consciousness*, anticipates a 'true' determination of the world just insofar as consciousness is the anticipation of itself; consciousness anticipates the world according to its own demand for coherence and integration. Thus consciousness, by definition, is never wholly given over to radical discontinuity and absurdity: "A truth seen against the background of absurdity, and an absurdity *which the teleology of consciousness presumes to be able to convert into truth*, such is the primary phenomenon [*phénomène originaire*]" (*PhP*, 296/342; my italics). The 'primordial level' that is on the horizon of all our perceptions, both as the conscious subject's natural, bodily, situation, and, correlatively, as the formal unity of a telos, is the objective correlate of a consciousness insofar as the latter is essentially characterized by a presumptive unity.

2) There is a discontinuity between the spatiality (or spatialities) of the primordial level(s) and consciousness as the 'field of presence,' and this discontinuity is what 'appears' as a threat of instability within the field of presence—as spectral depth, rather than merely the 'depth' of a background in relation to a foreground. It will take some time to explain what I mean here, and to develop the implications of this claim. We will need to consider what Merleau-Ponty says about spatial levels, and the spatiality of one's own body, in light of what he says about, on the one hand, the idea of a teleology of consciousness (stressing the continuity of experience) and, on the other hand, the idea of a past that has never been a present (stressing an irremediable discontinuity). Merleau-Ponty says that each of our experiences, 'including the first,' passes on an *already acquired* spatiality. John Russon has thus written of an "originary passivity" that is the condition of our being spatial, and that, further (because even the first of our experiences necessarily passes on an already acquired spatiality), is also at the same time a condition of our self-consciousness. He writes:

> What Merleau-Ponty's analysis of bodily spatiality demonstrates . . . is that action cannot be primary: our activity is necessarily rooted in a certain givenness, a certain passivity, a certain spatiality. Acting in general is a capacity *given* us by (as) our bodies: any specific actions we engage in—anything we "do"—draws upon this mysterious givenness of the specificities of this power, and thus all our activity is subtended by an original passivity.[13]

This 'originary passivity' is the condition of our being self-conscious *as* embodied subjects; the spatial form of our self-consciousness is originally determined as a sense of the *givenness* of one's own body. Merleau-Ponty writes:

My first perception and my first hold upon the world must appear to me as action in accordance with an earlier agreement reached between $x$ and the world in general, my history must be the continuation of a prehistory and must utilize the latter's acquired results. My personal existence must be the resumption of a prepersonal tradition [*la reprise d'une tradition prépersonelle*]. There is therefore another subject beneath me, for whom the world exists before I am here, and who marks out my place in it. . . . . Space and perception generally represent, at the core of the subject, the fact of his birth, the perpetual contribution of his bodily being, a communication with the world more ancient than thought [*une communication avec le monde plus vielle que la pensée*]. (*PhP*, 254/293–4)

This is why Merleau-Ponty says: "I never live in varieties of human space, but am always rooted in a natural and non-human space" (*PhP*, 293/339). This claim, as we have just seen, might appear to lend support to the thesis of a 'teleology of consciousness' insofar as the life of consciousness is characterized by a striving toward integration and self-grounding. The argument for this teleology appears to be premised on the determination of the embodied subject as a 'consciousness.'

Renaud Barbaras has suggested that the thesis of a teleology of consciousness thus betrays a certain limitation in Merleau-Ponty's critique of traditional metaphysical determinations of the subject.[14] The modern epistemologies that Merleau-Ponty criticizes have begun by assuming the existence of an objective nature and then have sought to find out how objectivity is constituted for a subjective consciousness. Merleau-Ponty's analyses of embodied perception have certainly led him to identify a more fundamental stratum of experience than the one thus assumed to be fundamental in such approaches, a stratum in which subjectivity and the world are constitutively intertwined and mutually dependent. But, according to Barbaras' interpretation, Merleau-Ponty retains the idea of a teleology of consciousness because he does not fully overcome the opposition between consciousness and a mute, objective, nature. If objectivity is, as Merleau-Ponty has shown, derivative of a more original stratum of perceived being, then Merleau-Ponty would have to show how teleology emerges on the basis of this more original stratum. By simply asserting the thesis of a teleology of consciousness, Merleau-Ponty seems to reinstate a fundamental opposition between consciousness and the world and to subordinate the being of the phenomenon to the subjective conditions of possible appearance. We would thus fall back into a mode of inquiry according to which perception is analyzed from the point of view of a consciousness's demand for objective knowledge rather than beginning from a description of the being of the phenomenon. It is difficult to evaluate the merits of this interpretation because Merleau-Ponty simply does not say enough, in *Phenomenology of Perception*, about this notion of a teleology of consciousness. Nevertheless, I would like to consider for a moment the plausibility of such a criticism because it will help us to bring out what I have described as a tension in Merleau-Ponty's thinking about the body and space, a tension between the themes of continuity and discontinuity.

If the thesis of a teleology of consciousness indicates that Merleau-Ponty's phenomenology remains in the orbit of a 'philosophy of consciousness,' then we might interpret that thesis as follows: the body is unified as *the* body of a subject whose essential nature (as a consciousness) requires that it strive to make *explicit* the grounds of the unity that it has always already *implicitly* presupposed—its 'primordial,' 'natural' basis. Merleau-Ponty's statement of the thesis of an original, unified, 'natural' space would also thus *presuppose* a 'teleology *of consciousness.*' To ground the unity of 'eyes, hands and ears, which [*qua* sensing] are so many natural selves,' the body, according to this interpretation, must be unified according to the regulative demands of the consciousness of a telos. The body would be reduced to the status of being the *means* by which a consciousness makes sense of itself in making sense of its world. And there are indeed passages wherein Merleau-Ponty speaks of the body in this way. Here are two examples: "I am conscious of the world through the medium of my body [*par le moyen de mon corps*]" (*PhP*, 82/97); "Consciousness is being-towards-the-thing through the intermediary of the body [*par l'intermédiaire du corps*]" (*PhP*, 138–9/161). If the body were not unified according to the demands of a teleology of consciousness then 'the perpetual contribution of [one's] bodily being' (i.e., the contribution of the many 'natural selves') would be a perpetual threat to the unity of conscious experience. Merleau-Ponty introduces the thesis of a 'teleology of consciousness' at the end of the chapter on space, in order to exorcise the phantoms discussed in the chapters on space and sensation, but in doing so, he perhaps elides the more profound (ontological) questions provoked by the insistent presence of these ghosts. These questions concern the *emergence* of consciousness (as, in its most basic form, the mysterious "communion" [*PhP*, 212/246] effected within, or, rather, effected *as* the sentient body), the very emergence of a sense (*sens*) of situations. The thesis of a teleology of consciousness occludes the ontological dimensions implied by these questions insofar as it too hastily dispatches the profound threat of instability and disunity haunting the present, not merely as a negativity, but as a 'constitutive emptiness' at the heart of the present. Let us consider the implications of this interpretation of the thesis of teleology in light of the thesis of the spatiality, or spatialities, of sensation and the problem of the unity of these incompossible 'spaces.'

Sensation, the 'primordial contact with being,' is already a becoming-spatial, or, to be more precise, each sensation is a certain 'making' of space:

> It would be contradictory to assert that the sense of touch is devoid of spatiality, and that it is *a priori* impossible to touch without touching in space, since our experience is the experience of a world. But this insertion of the tactile perspective into a universal being *does not represent any necessity external to touch*, it comes about spontaneously in *the experience of* touching itself, in accordance with its own distinctive mode [*selon son mode propre*]. Sensation *as it is brought to use by experience* is no longer some inert substance or abstract moment, but one of *our* surfaces of contact with being, *a structure of consciousness*, and in place of one single space, as the universal condition of all qualities, we have with each one of the latter, a *particular manner* of being in space and, in a sense, making space [*et en quelque sorte de faire de l'espace*]. (*PhP*, 221/256; my italics)

Recall that, according to Merleau-Ponty, "the spatial realm of each sense is an unknowable absolute for all the others" (*PhP*, 223/257). What would, nevertheless, subtend the (seemingly impossible) unity of all of these *singularities*, what would allow them to function, rather, as '*particular* manners of being in space,' is here said to be, on the one hand, 'not any necessity external to' each sense, but, on the other hand, their availability for being 'brought to use by experience,' i.e., by a consciousness. Without presupposing either the unity of a 'consciousness' or the physiological unity of a body, it is not obvious, on any a priori grounds, that the 'universal being' into which the 'tactile perspective' inserts itself should be the 'universal' of a unified bodily space. But in construing the body as an *intermediary* between consciousness and its world, the threat of radical disunity is overcome before it can take hold.

Two other threats would also appear to be mitigated by this thesis of a teleology of consciousness, in addition to the problem of the unity of the body and its various 'surfaces of contact with being.' 1) It would mitigate the threat of radical *temporal* discontinuity, which is also the threat of death:

> I am no more aware of being the true subject of sensation than of my birth or my death. Neither my birth nor my death can appear to me as experiences of my own, since, if I thought of them thus, I should be assuming myself to be pre-existent to, or outliving, myself, in order to experience them, and I should therefore not genuinely be thinking of my birth or my death . . . Each sensation,

being strictly speaking, the first, last and only one of its kind, is a birth and a death [*Chaque sensation, étant à la rigueur la première, la dernière et la seule de son espèce, est une naissance et une mort*]. The subject who experiences it begins and ends with it, as he can neither precede nor survive himself, sensation necessarily appears to itself in a setting of generality, its origin is anterior to myself [*elle vient d'en deçà de moi-même*]. (*PhP*, 215–6/249–50)

At the level of sensory experience, my "eyes, hands, and ears," are "so many natural selves," and their very plurality is a presentiment of my radical contingency, my birth and my death (*PhP*, 216/250). But 'consciousness,' as teleology, would already be a relation to itself; the body would be animated by a higher 'life' carrying the subject of perception beyond each of these births and deaths of the subject(s) of sensation. 2) The thesis of teleology thus also mitigates the threat posed by intersubjectivity. Let us cite the words immediately preceding Merleau-Ponty's remark about each sense having its own 'spatial realm': "*Like the perspective of other people making its impact on the world for me*, the spatial realm of each sense is an unknowable absolute for all the others" (*PhP*, 223/257; my italics). It turns out, however, that the very 'generality' and 'anonymity' of sense experience also attests to my already having overcome the threat to the unity of my experience implied by the possibility of other perspectives. If the plurality of (the) body, qua sentient, is able to be, at once, preserved and subordinated to the demands of a teleology of consciousness, then difference poses no threat to the unity of experience. In reflection, we find within ourselves, "along with the perceiving subject, a pre-personal subject *given to itself*" (*PhP*, 352–3/405; my italics). This means that the pre-personal subject (the subject of sensation) is already a consciousness-of-itself, and thus the plurality of 'natural selves' is already overcome by the formal unity of a teleology. Merleau-Ponty writes,

> In reality, the other is not shut up inside my perspective of the world, because this perspective itself has no definite limits, because it slips spontaneously into the other's, and because both are brought together in the one single world in which we all participate as anonymous subjects of perception [*sujets anonymes de la perception*]. (*PhP*, 353/406)

Consciousness, as the regulative structure subtending the unity of the sentient body, a unity which the body thus, in turn, bequeaths to consciousness in the form of a unified 'natural' or 'primordial' spatiality, would also make it possible for me to incorporate other perspectives into my own. Thus the doctrine of a teleology of consciousness would appear to signify a return of the modern epistemological subject and a somewhat dogmatic preference for continuity over discontinuity in Merleau-Ponty's philosophy.

Now, over the rest of this chapter I will argue that regardless of the validity or invalidity of the interpretation of the thesis of the teleology of consciousness that we have just considered, it is in fact not supported by the more general sense of the analyses of *Phenomenology of Perception* (and I will merely suggest here, because I mean to discuss it more directly in chapter 5, that this is why Merleau-Ponty subsequently devotes some effort to clarifying the status of the concept of 'consciousness' in his philosophy). This is *not* to say that Merleau-Ponty ends up rejecting the idea of teleology as such, but rather teleology comes to manifest an ontological dynamic that is, as it were, older than consciousness. We could say that Merleau-Ponty comes to see that consciousness is teleological, not because of its self-presence *per se*, but because its self-presence is also a relation to a certain non-presence (a 'non-presence' whose teleological implications can only be clarified as Merleau-Ponty further develops his thinking on the topics of intersubjectivity, expression, and language, matters that we shall address in chapters 4 and 5).

As we have noted, at the end of the "*Sentir*" chapter, Merleau-Ponty says that reflective consciousness, the consciousness that explicitly posits itself, "does not itself grasp its full significance unless it refers to the unreflective fund of experience which it presupposes, upon which it draws, and which constitutes for it a kind of original past [*un passé originel*], a past which has never been a present [*un passé qui n'a jamais été présent*]" (*PhP*, 242/280). This passage has provoked considerable discussion and debate among scholars of Merleau-Ponty. The passage *either* expresses the relation between sensation (with its anonymity and its multiple spatialities) and conscious experience (as *tacitly* or *explicitly* self-conscious) *or* it expresses the relation between an already unified, *tacitly* self-conscious, body, and an *explicitly* self-conscious subject. That is to say, there are (at least) two ways that we could interpret the passage. On the one hand, we could identify the 'unreflective fund of experience' with 'prereflective *consciousness*' and thereby conclude that the 'past which has never been a present' is simply a present (a *tacit* consciousness), or a past present, that has never been *explicitly* reflected upon. With this interpretation, we could affirm the teleology of consciousness (which is, again, grounded in the putative unity of the 'primordial,' bodily space, to which it always refers back) and conclude that explicit consciousness inherits a primordial spatiality, an original, unified, field of presence, but one that (for the explicit consciousness) has never been a present. On this interpretation, the original past is the prereflective past of consciousness, having its roots in the tacit reflexivity of the lived body.[15] Support for this reading could be found in Merleau-Ponty's oft-repeated acknowledgement that the act of reflection involves *a change in the structure of consciousness*, which entails that prereflective presence (consciousness) differs from reflective presence.[16] On the other hand, we could take the final phrase in the passage more literally, as referring to a past which has *never been* a present, as in, it has never been *any form* of consciousness or presence *to* a consciousness, tacit or explicit. After all, however general or anonymous our prereflective *experience* might be, Merleau-Ponty does not countenance the idea of a *consciousness* (in any form) that would not also be a *presence*.[17]

Leonard Lawlor has argued for the latter of these two interpretations. Or, rather, Lawlor has argued that, rather than interpret this originary past on the basis of the unreflective, we must "interpret the unreflective on the basis of the originary past."[18] He offers four textual arguments for this reading, three of which I will mention here. The first is based on a reading of the theme of the "trace" in the chapter on temporality. There Merleau-Ponty explains that, for example, our ability to recognize a carving on a wooden table as a trace of a past experience presupposes a *sense* of the past. Lawlor writes,

> The sense of the past, for Merleau-Ponty, is what allows us to differentiate between a present which is the present and a present which refers to the past. Since what Merleau-Ponty is calling the sense of the past establishes the difference between the present and the past, it cannot be dependent on the present or on perception.[19]

Second, also in the temporality chapter, Merleau-Ponty reproaches Bergson for holding the position (which it turns out, as Lawlor argues, the latter himself argues *against* in *Matter and Memory*) that duration "snowballs on itself" and that memories accumulate in the unconscious. According to Merleau-Ponty, Bergson thereby, "makes time out of the preserved present, evolution out of the evolved."[20] The position that Merleau-Ponty thus attributes to Bergson, and that he himself rejects, is "one that conceives the past as something caused by and dependent upon the present."[21] The position that Lawlor attributes to Merleau-Ponty (and to Bergson) is, on the contrary, formulated as follows: "Being caused by a present but not dependent upon it, this type of past ['a past which has never been a present'] amounts to a repetition without original."[22] It is not only the case that this past is not dependent on the present, but rather that the present is dependent upon this past. Third, Merleau-Ponty, in speaking of the 'past which has never been a present,' also uses the term "original past" (*un passé originel*). Lawlor writes,

> If it is the case that 'to be fully present to prereflective consciousness' means to be dependent on prereflective consciousness's present,

then it is impossible to explain why Merleau-Ponty would use the adjective "originel" to modify the word "passé." If the past is dependent on the prereflective consciousness's present, then it is derivative from that present and is not itself original, is not itself a sort of "origin."[23]

Let me add to these a fourth argument of my own for this reading. In the chapter entitled, "The Body as Object and Mechanistic Psychology," Merleau-Ponty says that time is able to re-integrate into personal existence "even that past of all pasts which the stereotyped patterns of our organic behaviour seem to suggest as being at the origin of our volitional being [à l'origine de notre être volontaire]" (PhP, 84–5/100). With the words, 'seem to suggest,' Merleau-Ponty says that our relation to the 'origin of our volitional being' is a relation *in* the present, but one that, far from being dependent on the present, is, like the 'traces' carved in the table, a presence that depends on a *sense* of the past. Clearly we have here another reference to embodiment as an 'originary passivity,' a givenness of spatiality on the basis of which we are alone able to be, for ourselves, an 'I can.' Merleau-Ponty continues:

> In this context even reflexes have a meaning, and each individual's style is still visible in them, just as the beating of the heart is felt as far away as the body's periphery. But this power naturally belongs to all presents, the old no less than the new. Even if we claim to have a better understanding of our past than it had of itself, it can always reject our present judgment and shut itself up in its own autonomous self-evidence. *It necessarily does so in so far as I conceive it as a former present [un ancien présent].* (PhP, 85/100; my italics)

The past shuts itself up in its autonomous self-evidence insofar as, in thematizing it, we fail to attend to the *sense* of the past. The specific past of our bodies is not merely reducible to a set of biological or anthropological facts; it is, first of all, a certain dependency, an originary passivity, that haunts the present of the 'I can.' The point that I have been particularly concerned to stress in this chapter concerns the way in which self-consciousness is accomplished as a certain spatio-temporal field that is held open to its own possible transformations. As embodied selves, we arrive at self-consciousness only on the basis of an originary passivity; we find ourselves in a present that is haunted by a past that does not fit into its order, a past that is not a 'former present.' This means, again, that this past cannot be determined according to the 'essential structures' of the 'field of presence,' the field of the 'I can.' This past, the original past, is a certain fecundity, generativity, or open-endedness, but for this very reason it is also a certain (paradoxical) sense of powerlessness of the subject *within* the field of presence.[24]

## The Depth of the Past

As we have seen, in addition to speaking of an 'original past,' Merleau-Ponty also speaks of depth as 'original.' And we have also seen that the field of presence is both a temporal and a spatial field, and that, for Merleau-Ponty, our situatedness has a spatial articulation *because* it is temporal. Now I would like to suggest that 'original' depth, or what I have been calling 'spectral depth,' is the spatiality corresponding to the temporal category of the 'original past.' In fact, in his later essay "Eye and Mind," Merleau-Ponty himself seems to combine these with his notion of "immemorial depth of the visible [*au fond immémorial du visible*]" (*EM*, 188/86). Spectral depth is precisely a core of un-presentability (a phantom) within the field of presence. This is the residue of non-meaning (*non-sens*) that is left over when the past is determined according to the order of sense inaugurated (as all orders of sense ultimately are) by a movement—i.e., as a 'motivation.' A motivation appears (if at all) only as enveloped by a decision (a 'tacit decision' concerning a certain determination of presence, a field of possibilities and motivations). Spectral depth, then, characterizes the spatiality of the field of presence insofar as the motivation necessarily appears, in a movement that articulates space, as a 'repetition *without original*,' as reliant on a ground that does not appear.[25] It is the presence/non-presence of an *Abgrund* within any 'tacit decision' concerning the relation of living movement to its *Grund*. Spectral depth is thus at once an openness of the present to an infinity of other determinations *and* an irrecusable demand for *some* structuration of the field in order that some determinate being might be able to 'appear'—it is, in this sense, precisely a demand for a decision. But this spectrality means that the present cannot quite be a '*determinate* structure' in the terms of which one would be able (as an 'I can') to anticipate further possibilities. Thus the necessity that any motivation only appear *within* a decision—which entails a discontinuity between consciousness as presence and the original past—means that we never *experience* the primordial contact with being as such. The primordial contact is precisely what cannot appear in any present determination of presence except as a phantom. This non-presence is manifested as a resistance from within the field to the enclosure of its own 'horizon.'

The whole discussion concerning the incompossibility of the spatialities of the various senses could be read in the light of this notion of an originary past. Explicit consciousness would not inherit, from its prereflectively self-conscious body, an already unified space; rather consciousness could be understood in terms of a more originary ontological dynamic. This would be the process of the enactment of the unity of the body and of the incompossible 'spaces' of the senses—an enactment that would always demand new enactments. The incompossibility of these spaces, the fact that each is a kind of 'unknowable absolute for all the others,' is a problem that consciousness, as presence, takes itself to have already overcome; but as an *original* past, as spectral depth, this problem is also never overcome. Consciousness is the field of presence in which a 'repetition without original' can appear as a kind of origin; but the very absence of the sensation (which is not a pure absence, but, again, a certain haunting of the field of presence) is precisely what allows for (and requires) the "communion" of a living body, and this then would be the condition of the emergence of a consciousness.[26] What is called consciousness could thus be understood as something like a patterned response (the very possibility of repetition announced in a 'repetition without original') to an original 'trauma.'[27] Thus, the decision(s) that determine(s) the present (as consciousness) could not be understood as the decision(s) *of* an already self-identical subject (even of a prereflective body). The *I* would, rather, be enacted on the basis of local 'decisions' (taking place 'on the periphery of my being') concerning the senses of sensations, the senses of incompossible spaces, and thus, the senses of situations. The *I* would not be the identical subject of a primordial contact with being, but the result of a certain original *breaking with* being, a distantiation, an opening-up of depths, of the spatiality of 'one's own body.' The reference of each spatial level (of each determination of the 'field of presence') back to an original space would subtend the unity of consciousness, but the *discontinuity, within* the present, *between* the present and 'primordial,' 'natural,' space would also be the mark of an original disunity (of the self)—its birth(s) and its death(s).[28]

In the next section, I will argue that this discontinuity entails that our identities are *enacted* in movement and, in particular, through the manner in which learning establishes the unity of our moving bodies. It is thus precisely because our situation is characterized by 'spectral depth' that we are subjects. We experience situations as the demand to learn to move ourselves, the demand to continue to 'decide' the shape of our present in learning ways of moving. The most basic form of subjectivity then is living movement.

## II. LEARNING

In the chapter entitled "'Attention' and 'Judgment,'" Merleau-Ponty notes that infants, in the first nine months of life, do not yet distinguish colors. They appear to distinguish globally between the 'colored' and the 'colorless' and only subsequently come to distinguish 'warm' and 'cold' shades, and then, later, to distinguish each of the colors of the spectrum. Psychologists had traditionally interpreted this inability to distinguish colors as reflective of an inability, on the part of infants, to pay sufficient attention to the phenomena. Merleau-Ponty claims, on the contrary, that the psychologists were hampered in their efforts to understand the infant's behavior because they themselves "were not yet able to conceive a world in which colours were indeterminate, or a colour was not a precise quality." Merleau-Ponty thus offers an alternate explanation:

> The criticism of these prejudices . . . allows the world of colours to be perceived as a secondary formation, based on a series of 'physiognomic' distinctions: that between the 'warm' and 'cold' shades, that between 'coloured' and 'non-coloured.' We cannot compare these phenomena, which take the place of colour in children, to any determinate quality, and in the same way the 'strange' colours seen by a diseased person cannot be identified with any colour in the spectrum. The first perception of colours properly speaking, then, is a change of the structure of consciousness, the establishment of a new dimension of experience, the setting forth of an *a priori* [*le déploiment d'un* a priori]. (*PhP*, 30/38)

We have already seen, in chapter 1, that this change of 'the structure of consciousness' is the acquisition of a new sensorimotor know-how, a new form of bodily movement, or rather, a new manner in which movement allows 'itself' to be moved. Merleau-Ponty writes that, "Apart from the probing of my eye or my hand, and before my body synchronizes with it, the sensible is nothing but a vague beckoning" (*PhP*, 214/248). The sensible "quality is revealed by a type of behaviour," that is, again, it appears in bodily movement (*PhP*, 211/245). What identifies vision as such is not "a collection of sensible qualities but . . . a certain way of giving form or structure to our environment" (*PhP*, 115/133). Further, in acquiring a new form of movement (what Merleau-Ponty here perhaps misleadingly calls "a change in the structure of consciousness") we no longer *see* the same phenomena—the 'colors' seen by the child cannot be *compared* 'to any determinate quality.' Learning new manners of moving oneself is thus a matter of effecting a passage between incomparables.

The problem of the identity-in-difference of the body requires that we think of the body not as a discrete entity but rather as a dynamic identity enacted across different phases of living movement. This is essentially what is meant by Merleau-Ponty's notion of 'body schema,' a concept that we shall discuss in detail in Chapter 4. To be sure, Merleau-Ponty's language remains, in various passages of *Phenomenology of Perception*, ambiguous on this point. For example, he writes that "the normal subject penetrates into the object by perception, assimilating its structure into his substance, and *through this body* the object directly regulates his movements [*et qu'à travers son corps l'objet règle directement ses mouvements*]" (*PhP*, 132/154; my italics). The words appear to say that the body's movements are regulated by the action of the object on the subject 'through,' or 'across,' the medium of his body. But Merleau-Ponty also, and much more consistently, says that the body is unified because, in moving, it "interprets itself" (*PhP*, 150/175), because, in moving, it is "an expressive unity [*une unité expressive*]" (*PhP*, 206/239) and he says that "the parts of the body are mutually implicatory within the Unity of the gesture" (*PhP*, 173n./202n.). Self-consciousness, these passages seem to suggest, is originally accomplished as learning, as the articulation of sense in movement.[29]

The sensible, we have argued, is the original demand for space. The articulation of our body, the differentiation, and the 'communion,' among its 'parts' is enacted in responding to a plurality of demands for space. Merleau-Ponty remarks that sensations, rather than merely appearing as immanent data, or *hyle*, are always already intentional—directed toward a transcendence—in that they announce a certain "*rhythm* of existence":

> Sensation is intentional because I find that in the sensible a certain rhythm of existence is put forward [*je trouve dans le sensible la proposition d'un certain rhythme d'existence*]—abduction or adduction—and that, following up this hint, and stealing into the form of existence which is thus suggested to me, I am brought into relation with an external being, whether in order to open myself to it or to shut myself off from it. (*PhP*, 213–4/247)

The body enacts a certain 'rhythm' of the sensible, a rhythmic repetition of the event of sensation. In movement, a body differs from itself, it extends outward from itself, or coils back upon itself, articulates itself into parts and phases. And, as we have said, movement makes sense insofar as, across these differences and articulations, an aim or orientation is established—the emergence of the *sense* of movement involves the annunciation, within the movement, of a certain logic of parts and wholes. The retroactive determination of a sense in movement is the retroactive determination of a certain rhythm. It is as though the movement would be able to declare of itself: in each of these phases, across each of these differences and spacings, one thing, one meaning, is repeating itself. A rhythmic movement opens up spatio-temporal gaps that are traversed by the sensible insofar as the event of sensation is, as it were, echoed in the responsive movement. But insofar as movement also spatializes an event that is itself only the 'call' for space, the echo of the sensible is also inevitably a creative operation of the body. If it is true that all sense begins in this rhythmic enactment of a logic of parts and wholes within a movement, then it is not surprising that recent research on intersensory perception in infants has shown that infants are highly attuned to what can be called rhythmic aspects of perceptual events. And this is especially so when these rhythmic aspects are *synchronized* across different sensory modes, for example, as in one study, when a rhythmic pattern of audible pulses is synchronized with a pattern of flashing lights.[30] In fact, much recent research has been aimed at discerning so-called 'amodal' features of perception. This research program reflects Gibson's view that the development of intersensory, or 'intermodal,' perception is not so much a matter of 'integrating' information from independent sources, as of developing abilities for more finely 'differentiating' invariants within the flow of sensory 'information'—'information' that, in Gibson's hypothesis, is originally largely undifferentiated with respect to sensory modes.[31] This view would also be consistent with the sensorimotor approach advocated by O'Regan and Noë. As we saw in chapter 1, what differentiates the sensory modes, in their view, are differences in the dynamic structures of sensorimotor invariants. Since dynamic structures appear by virtue of the movement of the body, there is only a relative difference between, say, touching and seeing. Accordingly, the development of perceptual skills is a matter of learning to *differentiate* among structures of invariants rather than of learning to *integrate* sensory information from discrete sources.

This also seems to be Merleau-Ponty's view. He claims that perception is originally "synaesthetic." He writes, "The senses intercommunicate by opening on to the structure of the thing. One sees the hardness and brittleness of glass, and when, with a tinkling sound, it breaks, this sound is conveyed by the visible glass." He thus argues that:

> Synaesthetic perception is the rule, and we are unaware of it only because scientific knowledge shifts the centre of gravity of experience [*déplace l'expérience*], so that we have unlearned how to see, hear, and generally speaking, feel, in order to deduce, from our bodily organization as the physicist conceives it, what we are to see, hear and feel. (*PhP*, 229/265)

The traditional assumption that the senses constitute so many discrete pathways by which information is transmitted through the nervous system is a prejudice supported by a scientific construal of the body as an assemblage of 'parts and processes.' Why then does Merleau-Ponty make so much of the incompossibility of the 'worlds' of the various senses, and why have we been at such pains to understand this problem? Why do we find, in this incompossibility, at once such a profound threat to the unity of the subject, and the key to explaining its transcendence and the transcendence of things? In fact, the temptation to hypostasize the subject of perception, whether to reduce it to its physiological *body*, or to view the body as an intermediary between a *consciousness* and its objects, results in an occlusion *both* of the nature of the subject's unity *and* of the threat of disunity that also characterizes its mode of being. The tension between unity and disunity is most evident in the phenomenon of learning wherein the tension proves to be essential.

What distinguishes the senses from each other, for Merleau-Ponty, are not the physiological differences between organs or nerve pathways, but, as we have seen, the differences between manners of 'making space.' Each sensation, as a certain motor response to a call for space, articulates a 'total being.' Sensations are, to use again the language of 'motivation' and 'decision,' so many motor enactments of local 'decisions' that allow 'worlds' to appear as motivational nexuses. But, as we have said, these calls, each of which lays claim to being a 'total being'—absolute, incommunicable, and singular—never 'appear' in the original. The sense (*sens*) of the movement thus vouchsafes the appearance of the sensible only in the mode of a 'repetition without original,' a 'past which has never been a present.' In other words, as manners of movement, the senses allow these singularities to appear, but only by means of an overcoming of their singularity. That is to say, the sensible only appears *as meaning*: "If, then, taken as incomparable qualities, the 'data of the different senses' belong to so many separate worlds [*de mondes séparés*], each one in its particular essence being a manner of modulating the thing, they all communicate through their significant core [*par leur noyau significatif*]" (*PhP*, 230/266). What we could thus call the *singularity* of the sensible is sublimated by the very manner of its appearance. If what motivates a movement is a singularity, what is manifested in movement is a certain rhythm, a *style* of movement. Correlatively, the organs of the body, as so many 'natural selves,' become a *subjectivity* by the manner in which these organs, considered as *particular* manners of movement, stylize their corresponding 'worlds.'[32] As Merleau-Ponty writes in "Eye and Mind":

> My movement is not a decision made by the mind [*une décision d'esprit*], an absolute doing which would decree, from the depths of a subjective retreat, some change of place miraculously executed in extended space. It is the maturation of vision. I say of a thing that it is moved; but my body moves itself, my movement deploys itself [*mais mon corps, lui, se meut, mon mouvement se déploie*]. It is

not ignorant of itself; it is not blind for itself [*pour soi*]; it radiates from a self.(*EM*, 162/18)

Thus, when Merleau-Ponty says that in acquiring habits we appropriate 'fresh instruments,' we can take this also to mean that, in moving, in learning to move, the body appropriates itself. The event of sensation is the call for a certain spatio-temporal rhythm, a return of the sensible as a certain sense. This, then, is the significance of rhythm and amodal perception for the development of the child. Synchronized rhythms, announcing themselves at once to the eyes and to the ears, also organize the *living body* around a 'significant core.' They synchronize the body. In harkening to the call for a certain 'rhythm of existence,' put forward (as in the experiments to which we referred above) by a flashing light and a corresponding pulsation of sound, the 'eye' enacts a rhythm of the visible by also harkening to the rhythm of the audible. Two manners of making space answer to each other's demands; each provides the completion that the other was looking for in order to be able to constitute its 'total being.' In movement, the various surfaces and organs of our body, the fingers, the mouth, the eyes, first of all appropriate *each other* in embodying a certain rhythm, or style, of the sensible, that is, in learning.

Conceiving these 'natural selves' as manners of movement thus allows us to grasp how the 'parts' of the body are open to each other. The 'parts' of the body are, as Merleau-Ponty says, "dynamically acquainted with each other [*se connaissent dynamiquement*]" (*PhP*, 232/269):

It is not the epistemological subject who brings about the synthesis [of the perceptual phenomenon], but the body, when it escapes from dispersion, pulls itself together [*se rassemble*] and tends by all means in its power towards one single goal of its activity, and when one single intention is formed in it through the phenomenon of synergy. (*PhP*, 232/269)

Strictly speaking, the 'parts' of the sentient body are, as we have been saying, neither unified nor dispersed—each 'part' is a kind of absolute, each constituting a singular spatial domain. Speaking of the 'parts' of the body is an unavoidable concession to the demands of language; it reflects the demands of a grammar that tends to reify 'subjects' and 'objects.' In attempting to grasp the nature of the 'unity' of these 'parts' we have been considering the manner in which movement that makes sense is necessarily *expressive* movement. Thus we see how the body, as an ensemble of movements, 'interprets itself' and implies its own unity only in being foreign to itself, as the unity-across-difference of the expressive gesture. Movement allows some*thing* to appear in exactly the same way as it lets the moving body appear—as the always partially absent prehistory of the sense that it inaugurates, or to which it conforms. When we said earlier that the doctrine of an original past implies the non-presence of the 'sensation,' we noted that this non-presence has both a subjective and an objective aspect. In responding to the sensation, the body also responds to itself, but also preserves the non-presence of itself.[33] Thus the 'unity' of the body is that of a dynamic 'schema' that remains "open and limitless [*ouverte et indéfinie*]" (*PhP*, 233/270).

In this connection, developmental psychologists have observed that the development of spatial cognition in infants is crucially affected by 'locomotor experience.' One set of studies, conducted by Rosanne Kermoian and Joseph Campos, has revealed significant variation among infants (8.5 months of age) on the basis of locomotor experience, in their abilities to locate (hidden or partially hidden) objects while seated on the caregiver's lap.[34] In light of the fact that the search tasks used in these studies did not themselves involve locomotion (aside from the necessity of reaching for the object) it does not seem obvious why locomotor experience should make a decisive difference here. After all, the 'experience' in question (crawling, moving about in a walker) is not directly related to the task. But it is precisely in *moving* our bodies that we articulate the *spatiality* of our bodies. The experience of moving affects the spatio-temporal *form* of our experience. And it is in terms of this spatio-temporal form that we are able to locate things *in* space.

One crucial development of spatial cognition in infants is the transition from 'egocentric,' body-oriented, localization of objects to 'allocentric' localization based on spatial landmarks. This transition has been observed, to take one example, in studies in which infants have been habituated to respond to a signal indicating that a stimulating event is about to occur in a certain corner of a room.[35] Researchers can test the infant's manner of locating the site of the event (whether by means of egocentric or allocentric localization) by turning the infant around and then producing the signal that would alert the infant to the imminent event. An infant who localizes by means of egocentric coordinates will, at first, look in the 'wrong' direction. There is not an obvious 'stage' in which the transition from egocentric to allocentric localization occurs, but there is some evidence to suggest that this development is also affected by varying degrees of locomotor experience.[36] The transition from egocentric to allocentric localization then is a development in the way in which a self-moving body is open to itself in being open to otherness. Rather than construing these developments as 'stages' (reflecting the unfolding of a developmental program), evidence of the decisive role of locomotor experience would again suggest that movement is crucial to this kind of development because it articulates the circuit of body and world—this experience is the *becoming* of an a priori, a new habitual way of 'making space.'

Merleau-Ponty says that the acquisition of a 'habit' (a new sensorimotor know-how) is the acquisition of a new *form* of behaviour. It is a new *meaning*, but one which is also, at the same time, a new way of discerning meaning in the world and in the movements of one's own body. As Merleau-Ponty says, "the acquisition of a habit is indeed the grasping of a new significance, but it is the motor grasping of a motor significance [*la saisie motrice d'un signification motrice*]" (*PhP*, 143/167). That is to say, the acquisition of a habit is not exactly the acquisition of a new 'knowledge'; rather it is a new way in which living movement lets 'itself' be moved. Merleau-Ponty illustrates this with (among others) the example of an organist. A skilled organist, he says, can play an unfamiliar organ, one with more or fewer manuals and stops than the ones with which he is familiar, and only needs a very little time to be prepared to play his program:

> During the rehearsal, as during the performance, the stops, pedals and manuals are given to him as nothing more than possibilities of achieving certain emotional or musical values, and their positions are simply the places through which this value appears in the world . . . There is here no place for any 'memory' of the positions of the stops, and it is not in objective space that the organist in fact is playing. In reality his movements during rehearsal are consecratory gestures [*des gestes de consécration*]: they draw affective vectors, discover emotional sources, and create a space of expressiveness [*ils créent un espace expressif*] as the movements of the augur delimit the *templum*. (*PhP*, 145–6/170)

In acquiring the skill of playing the organ, the body of the organist has become a new kind of expressive unity. It is certainly true that, in the process of learning to play a musical instrument, one must attend carefully to what one is doing. One must practice the scales repeatedly, stopping to correct mistakes. But the goal of this process is not to develop a more finely honed attentiveness to the movements of one's fingers, but rather to achieve a kind of fluidity of expressive motion in which one can ignore one's fingers and adhere to the demands of the music. If we recall what Merleau-Ponty says in the "*Sentir*" chapter about the distinct spatiality demanded by the *sound* of music, the way it 'besieges' the visible space of the concert hall, we can see that learning to play an instrument, learning to adhere to the 'affective vectors' of the music, is also learning a new manner of 'making space.' What the accomplished player is able to do, and what the beginner generally is not, is to let music, as a kind of coherent and compelling reality, emerge from the movements of her own body, to move in such a way as to let something *other* than her own movements show itself. And this means opening up a 'space' that is, at least in its initial emergence, irreconcilable with the 'space' of the visible. It is then that the musician can begin to answer to the demands of the music rather than to the necessity of coordinating the movements of her own (visible) body. Later, the two 'spaces' will transform one another and achieve a common level (but not without thereby introducing a certain spectrality that can never quite be located within the field of presence). We can see that the development of this skill is a restructuration of the body, provided that we understand the body as a dynamic reality, rather than a thing, or an ensemble of organs. "Habit," Merleau-Ponty says, "expresses our power of dilating our being-in-the-world, or changing our existence by appropriating fresh instruments" (*PhP*, 143/168). Again, the fresh instruments here are new *forms* of movement.

I want to highlight two implications of this notion of habit. First, if our bodies were not in some sense, as it were, an ensemble of discrete spaces, this development would not be possible. Again, it is true that we have to learn the skill of playing an instrument by attending to it, by consciously coordinating our various motions, but at a certain point, the immanent logic of our movements begins to unfold *itself*. It is only insofar as the 'parts' of our bodies are *not* synthesized by a consciousness (using the body as its intermediary) that they can become obedient to the initially irreconcilable demands of the sensible. Second, the 'communion' among the 'parts' of our bodies is effected as sense (*sens*) in relation to a transcendence (the compelling reality of the music, with its own demand for space), but in order to adhere to the demands of this transcendence, they must *remain* open to new figurations. This is why the organist, when confronted with an unfamiliar instrument, is not stopped short. Habit is a kind of determinacy of the body that is also a new way of opening itself to restructuration.

This dialectic of determinacy and unity on the one hand and openness to difference and further determination on the other is highlighted in Kirsten Jacobson's account of learning as fundamentally a matter of "learning to dwell." Jacobson uses the Heideggerian language of 'dwelling' in connection with Merleau-Ponty's analysis of spatial levels to develop an account of the habituated, situated character of subjectivity as *being-at-home*. Home is, so to speak, the *sense* of an original determinacy, a more or less stable background to our unfolding experience, a fundamental level to which our developing situation implicitly refers back:

Home—our foundational level—can be a force of shutting down our freedom, of closing the doors to other possibilities for seeing, thinking, and acting. Yet, home is also the very situating foundation that allows us the power to strike out into the foreign and to be open to the world. Though the experience of home is thus inherently structured by an almost self-contradictory tension, the exercise of our freedom in fact requires this dual nature of our existence as open and closed, as vulnerable and secure.[37]

This paradoxical character of 'home' expresses the ambiguity of the sense of habit in our example of the organist. The organist is already 'familiar' with the new instrument insofar as she is able to assume the stance developed in her initial involvements with organs and let this stance open itself to novel circumstances. For better or for worse, we take 'home' with us into new situations and this is key to the phenomenon of learning. Being-at-home is accomplished only insofar as it is never *fully* accomplished.

Earlier, when we spoke of Merleau-Ponty's interpretation of Wertheimer's experiments (in which the latter used a mirror to show a subject only an oblique image of the room in which he was situated), we noted that, according to Merleau-Ponty, it is possible for a subject to adjust to new 'levels' because each new level is, for the subject, simply a new way of being situated. Our bodies are oriented by the senses of tasks. For Merleau-Ponty, a re-orientation is thus not a radical break with a previous spatial level; rather, the new level seems strange, at first, because it refers back to the one preceding. Thus, rather than being radically discontinuous, the spatiality of our experience is open to infinite possibilities for being spatial. Our discussion of sensation has also taught us that the multiplicity of spatial levels is not simply experienced sequentially, and that the spatial levels of our experience are not, at any given time, absolutely exclusive of each other. Alphonso Lingis has expressed this point in connection with the plurality of the 'spaces' of sensation:

The world in which we perceive extends in space-time that is not a priori apprehendable in the formula for Euclidean or non-Euclidean geometrical dimensions and the objective time of successive moments. It extends on *levels*—the level of the light that our gaze adjusts to and sees with as it looks at the illuminated contours that surface as reliefs on the level, the level of sonority our hearing attunes to as it harkens to sounds and noises that rise out of it, the level of the tangible our posture finds as our limbs move across the contours and textures of tangible substances, the levels of verticality and of depth and of rest that emerge as our position becomes functional in a layout of tasks. The level is found sensorially, by movement that does not grasp at the objective but adjusts to it, is sustained by it, moves with it and according to it.[38]

Thus, as we have seen, the spatio-temporal coherence of our world, and of our bodies, is found only by way of a multitude of local adjustments, the adherence of our gaze, our touch, our hearing, to the manifold levels in which things beckon to appear. To adhere to these levels is thus to learn what the spectacle demands of us in order that something might be able to appear, and thereby to learn our bodies through the acquisition of habits.

As Alphonso Lingis' description of our adherence to multiple spatial levels implies, perception is not simply something we do. Our bodies are, we could say, *inspired* unities. Learning our bodies is, in part, a process of inspiration. This is what is suggested in a relatively long passage from *Phenomenology of Perception* that I would like to quote in full. Right after saying that the subject of sensation is "synchronized" with his environment, Merleau-Ponty writes,

The relations of sentient to sensible are comparable with those of the sleeper to his slumber: sleep comes when a certain voluntary attitude suddenly receives from outside the confirmation for which it was waiting. I am breathing deeply and slowly in order to summon sleep, and suddenly it is as if my mouth were connected to some great lung outside myself which alternately calls forth and forces back my breath. A certain rhythm of respiration, which a moment ago I voluntarily maintained, now becomes my very being, and sleep, until now aimed at as a significance, suddenly becomes a situation. In the same way I give ear, or look, in the expectation of a sensation, and suddenly the sensible takes possession of my ear or my gaze, and I surrender a part of my body, even my whole body, to this particular manner of vibrating and filling space known as blue or red. Just as the sacrament not only symbolizes, in sensible species, an operation of Grace, but is also the real presence of God, which it causes to occupy a fragment of space and communicates to those who eat of the consecrated bread, provided that they are inwardly prepared, in the same way the sensible has not only a motor and vital significance, but is nothing other than a certain way of being in the world suggested to us from some point in space, and seized upon and acted upon by our body, provided that it is capable of doing so, so that sensation is literally a form of communion. (*PhP*, 211–2/245–6)

Now, there are a number of important themes in this passage, some of which I will return to in chapter 4, but I particularly want to stress again here the way in which sentient subjectivity is not *simply* to be understood as an 'I can.' When Merleau-Ponty says that the sensible has 'not only a motor and vital significance,' he is suggesting that a certain supplement, not yet determinable in terms of the 'essential structures' of the field of presence, is necessary to our being in the world. That supplement, thought here on the analogy with the theological category of Grace, is not itself a sense (*sens*), but that which is needed for the emergence of sense—a singularity that is already absent by the time anything appears, but whose spectral non-presence continues to haunt the field of presence. This singularity opens up a field of presence (a field of the 'I can') only because it has no 'place' within it.

Merleau-Ponty says that each sensation is a birth and a death of the sentient subject. The perpetual contribution of our bodies to our conscious experience is thus also an intimation of our radical contingency and, thus, our dependence. Our bodies 'contribute' a natural basis, and a historicity, insofar as our present is haunted by an 'original past.' Learning presupposes that we are natural bodies, mortal bodies—and that our self-consciousness (the sense of the 'I can') is haunted by the specters of this contingency. We are exposed to this contingency (our birth, our death) each time that the movements of our bodies announce an order of sense, but fail to absorb their own beginnings into the order of sense that they announce. This very 'failure,' the persistent intimation of non-sense in every order of motor sense, is also what lets things appear as unanticipated and inexhaustible realities. Reality *requires* 'decisions' of our bodies in order to be able to appear, and it thus also requires learning.[39] Learning is not merely an overcoming of a certain discontinuity of our experience (it is not simply the deployment of a 'power'), but a kind of mysterious transubstantiation of our bodies through the adherence of its organs and surfaces to a plurality of demands for space.

The discontinuity within the field of presence, between the 'essential structures' of the field, and the originary past (which has no real 'place' in the field but nevertheless subtends the field insofar as the latter is an open-ended structure) thus points to an ontological character of the situated self. In the next chapter, we will return again to the sensorimotor and ecological accounts of cognition that we explored in chapter 1, to investigate more directly what they can teach us about situated subjectivity. But the very things that we have learned in this chapter will also help us to see the limits of 'naturalistic' accounts of situated subjectivity.

THREE

# SUBJECTIVITY AND THE
# 'STYLE' OF THE WORLD

The natural world is the horizon of all horizons, the style of all possible styles [*le style de tous les styles*], which guarantees for my experiences a given, not a willed, unity underlying all the disruptions of my personal and historical life. Its counterpart within me is the given, general and pre-personal existence of my sensory functions in which we have discovered the definition of the body.

—Merleau-Ponty

## I. THE 'SUBJECT' AND THE 'WORLD' OF SITUATED COGNITION

Gibson's ecological psychology, like O'Regan and Noë's sensorimotor approach, seems able to offer us an account of the appearance of a world-in-depth. It is a world whose phenomenality involves a kind of solicitation of our self-moving bodies—it appears to us insofar as it appeals to us to explore and move and thereby to involve ourselves in the spectacle that it offers. Appearance is thus construed in these accounts as inherently a matter of *dynamic* structures constituting a *situation* for our bodies. That is to say, appearance is conditioned by motor possibilities having to do with the perceiving organism itself—its morphology, its musculature, its sense organs, its characteristic behaviors with regard to eating, or to avoiding predators, as well as more sophisticated learned behaviors, including modes of work, play, language, and so forth. Both of these accounts, in many ways, overcome the limitations that Merleau-Ponty finds in traditional epistemologies: they seem to overcome the prejudice according to which perception putatively picks out, or constitutes, discrete objects on the basis of raw data; they seem to overcome the subject-object duality that requires modern epistemologies to imagine a fixed (objective) reality beyond (merely subjective) appearance and then to wonder how the subject gains epistemic access to this reality; thus, they both seem to avoid the tendency of modern representationalist theories of cognition to try to reduce experience to objective 'parts and processes.' But I am not convinced that these approaches are completely successful at all of this. The problem, as I indicated in chapter 1, concerns the metaphysical assumptions made by the advocates of the sensorimotor and ecological accounts of perception in the course of formulating their epistemological claims. These assumptions have significant implications for our understanding of the situated self.

In this chapter, I will make use of what we learned in chapter 2 to examine these approaches critically. I will show that, without a fundamental ontological investigation of the modes of being of environments and selves, no challenge to the epistemology of representation can be complete. That epistemology is essentially linked to a certain set of ontological commitments that remain as presuppositions in the idea of a 'naturalized' phenomenology. By critically examining these approaches we will be able to see more clearly what would be demanded of a theory of situated subjectivity. Merleau-Ponty, in my view, goes much further than these scientific approaches in disclosing the character of such a subjectivity. But I will also continue to develop a certain line of critical inquiry that we initiated in chapter 2 concerning Merleau-Ponty's notion of a tacit, or prereflective, self-consciousness. Some thinkers have deployed this notion in order to overcome the perceived short-comings of the sensorimotor and ecological accounts of cognition. It has been pointed out that the sensorimotor and ecological accounts of cognition do not sufficiently distinguish between self-consiousness and the forms of intentionality involved in the perception of objects. Taking their inspiration from phenomenologists like Husserl and Merleau-Ponty, Dan Zahavi, Evan Thompson, and others have pointed to an implicit, or tacit, bodily sense of self-consciousness subtending the explicit or reflective sense of self. But the analyses that we have explored so far have also already given us reason to be wary of the notion of a tacit *consciousness*. In this chapter, then, I will begin to set out an interpretation of this notion of a tacit cogito, as it is deployed by Merleau-Ponty, that I believe is more consistent with the interpretation that we have been developing of Merleau-Ponty's concept of subjectivity.

*Sensorimotor Laws*

In an article on perceptual consciousness, Erik Myin and Kevin O'Regan acknowledge the similarities between the sensorimotor approach and the phenomenology of Merleau-Ponty. But they also claim that their approach holds out a further possibility for future (scientific) research:

We concur with the criticism, present in this tradition [phenom-
enology], that a reductionist approach, in which direct identification of the phenomenal with the neurophysiological is attempted,
is doomed to perennial failure. On the other hand, we think a
skill-based approach, which orients the science of perception instead
towards *capacities* deployed by organisms, rather than to momentary
internal events in their brains, holds out the promise of turning the
phenomenologist's insights into a successful, yet *broadly naturalistic*
[my italics] research programme.[1]

The notion of sensorimotor 'laws' is crucial to this project of 'naturalizing
phenomenology.' We have already encountered, in chapter 1, some examples
of O'Regan and Noë's use of the concept of 'law': "the distribution of information sensed by the retina changes drastically, but in a *lawful* way, as the
eye moves"; "We therefore suggest that a crucial fact about vision is that
visual exploration obeys certain *laws* of sensorimotor contingency"; "the *laws*
of sensorimotor contingency might actually *constitute* [italics in original] the
way the brain codes visual attributes."[2] Now, one can speak of 'laws' in this
context only if it is assumed that motor actions (involving some sense organ,
or some combination of them) discover correlations between stable features
of the world (of the sensory apparatus itself, of the sensible attributes of
objects). The laws governing this correlation must, according to O'Regan
and Noë, come to be 'known' by a perceiver in order for there to be an
experience of the corresponding properties. The typical changes in the flow
of information produced by movement are taken to be lawful because it is
assumed that they reflect *realities* that are transcendent to the experience,
as, for example, when O'Regan and Noë write that "the sensation of red
comes from the *structure of changes* that is caused by red."[3] In putting it
this way, they do not mean to advocate any naive realism of color—they
are not suggesting that some real redness in the world directly causes the
experience of red—rather, they are saying that some surface in the world
possesses properties that, when properly illuminated, and when explored by
the right kind of sensorimotor perceptual system, manifest themselves as a
definite structure of changes in the flow of sensory information and that *this*
occasions the experience of red. As they put it, visual exploration "provides
ways of sampling" the "properties" of "real objects" that "can be positioned
in the three-dimensional world at different distances and angles with respect
to an observer."[4] There are sensorimotor laws because motion is a mediating
term that does not itself alter the objective realities (e.g., retina, illuminated
visible object) between which it adumbrates the possible correlations.

Let us consider how this notion of sensorimotor laws applies to a
specific example. O'Regan and Noë claim that,

Your visual apprehension of the roundness of a plate consists in part in your knowledge that changes in your relation to the plate (movements relative to the plate) will induce changes in the plate's profile. That it looks round to you now, despite its elliptical profile, is constituted by your application, now, of skillful mastery of the appropriate rule of sensorimotor contingencies.[5]

Again, we see here how the sensorimotor approach's challenge to representationalism works: the perceptual system need not construct an internal map of the visible world (containing information on the basis of which it would infer the latter's three-dimensional geometry). Rather, on the sensorimotor account, the perceiver actively explores the object, and its brain abstracts from the resultant dynamic flow of sensory information the laws correlating its own movement to the sensible properties of the object. In this case, for example, the elliptical profile would approach roundness as the plate is moved to a position beneath the eyes and closer to the observer's chest.

Notice that, like Merleau-Ponty's, O'Regan and Noë's account addresses the problem of depth in terms of the *temporality* of experience. The perceiver's skillful mastery of the appropriate rule allows her to experience 'now' how the plate *would* look at some point in the future (though it is not clear why the overhead view should, in this case, be privileged). Sensorimotor laws are rules abstracted by a sensorimotor perceptual system from 'samples' of the flow of sensory information. These laws are in effect rules for making absent contents present to the perceptual system. But if O'Regan and Noë's description of this phenomenon is part of an effort to naturalize phenomenology, we may legitimately submit it to the test of a certain skepticism about the phenomenological description: does the plate viewed from an oblique angle really 'look round'? Is it not possible that an idealized construction has been substituted here for our actual experience?

The contrast between O'Regan and Noë's approach and that of Merleau-Ponty is evident in the latter's description of the very same phenomenon: a plate, or a disc, viewed from an oblique angle. There are at least two places where Merleau-Ponty refers to this example. In *Phenomenology of Perception*, he writes that "the apparent shape of a disc turning round one of its diameters does not vary as one would expect according to geometrical perspective," and then, a little later, adds that "a disc placed obliquely to our face *resists geometrical perspective* [*résiste à la perspective géométrique*], as Cézanne and other painters have shown by depicting a soup plate seen from the side with the inside still visible" (259–260/300–301; my italics). Further, in "Cézanne's Doubt," Merleau-Ponty writes: "To say that a circle seen obliquely is seen as an ellipse is to substitute for our actual perception what we would see if we were cameras: *in reality we see a form which oscillates around the ellipse without being an ellipse*" (SN, 14/24; my italics). Merleau-Ponty is in agreement with O'Regan and Noë that we are not cameras, that we do not in fact see an ellipse; but where they claim that the plate 'looks round to you,' Merleau-Ponty claims that it 'oscillates around the ellipse,' that it 'resists geometrical perspective.' There is a lot at stake in this difference. If, from where you are situated, the visible profile of the plate is elliptical, and yet thanks to your mastery of sensorimotor contingencies the plate 'looks round to you' when you see it, then we surely need to account for the *lawful* character of these sensorimotor contingencies if we are to explain your experience. But Merleau-Ponty's account requires no such thing because, according to his description, the appearance of the plate remains open-ended, undecided, inexhaustible.[6] The difference compels us to ask whether or not we ought to say that sensorimotor perception *discovers* a reality or is somehow the ongoing *enactment* of one. If we adopt the latter position, which is, I believe, Merleau-Ponty's own position, then we are not permitted to explain the character of perceptual experience on the basis of a presumed objective reality, a reality in itself (i.e., we may not appeal to the objective 'roundness' of the plate, the objective features of the eye, etc.). Rather, having noticed the self-articulating movement that lets something appear, we are compelled to describe a movement that articulates a relation to what differs from, but is not foreign to, the movement itself. And, again, however we describe this wonder, our description will surely have important implications for how we construe the situatedness of the subject.

O'Regan and Noë's claim that perceptual experience involves the mastery of sensorimotor laws may sound similar to Merleau-Ponty's interpretation (which we cited in chapter 1) of the experiments by Goldstein and Rosenthal: "In these various experiments each colour always acts with the same tendency, with the result that *a definite motor value (valeur motrice définie)* can be assigned to it" (PhP, 209/242; my italics). But a crucial difference lies in the way in which the term '*valeur motrice*' cuts across the difference, so crucial in O'Regan and Noë's description, between 'information' and 'law.' When Merleau-Ponty says that a definite motor value can be assigned to the color, he does not mean that a fixed law governs the structure of relations between sensory information and movement; rather he means that perception, as movement, is itself the assignation of a value. We saw this, in chapter 2, with the definition of habit as 'the motor grasping of a motor significance.' It is as certain motivational values, then, rather than as 'information,' that living movement encounters the features of its world. Perception happens, as we saw in Merleau-Ponty's account of depth, not when a law is (tacitly) known, but when a 'decision' envelops a 'motivation': "The motive is an antecedent which acts only through its significance [*sens*], and it must be added that it is the decision which affirms the validity of this significance [sens] and gives it its force and efficacy" (PhP, 259/299). In other words, it is not merely the case that the motive is an antecedent (a cause) whose effectiveness is mediated by some information-value that it also has for a sensorimotor system; rather, the motive is an antecedent only for the decision that affirms it as such. Perception, Merleau-Ponty seems to suggest here, is not a type of knowledge, but a movement *discriminatingly allowing itself to be moved*.

The difference between the two positions is made further evident when Merleau-Ponty writes that motility and sensation must not be understood in such a way as to leave "unaffected the terms between which [the relation] stands":

> The motor significance of colours is comprehensible only if they cease to be closed states or indescribable qualities presented to an observing and thinking subject, and if they *impinge within me upon a certain general setting through which I come to terms with the world*; if, moreover, *they suggest to me a new manner of evaluating*, and if motility ceases to be the mere consciousness of my movements from place to place in the present or immediate future, and becomes the function which constantly lays down my standards of size and the varying scope of my being in the world [*l'amplitude variable de mon être au monde*]. (PhP, 210/243; my italics, translation slightly modified)

We could say that, in Merleau-Ponty's view, the motor significance of colors must be understood in terms of an embodied dialectic in which sensation (as 'motivation,' or 'value') and movement (as 'decision,' or 'evaluation') are co-implicated and *mutually* transformative. The motor *values* of colors only reveal themselves within acts of *evaluation*, and those acts will themselves take the form of movement. This is why Merleau-Ponty (in contrast to O'Regan and Noë) insists on the indeterminacy of the phenomenon. The relation between sensory 'information' (a term that would no longer seem appropriate here) and subjective movement is, again, not a matter of determinate 'laws' but rather of a situation of 'living significance' which is intrinsically open to its own development. Each of my involvements with the color red (each involving a host of contextual factors) would reconfigure the sensorimotor body (awakening ever 'new manners of evaluating' situations in which I am again confronted with the color red)—and each experience of red—the red of a Caravaggio painting, the red of blood from a wound, the red of a Soviet flag—will involve the further articulation of that history of involvement.[7] This would mean that the 'laws' of sensorimotor contingencies are themselves subject to the vagaries of historicity—that of cultures and of the lives of individuals—and thus to a certain irreducible element of contingency.[8] This is, I believe, Merleau-Ponty's own view (and it means that the concept of 'decision,' which, in connection with 'motivation,' is so important in *Phenomenology of Perception*, anticipates the later concept of 'institution,' which we shall consider in chapter 5). The sensorimotor account's appeal to the lawfulness of sensorimotor contingencies commits it to a metaphysical realism which makes it unable to adequately account for this element of historicity and contingency in our experience. This, as we have said, has profound implications for an understanding of subjectivity.

*Sensorimotor Subjectivity*

We noted earlier that perceptual experience is characterized by a kind of two-sidedness: in typing on the computer keys, I am able to feel the sensations in my fingers *and* to see my fingers as visible parts or surfaces of my own body. My body is, in this experience, both subject and object. Evan Thompson writes that "The challenge for any scientific account of consciousness is to preserve this unique double character of bodily self-consciousness."[9] As we also noted earlier, in the act of looking at something, including my own hands, I am generally not *explicitly* self-aware—I need not be actively reflecting on my own experience in order to see an object. But the very possibility of reflecting on my experience is itself apparently grounded in a kind of *tacit* self-awareness that was always already underway in my experience, a self-awareness that, according to many phenomenologists, necessarily subtends the *unity*-in-difference of the experiential 'field of presence.' Thompson describes this as "non-intentional self-awareness."[10] For Thompson, the requirement imposed upon 'any scientific account of consciousness,' that it be able to account for this non-intentional self-awareness, is particularly pressing for the advocates of the sensorimotor approach:

> The dynamic sensorimotor approach needs a notion of selfhood or agency, because to explain perceptual experience it appeals to sensorimotor knowledge. Knowledge implies a knower or agent or self that embodies this knowledge. But what organization does a sensorimotor system need to have in order to be a genuine sensorimotor agent with a correlative sensorimotor environment . . . ?[11]

Thompson is of the view that the sensorimotor account does not in fact offer a satisfactory answer to this question. He refers to a 2002 article in which Erik Myin and Kevin O'Regan explicitly address the questions of subjectivity and agency in the terms of the sensorimotor approach. They claim that sensorimotor experience is characterized by a number of qualitative properties among which are 'forcible presence' and 'subjectivity.' They write:

> Forcible presence is the fact that, contrary to other mental states like my knowledge of history, for example, a sensory experience imposes itself upon me from the outside, and is present to me without my making any effort, and indeed is mostly out of my voluntary control. . . . Subjectivity indicates that the experience is, in an unalienable way, my experience. It is yours or mine, or his or hers, and cannot be had without someone having it. But subjectivity also indicates that the experience is something for me, something that offers me an opportunity to act or think with respect to whatever is experienced.[12]

With the idea of 'forcible presence,' Myin and O'Regan seem to add a significant qualification to the notion of sensorimotor contingencies. A sensorimotor system does not merely 'sample' at random from a flow of sensory information and thereby discover structures of co-variants between sensation and movement; rather, the notion of 'forcible presence' implies that some types of information distinctly possess more 'grabbiness' than other types. Changes in the visual scene, for example, are particularly likely to immediately attract our attention.[13] To use O'Regan and Noë's example, if I am holding a book in my hand (rather than merely thinking of a book), "the book forces itself on [me] as present because any movement of the book *causes* [me] to direct [my] attention ([my] processing resources) to it."[14] The notion of 'forcible presence' is obviously related to that feature of our sensory experience that Myin and O'Regan call 'subjectivity,' i.e., the way in which things are experienced as offering *me* an opportunity 'to act or think.'[15] These two concepts (among others) are developed by the advocates of the sensorimotor approach in order to explain how it is that a sensorimotor system can have a phenomenal consciousness. There is, for Myin and O'Regan, a kind of subjective, or first-personal, quality to our sense experiences because they happen *as* more or less forceful solicitations; sensations are *experienced* only insofar as they grab one's attention and offer one an opportunity to act. Keeping in mind our earlier discussion about valuation, motivation, and decision in Merleau-Ponty, we could ask (modifying Thompson's question): what organization does a sensorimotor system need to have in order for some sensations to *matter* to it, or for some sensations to *matter more* to it than others? An answer to this question seems to be required as soon as the notion of sensorimotor invariants is qualified by the claim that some sensory information is 'grabbier,' or that contents of (sensory) experience 'offer' *me* an opportunity to act. The language of 'processing' and 'causation' seems to obscure the issue, as does O'Regan and Noë's analogy (highlighted by Thompson) between a sensorimotor perceptual system and a missile guidance system:

As the missile zigzags around to evade enemy fire, the image of the target airplane shifts in the missile's sights. If the missile turns left, then the image of the target shifts to the right. If the missile slows down, the size of the image of the airplane decreases in a predictable way. The missile guidance system must adequately interpret and adapt to such changes in order to track the airplane efficiently. In other words, the missile guidance system is 'tuned to' the sensorimotor contingencies that govern airplane tracking. It 'knows all about it' or 'has mastery over' the possible input/output relationships that occur during airplane tracking.[16]

Now it must be repeated that the notions of 'forcible presence' and 'subjectivity' seem to add something to this mechanistic picture of the perceptual system; namely, they point to the fact that, at least with respect to *our* (human? living?) sort of perceptual system, certain things appear in experience because they 'grab' the system's attention and call on it to act. But these additions seem arbitrary. Nothing in the sensorimotor account helps us to understand what it is about *this* sort of sensorimotor system that would allow for any particular thing to be more or less able to 'cause' it to direct its 'processing resources' to it—in contrast to the guided missile, which would presumably have been designed and programmed to detect only relevant information. Furthermore, there is an important difference between saying that salient sensible features of the world 'cause' the system to act (forcible presence) and that such features 'offer' the system an opportunity to act (subjectivity). We may be able to see how 'forcible presence' might apply to the guided missile example, but not how 'subjectivity' would apply. What would account for this difference?

Thompson suggests that two things are lacking in the sensorimotor approach. First, it needs to be recognized that a perceptual system must also be an 'autonomous system,' it must be *autopoietic*.[17] As Thompson writes:

An autonomous system is a self-defining or self-determining system, by contrast with a system defined and controlled from the outside or a heteronomous system. . . . Its individuality and agency are based on its having a self-producing or *autopoietic* organization: it is organized as a self-producing and self-maintaining network that constructs its own membrane boundary and actively regulates its background or boundary conditions so as to remain viable in its environment.[18]

Thus, unlike the missile guidance system, which "does not produce and maintain its own sensorimotor identity as an invariant of its sensorimotor interactions with the environment," an autopoietic system is a system that encounters 'information' about the outside world only as certain *values* determined with reference to its own project of self-organization and self-maintenance.[19] Without being too hasty in identifying this *autopoietic* approach with the approach that Merleau-Ponty ends up pursuing, let us note that Thompson's proposal does address the very issues that we have claimed distinguish Merleau-Ponty's phenomenology from the sensorimotor approach: Thompson explicitly addresses the question of 'value' (i.e., he replaces the notions of sensorimotor 'information' and 'invariants' with something like sensorimotor 'evaluation') and he recognizes that this move implies an *ontology* of the situated self rather than merely a psychophysical epistemology of situated cognition. The ontology of autopoiesis would have to found the epistemology of sensorimotor cognition if the latter were to be able to address the problems that it is intended to address.

The second thing lacking in the sensorimotor approach (which seems very much related to the first) is, according to Thompson, an account of "subjectivity in the sense of a phenomenal feeling of bodily selfhood linked to the correlative feeling of otherness":

> What [Myin and O'Regan] write about subjectivity does not address the first-personal character and non-object-directed or intransitive self-awareness constitutive of experience (or experiencing), but instead the conscious access the subject has to the intentional objects of perceptual experience.[20]

In making perception depend on the knowledge of sensorimotor co-variants, the sensorimotor account must be able to offer an account of how I can be (tacitly) conscious of the position of my own body, the difference between my body and other things, as well as *my own* possibilities for moving in relation to those things. I must in some sense be alive to my own 'I can' in order to be able to discover meaningful correlations between sensation and motion ("motor *values*," to use Merleau-Ponty's terminology). Thompson here raises the question of prereflective self-awareness. I would like to set this aside for the time being as it will come up again in connection with the ecological approach, which, it turns out, motivates, among some contemporary phenomenologists, a very similar objection.

*Ecological Laws*

Gibson, as we have seen, also believes that perception is dependent on invariants that are discernable in the environments of moving organisms.

And he also maintains that it is possible to develop a scientifically useful body of "ecological laws" specifying conditions under which 'affordances' appear.[21] (Though ecological perception is made to depend upon a perceiver's coming to *know* these laws, Gibson, like O'Regan and Noë, insists that this is not a propositional but a "*tacit* knowledge."[22]) Thus, though ecological psychology poses a profound challenge to the epistemologies that have been generated in connection with the modern natural sciences, it is able to offer its own grounds for an empirical-scientific research program.

M.T. Turvey, a leading contemporary figure in the field of ecological psychology, has recognized the possibility for ecological psychology to articulate its own ontology. In this way it would be able to properly ground its claim to being a natural science.[23] He sets forth a proposal for what he terms a "realist" ontology of affordances. The difficulty in carrying out such a proposal is that the fundamental category of ecological psychology (affordance) is, in principle, perceiver-relative. There would appear then to be no obvious way to describe the ecological 'world' in terms that would be universal—i.e., in a manner that would be adequate to a scientific sense of the term 'world' as an objective totality. For Turvey, an important step in overcoming this problem is to find some way of defining and quantifying the possibilities available to specific animals such that their "dispositional properties"[24] could be investigated systematically in terms of their (lawful) correlations with the "dispositions" of things within their environments. This would necessarily involve initially construing environments in terms of quite different "reference frames" (corresponding to different organisms); but in allowing for the quantification of the relevant features of organisms and environments such an approach would, in principle, allow the different frames to be described according to a single common frame.

For the correlation of the dispositional properties of an organism and its environmental affordances, Turvey employs the term "prospective control." This is to be understood as "control concerned with future events, usually interpretable as goals to be realized":

> To be specific, conducting an act requires that one perceive whether the act as a whole is possible, what subacts are possible with respect to surface layout, and the possible consequences of current subacts if current (kinetic, kinematic) conditions persist.[25]

'Prospective control' is thus the proper object of ecological psychology because it is, in a sense, the proper object of perception; the 'object' of perception is the correlation of the dispositional properties of the perceiver and the features of the environment making the latter a totality of affordances. Perceivers and environments are thus "distinguishable yet mutually supportive realities."[26] Ecological psychology can incorporate subject-relative possibilities into its description of a single 'reality' through its understanding of the 'laws' governing prospective control. As Turvey writes: "Laws and circumstances (auxiliary conditions, boundary conditions, initial conditions) yield actual states of affairs." Thus, with respect to affordances and prospective control, he is able to conclude that: "real possibility is identical to lawfulness."[27] Ecological laws are thus grounded in actual states of affairs.[28] So there is, for ecological psychology, indeed something 'objective' about the perceived world. Though ordinary perception proceeds according to a kind of 'tacit knowledge' of ecological laws, it is possible, in Turvey's view, to develop an objective science of the "I can." This seems to hold out the promise, in another form, of a reduction of the first-person perspective to a third-person description of the world. But, again, as we have suggested, such an approach would seem to overlook an essential feature of our experience: the first-person perspective.

*Ecological Subjectivity*

This reduction is considered possible, in principle, by ecological psychology in part because it denies that there is any radically distinct form of awareness implied by the expression "first-person perspective." For ecological psychology, perception, as the perception of affordances, always includes a "co-perception" of the self. In order for an organism to pick out the invariants relevant to its own activities, it must be the case that "the moving self and the unmoving world are reciprocal aspects of the same perception."[29] In Gibson's terminology, perception must make available, to the subject, information about the environment ("exterospecific information") as well as information about the self ("propriospecific information").[30] For example, as I move toward an object, the entire optical array, including the object and its surroundings, expands toward the outside of my field of vision (though the rate of expansion will of course vary for objects at different distances). If, on the other hand, an object or person is moving toward me, only the object expands while the layout of the background remains fixed. This difference specifies a difference between my own movement and the movements of other things. Information about the self is thus co-perceived in the perception of the environment. Ecological self-awareness is entirely based upon this co-perception of the self. In overcoming the traditional epistemology of representation, Gibson also rejects the traditional notion that self-awareness (*ex hypothesi*, self-representation) presupposes discrete sources of information about the self (e.g., special proprioceptive nerve pathways). Gibson writes that:

In my view, proporioception can be understood as egoreception, as sensitivity to self, not as a one special channel of sensations or as several of them. I maintain that all the perceptual systems are propriosensitive as well as exterosensitive, for they all provide information in their various ways about the observer's activities.[31]

In other words, self-awareness is distinguished from the perception of objects (as affordances) on the basis of the different *meanings* attaching to different bits of information with respect to the observer's own activities. Once again, the ecological subject is not passively receptive, but an active interpreter.

George Butterworth[32] and Ulric Neisser[33] have each developed this Gibsonian notion of 'egoreception' into explicit accounts of the forms of self-awareness implied by an ecological psychology. They recognize that the 'ecology' of human beings clearly includes more than just affordances for walking, grasping, climbing, and jumping; it includes other human beings along with all of the institutions, texts, practices, ideologies, historical records, folk-psychology, myths, etc., that are constitutive features of social life. The human ecology includes affordances for walking, grasping, etc., in such a way as to *directly imply* my co-existence with others. A chair, for example, is an affordance for sitting only for people who live in a culture that manufactures chairs for this purpose, and only for individuals who have been taught that chairs are for sitting and not, say, for climbing on. Ecological theories of perception, then, must take the socio-cultural dimension of human ecology into account. And these socio-cultural dimensions are also crucial for understanding how information about the self is specified and rendered meaningful for a human perceiver. But, as with Gibson, rather than starting from some privileged form of self-access, these ecological accounts of self-awareness rely exclusively on 'information' that is made available through interaction with the environment.

Neisser offers an account of five "distinct" selves that are specified in the human ecology and that come to form the basis of our ordinary self-knowledge: 1) the *ecological self*, specified by information about our relationship to the physical environment; 2) the *interpersonal self*, specified by "species-specific signals of emotional rapport and communication"; 3) the *extended self*, based on personal memories and anticipations; 4) the *private self*, arising from a child's recognition that others do not directly share its experiences, and; 5) the *conceptual self*, "which draws its meaning from the network of assumptions and theories in which it is embedded," which may include theories about the self (about minds, souls, the unconscious, etc.) and which may also specify socio-cultural roles (husband, artist, employee, etc.). The unity of these five selves in our everyday self-knowledge itself depends upon "stimulus information to specify their cohesion."[34] Ultimately this last form of stimulus information will rely directly on the co-perception of myself in my environment—"I can usually see that it is I, here, who am engaging in a particular social interaction."[35]

One problem with this Gibsonian account of the self is that it ultimately appeals to perception (or co-perception) to explain the very thing that ecological perception seems necessarily to presuppose: non-intentional self-awareness. In order to be able to differentiate data pertaining to my body, with its motor possibilities, from data pertaining to the environment, I would need to have some prior (non-intentional) sense of my body as myself. This objection has been voiced by Dan Zahavi,[36] Shaun Gallagher,[37] and Maxine Sheets-Johnstone.[38] They share Gibson's criticism of the empiricist view of self-awareness as exclusively dependent on specific proprioceptors. And they share the view that the sense of self is open to development through perception and learning in precisely the sorts of interactive contexts that Neisser's account highlights. Lastly, they share the view that this development in many ways directly concerns the sense of being an embodied self in a concrete situation. The problem, as Zahavi puts it, is that ecological theories "conceive of the embodied self as an object, and of embodied self-awareness as a kind of object-awareness."[39] The real problem is that the ecological accounts of self-awareness offered by Gibson, Butterworth, and Neisser, do not live up to the demands that their ecological psychology implies.

An organism, Dan Zahavi argues, does not merely need to know its own dispositional properties in order to be able to discover affordances in its environment; it needs precisely to know that these properties are *its own*. In order to be able to make sense of the information available to it, the animal must know that some of the information it picks up applies *uniquely* to itself. Variations in movement patterns in the optical array could never provide me with self-specifying information if I did not already have a nontransitive awareness of my body's agency and movement. As Zahavi writes, "To put it another way, the question of self-awareness is not primarily a question of a specific *what*, but a unique *how*. It does not concern the specific content of an experience, but its unique mode of givenness."[40] The "I can" of ecological (and sensorimotor) subjectivity must first of all be genuinely subjective. This condition, Zahavi argues, cannot be satisfied by a hypothesized 'co-perception' of the self. Gallagher makes this same point when he says that any kind of object-directed awareness necessitates a nontransitive awareness of self. He claims that "to understand ecological, proprioceptive, or nonconceptual awareness as an instance of perception in the strict sense of object-perception, *or as a juxtaposed co-perception*, results in a certain kind of infinite regress."[41] Gallagher demonstrates this by having us consider the function of the body in providing the basis for an egocentric spatial frame of reference:

The fact that perception is perspectivally spatial is a fact that depends precisely on an implicit reference to the spatiality of the perceiving body. If one accepts the premise that sense perception of the world is spatially organized by an implicit reference to our bodily framework, the awareness that is the basis for that implicit reference cannot depend on perceptual awareness without threat of infinite regress. To avoid infinite regress one requires a prereflective bodily awareness that is built into the structures of perception and action, but that is not itself egocentric.[42]

At some point, Gallagher argues, we must arrive at the self-appearance of a subjectivity *subtending* the appearance of the perceived. Gallagher and Zahavi both insist that self-awareness cannot be separated from hetero-awareness, but they also insist that there are different forms of awareness implied here. The attempts made by the ecological and sensorimotor approaches to ground perception in the law-governed correlation of a sensorimotor body with its environment founder on the problem of subjectivity because, while they entail bodily self-awareness as a condition of perception, they place the body entirely into the order of the perceived. What they seem to miss is the way in which bodily *self*-awareness fundamentally *structures* appearance—including the appearance (as object) of one's own body. By placing the body wholly into the order of the perceived, by failing to account for the way in which the body is both subject *and* object of perception, they, in effect, revive the mind-body problem.

This problem is particularly evident if we consider the fact that the subject, in both accounts, is said to possess a (tacit) *knowledge* of the laws correlating her bodily possibilities to features of the environment, knowledge that can putatively be made explicit using the methods of empirical science. But we are not told how an ecological subject, whose forms of self-awareness are grounded in a *co-perception* of herself along with other perceivable features of her environment, could ever come to know her own body as the unique incarnate principle of her *own* possibilities. The body is the principle of possibilities only insofar as it is an ensemble of powers, skills, capabilities, and so forth. We can begin to discover what hands (in general) are capable of only because we first of all know what *our* hands can do. And we can know *this* only because our hands incarnate our own possibilities—we, so to speak, live through the deployments of these possibilities. Only an ecological subject would ever be able to recognize the lawfulness of environments (even those of other species) because only an ecological subject can know the meanings of 'possibility' and 'affordances.' She knows this because she is first of all aware of her own situation as alive with powers and possibilities, as a certain way of being open to futurity.

But, in fact, we cannot see how an ecological or sensorimotor subject would ever be able to discover this because the form of her bodily self-awareness is indistinguishable from that of her apprehension of third-personal facts and laws of the environment. The very notion of 'possibility' (as it is used by ecological psychology) thus becomes incomprehensible; possibility comes to be indentified with third-person facts and detached from the very being whose dynamic structures of behavior are the very principles of that possibility. Insofar as they claim to found new *scientific* approaches to perception, the sensorimotor and ecological approaches entail a subject who must be able to grasp, from the outside (i.e, from a third-person point of view), the principles organizing her own ecological situation. To put the problem another way: if an ecological psychologist is not *at once* wholly a body and wholly an 'I can' (a unity that phenomenology affirms but that remains ultimately unexplained in both the sensorimotor and ecological accounts), then we can only imagine that she discovers the identity between 'real possibility' and 'actual states of affairs' in pure thought (if she can discover it at all). Thus, with regard to the subject, the sensorimotor and ecological approaches to perception, in spite of all their advances beyond traditional epistemology, end up oscillating between the alternatives of empiricism and intellectualism.

## II. PERCEPTION AND SUBJECTIVITY BEYOND METAPHYSICS

Merleau-Ponty observes that "A psychology is always brought face to face with the problem of the constitution of the world." But, precisely insofar as it does not directly confront this metaphysical dimension, "Psychological reflection, once begun . . . outruns itself through its own momentum":

> Having recognized the originality of phenomena in relation to the objective world, since it is through them that the objective world is known to us, it is led to integrate with them every possible object and to try to find out how that object is constituted through them. (*PhP*, 60/73)

Merleau-Ponty makes this observation with particular reference to Gestalt theory and its claim, which we encountered above, that perception originally discloses form, meaning, or structure, and not discrete impressional data. Gestalt psychology 'outruns itself' insofar as it expresses its findings in terms of the psychological 'laws' governing the appearance of forms. The appearance of forms, Merleau-Ponty cautions, "is not the external unfolding of a pre-existing reason":

It is not *because* the 'form' produces a certain state of equilibrium, solving a problem of maximum coherence and, in the Kantian sense, making a world possible, that it enjoys a privileged place in our perception; it is the very appearance of the world and not the condition of its possibility; it is the birth of a norm and is not realized according to a norm [*elle est la naissance d'une norme et ne se réalise pas d'après une norme*]; it is the identity of the external and the internal and not the projection of the internal in the external. Although, then, it is not the outcome of some circulation of mental states in themselves, neither is it an idea. (*PhP*, 60–1/73–4)

We can see then that Merleau-Ponty's challenge to Gestalt psychology also applies to the sensorimotor and ecological accounts of perception. Sensorimotor and ecological accounts of perception, like Gestalt psychology, offer rich insights into the phenomena of perception, but their aim differs essentially from that of phenomenology. They want to tell us how perception is possible, and this is not equivalent to describing how it actually happens. The analysis of perception must first of all be freed from the hidden prejudices of realism *and* idealism or it falls prey to the very limitations that the ecological and sensorimotor approaches identify and seek to overcome. Perception, in Merleau-Ponty's view, does not proceed according to preexisting laws nor is it guided along the contours of a ready-made world; rather, the world of perception *emerges* along with its own immanent norms. This means that the norms guiding perception must remain open-ended, to-be-decided. Or, to put it in the Husserlian terms that we used for speaking of horizon in chapter 1, we are not merely speaking of an indeterminacy within a determinate structure, but a structural indeterminacy.

In this connection, let us note that the concept of 'tacit' or practical knowledge is sometimes used in a manner that makes it difficult to distinguish from propositional knowledge. The moment we say that sensorimotor or ecological perception involves the *tacit* knowledge of psychophysical *laws* it seems to me that we risk losing sight of what distinguishes sensorimotor know-how (implying an 'I can') from propositional knowledge (implying an 'I think'). I believe we find in Merleau-Ponty a form of tacit knowledge that is open to contingencies of a different order than the sensorimotor contingencies identified by O'Regan and Noë. That is to say, there is a form of know-how that is not merely an unconscious 'knowledge' of a series of if/then co-variants (sensorimotor contingencies in O'Regan and Noë's sense), but that is precisely *tacit* in the sense that it *cannot* be made exhaustively explicit. And it cannot be made explicit because it is a kind of skillfulness that remains open to possible transformations. Merleau-Ponty's analysis of depth perception, and the categories of 'motivation' and 'decision' that he introduces in the course of that analysis, already exemplifies this sense of open-ended know-how.

O'Regan and Noë's example of the guided missile exemplifies the limitations in their conception of 'practical knowledge.' When we say that a guided missile has 'mastery' of sensorimotor contingencies we mean that it processes information in terms of a set of if/then co-variants. It embodies a rule for 'making sense' of what it 'sees' by translating visual information directly into actions. This knowledge is said to be tacit, or practical, because the sensorimotor system does not know explicitly the rules that it nevertheless follows in performing this task. Human perceivers may have more complex tasks to perform, but O'Regan and Noë use the guided missile example because, in their view, it illustrates, in simplified form, the basic principle of sensorimotor perception, including human perception. Perception is practical knowledge of the relevance of sensory information with regard to possible movement (and vice-versa). Thus, they add, the perceiver "must be *actively exercising* its mastery of [sensorimotor] laws . . . the notion of being tuned, or having mastery, only makes sense within the context of the behavior and purpose of the system or individual in its habitual setting."[43] In other words, it is only with reference to a purpose or a task to be performed that one is able to perceive.

The notion of habit is crucial here. In many ways O'Regan and Noë's account of sensorimotor know-how is similar to Merleau-Ponty's understanding of habit as 'a motor significance.' The mastery of the laws of sensorimotor contingencies is a habit in this sense, and it is the habit, as a *form* of responsive behavior, that allows a perceiver to, as it were, see 'beyond' the currently 'sampled' information from the perceptual field. The perceiver knows what to do with the sampled information, both because the information is patterned, and because the perceiver ('in its habitual setting') has some habitual way of making use of these patterns for its own behavior. And this, again, is similar to Merleau-Ponty's claim that the 'essential structures' of the present allow us to anticipate what lies beyond the immediately given. But Merleau-Ponty's observation (which we discussed in chapter 2) that a child must *learn* to see colors, and that the 'colors' the child initially sees are incomparable to any determinate quality in the adult's world, requires that we make an important distinction with regard to the ways in which movement makes sense, or manifests a form in movement. The child cannot have clearly anticipated the 'colors' that she was eventually to see. And her sensorimotor know-how would not have been able to subtend this appearance without undergoing a transformation.

Let us distinguish between two kinds of movement. On the one hand, there is movement by which we make sense of 'information' from the perceptual field, and, on the other hand, there is movement by which we *learn* ways of making sense of the perceptual field. A completely habitual movement would make sense insofar as, in each of its phases, it adheres precisely to its own form. In this sense, a movement makes sense because there is no need to *make* sense. There would already be a form (perhaps as a kind of motor-program in the 'mind' of a subject, or somehow embodied as 'practical knowledge') to which the movement would adhere in all of its phases. This is the kind of movement that is implied in what Merleau-Ponty speaks of as "second-order" expression (which he thinks of, in connection with language, as the deployment of already instituted meanings). When, for example, I make a conventional gesture of pointing by extending my arm and index finger in a certain direction, my movement is the redeployment of a gestural meaning that is ready-made and already available for use, it is, precisely, a conventional gesture. But other kinds of movements—for example, someone's spontaneous 'dancing for joy'—may be quite ambiguous, or may even appear to lack any sense (even to the subject who 'initiates' them). They generate their own meaning in the course of their own unfolding. They may, then, even signal the emergence of a new habitual form of behavior, a form of behavior that can be repeated on other occasions. These movements make sense precisely insofar as they *make* sense. But the point here is that such movements do not start off 'knowing' what they are aiming at. The dance for joy is 'spontaneous' precisely to the extent that it is the very enactment of joy, it is someone's way of being joyful, or, we could also say, it is joy's way of enacting itself in a body.

The sensorimotor know-how of the infant who distinguishes only between 'colored' and 'not-colored' is the *form* of the behavior which lets these phenomena show themselves. It is, insofar as it manifests a sensible quality, an acquired habit in the sense of 'a motor grasping of a motor sense.' The movements involved in looking also let themselves be moved in a certain way. We know that eventually the child will learn to see the full range of the colors of the spectrum, but the habitual movements of, say, the ocular muscles, did not 'grasp' what they were aiming toward when the child differentiated only between colored and not-colored. The two sets of qualities are, again, 'incomparable.' But the motive for the transition cannot have come entirely from outside the child's perceptual experience either. What is required, then, for a transition to a new way of letting 'color' show itself is an element, *within* the sense of movement, of contingency—that is, an element of non-sense. So we must distinguish between know-how in the sense that, I think, is often implicit in O'Regan and Noë's use of the concept, as a knowledge (of rules, or laws) that I simply do not know that I possess, and know-how in the sense that Merleau-Ponty's has in mind when he indicates a form of behavior, a manner of making sense, that is open to *its own* transformation from within.

If we wanted to teach O'Regan and Noë's missile guidance system to move in a different way, or to sample different information from its 'visual' field, we would need to program these changes into it. But what we need to see, in the case of the development of a living perceptual system, is how the very appearance of the sensible is also the appearance of a demand to see otherwise. Such a perceptual system must not merely 'know' a sensorimotor rule; rather, it must also 'know' the impossibility of a rule. It must 'know,' in short, that what it makes appear is, to use Lawlor's phrase, a 'repetition without original.' And, at least for human perceivers, this 'knowledge' (the haunting of the present by 'a past which has never been a present') is precisely what vouchsafes the sense of the 'reality' of things:

> If the thing itself were reached, it would be from that moment arrayed before us and stripped of its mystery. It would cease to exist as a thing at the very moment when we thought to possess it. What makes the 'reality' of the thing is thereby precisely what snatches it from our grasp. The aseity of the thing, its unchallengeable presence [*presence irrécusable*] and the perpetual absence into which it withdraws [*et l'absence perpétuelle dans laquelle elle se retranche*], are two inseparable aspects of transcendence. (*PhP*, 233/270)

What O'Regan and Noë's missile guidance system fundamentally lacks, then, is a sense of 'reality.' This is because it lacks a sense of presence; and it lacks a sense of presence because it lacks the sense of non-presence, within the present, upon which the very *sense* of presence depends. As we have argued, the concept of 'law' as it is used in the sciences, and as it is thus used by the advocates of the sensorimotor and ecological accounts of perception, entails a certain conception of temporality. To achieve mastery of a law a subject must have a certain relation to its own future—it must somehow embody, in the present, the structures according to which its future will, according to a strict necessity, unfold. In this sense, the future must already be present as a determinate field of possibilities. Insofar as perception is made to depend on the mastery of sensorimotor or ecological laws, the subject must either be understood as a pure consciousness, able to understand itself as the transcendental condition for all possible appearance, or it must be a machine whose operations are strictly governed by lawful third-person processes. We are faced either with a pure being-for-itself, or a being in-itself. The sensorimotor account is inadequate to the problem of subjectivity because it does not criticize the prejudice in favor of presence that characterizes modern science and so it ends up conflating the subject of perception with a machine.

Now, arguably, we are placing too much of a burden on O'Regan and Noë's guided missile example. That is to say, it may be that this example is merely intended to show us one particular feature of the dynamics of perception—i.e., its reliance on structures of co-variants. But we can see the same limitation in the sensorimotor approach if we consider one of its more general claims pertaining to perceptual systems, including human ones.

O'Regan and Noë differentiate between sensory information that is simply registered by the nervous system, or the brain, and sensory information that the perceiver becomes aware of. You become aware of things, they claim, insofar as you "turn your attention" to them—that is, insofar as you are actively making use of information "for thought and action-guidance." They insist that "in the complete absence of *current access*, there is no perception."[44] In other words, the structure of the perceptual field (*ex hypothesi* the field of which you are currently, attentively, aware) is governed both by the laws of sensorimotor contingencies *and* the sense of a task—'thought and action-guidance.' But, as Evan Thompson points out, this approach involves equating all consciousness with attention and this equation prevents us from understanding how the transitions between not noticing and then noticing something actually occur within our experience:

> The experiential difference between not noticing and then noticing a noise is treated statically, as if it were a discrete state transition, with no extended temporal dynamics, and there is no differentiation within the temporal dynamics of the experience between implicit and explicit aspects. One may notice a noise in an implicit way, in which case one lives through the sound without grasping it as a distinct object.[45]

This brings us back to the phenomenological problems of depth, of the relationships between indeterminacy and determinacy, presence and non-presence, prominence and background. And, again, Merleau-Ponty approaches the phenomenon of depth through the categories of motivation and decision, of a 'tacit decision' that is also, at the same time, the affirmation of what motivates it. The field of awareness, with its prominences and occlusions, its nearness and farness, its surfaces and levels, is not structured by third-person processes—rather, it must be understood as the meaningful situation of a being who moves, values, acts, and responds. Thompson worries that O'Regan and Noë's account of attention seems to attribute the causes of "attentional shifts" to "subpersonal dispositions," to third-personal processes—their description thus overlooks the first-personal character of these transitions.

Thompson's own description seems to overcome the stark opposition between first-person and third-person by invoking the concept of "affection":

> "Affection" means being affectively influenced or perturbed. The idea is that whatever becomes noticeable must have already been affecting one and must have some kind of affective force or allure (affective grabbiness) in relation to one's attention. . . . Affective allure or grabbiness thus implies a dynamic gestalt or figure-ground structure: Something becomes noticeable, at whatever level, due to the strength of its allure or grabbiness, emerging into affective prominence, salience, or relief, while other things become less noticeable due to the comparative weakness of their allure.[46]

I am motivated to shift my regard because something affects me. Something that had not been prominent in my consciousness *becomes* prominent. Affection is not itself a matter of my own volition, and yet, if the affection did not have a "subjective or first-personal character," it would never be able to motivate the turning of my regard.[47] For Thompson, then, the temporal dynamics of experience are first of all the temporal dynamics of a prereflective consciousness. Alterations of the field of presence are transitions from tacit, or horizonal, consciousness to active noticing. They are possible because consciousness is a dynamic structure: it is the incarnate consciousness of a bodily 'I can.' Merleau-Ponty says something similar when he writes that, if we are to understand the act of attention and its possible modifications, "Consciousness must be faced with its own unreflective life in things [*Il faut mettre la conscience en présence de sa vie irréfléchie dans les choses*] and awakened to its own history which it was forgetting: such is the true part that philosophical reflection has to play, and thus do we arrive at a true theory of attention" (*PhP*, 31/40). Here Merleau-Ponty *seems* to be saying that philosophy can develop a true theory of attention because it remains with the first-person perspective; it helps consciousness to discover (to reflect upon) its own first-personal, prereflective, life. Thus we could say that Merleau-Ponty differs from O'Regan and Noë because, like Thompson, he pays heed to the demand to assert the primacy of the first-personal dimension.

And yet, as we have seen, this is not the whole story for Merleau-Ponty. Thompson says that even when I am only horizonally conscious of a sound, the "sound's appearance and affective influence have a subjective or first-personal character."[48] But Merleau-Ponty says that "Every perception takes place in an atmosphere of generality and is presented to us anonymously. . . . So, if I wanted to render precisely the perceptual experience, I ought to say that *one* perceives in me [*je devrais dire qu'on perçoit en moi*], and not that I perceive" (*PhP*, 215/249). Merleau-Ponty's description of affection here does not presuppose first-personal givenness; rather, he seems to want to show how the first-person *emerges* within a field of manifestation that is neither first-personal nor third-personal. If an 'affection' is a 'motivation,' it is because it is taken up into a 'tacit decision,' but this means that the affection does not originally happen in the mode of first-personal givenness. (This is not to say that there are not many things in our ordinary experience of which we are already marginally conscious and to which, at a certain point, we deliberately turn our full attention, but recall that, for Merleau-Ponty, our explicit, conscious, decisions always presuppose those 'tacit decisions' whereby our bodies have already marked out a field of possibilities, of affective motor values.) In fact, we must also say that the *decision* does not begin as a first-personal process: *I* am not the decider. In short, the decision that allows something to function as a motivation for my seeing is also a decision concerning the 'I can.' While I am in agreement with Thompson that the sensorimotor theory's account of subjectivity is inadequate insofar as it lacks an account of affection-as-motivation, I think that it can be misleading to think of affection in terms of first-personal givenness. This does not mean that the motivation and the decision are merely anthropomorphisms designating third-personal processes. What we need to understand is the *process* by which living movement enacts the identity of a self precisely by responding to a call of the sensible—this response would always be belated, and this belatedness would form a part of the structure of self-consciousness.

What appears in my experience appears in *my* field of presence, in what we could call a field of first-personal givenness. But it appears therein as a repetition without original. And this is why it can appear 'in an atmosphere of generality.' As we saw in chapter 2, the spaces opened up by our sentient bodies, as, say, our eyes harken to the demands of the visible, are singularities; each one is an absolute, a 'total being.' But the sensible appears *in* our experience as a certain generality because the contact between the organs of our sentient bodies and the world, a contact which beckons the motor powers of our bodies to begin to articulate the space in which something can appear, is always already in the past. This past, the time in which these singularities made their demands upon our bodies, appears in the present (which is why we can speak of all this in the terms of a 'phenomenology'), but only as 'immemorial depth,' as a constitutive non-presence *within* the present. Thus the singularity of the sensible is always already a generality, or, to use Merleau-Ponty's concept: a style. Style, like the concept of 'motor value,' which we discussed earlier, cuts across the dyadic opposition of 'information' and 'law' that we have found operating throughout both the sensorimotor and ecological accounts of perception.

Style is, as Merleau-Ponty says, a certain 'manner' in which things show themselves. The concept at once designates that which individuates things and persons, that which allows them to show themselves as *identities*, and that which reveals a certain *typicality* cutting across things and situations. As Merleau-Ponty writes,

> A style is a certain manner of dealing with situations, which I identify or understand in an individual or in a writer, by taking over that manner myself in a sort of imitative way, even though I may be quite unable to define it: and in any case a definition, correct though it may be, never provides an exact equivalent, and is never of interest to any but those who have already had the actual experience. I experience the unity of the world as I recognize a style. (*PhP*, 327/378)

We are not able to define a style, the style of a writer or painter, because precisely what is stylized in our own experience is a certain singularity. I cannot really define Merleau-Ponty's style of philosophizing by saying it is like, or unlike, someone else's style, nor can I do so by itemizing his persistent themes and concepts, or his preferred phrasings—I can only read it, let myself adhere to its unique demands. But adhering to these demands will also enable me to discern his influence, to discern imitations of his manner, and echoes of his concerns, in other writers and thinkers. The point is that I cannot say *what* enables me to move between the singularity on the one side, and the generality on the other. This is because there is necessarily some contribution of the sensible involved in the apprehension of a style. And, for this reason, there is a sense in which I can recognize a style only by directly experiencing it because only my body, through the manners by which it adheres to the demands of the sensible, can make this decisive contribution to my experience of a style. Only the mysterious 'communion' of incompossible spaces that is enacted *in*, and *as*, the unity of my sentient body, can envelope the singularity of the sensible in the generality of a style. As Merleau-Ponty writes:

> What unites 'tactile sensations' in the hand and links them to visual perceptions of the same hand, and to perceptions of other bodily areas, is a certain style informing my manual gestures and implying in turn a certain style of finger movements, and contributing in the last resort, to a certain bodily bearing. The body is to be compared, not to a physical object, but rather to a work of art [*Ce n'est pas à l'objet physique que le corps peut être comparé, mais plutôt à l'oeuvre d'art*]. (*PhP*, 150/175–6)[49]

The body can be unified in the manner of a work of art because each of its sensations of itself is also a 'repetition without original,' its unity is neither a *necessity* nor a *fact*, even if this unity *imposes itself* on a consciousness *as* something necessary, something *given*. The body 'appears' with a certain residue of non-presence, of spectral depth, and it is for this reason that it can appear to itself only according to a style. (We shall consider this issue in greater detail in chapter 4 when we speak of 'auto-affection').

The anarchic presence/non-presence of the sensible in our most fundamental awareness of the typical is precisely what intellectualism is not able to grasp:

Intellectualism is unequal to dealing with . . . perceptual life, either falling short of it [or] overshooting it; it calls up as limiting cases the manifold qualities which are merely the outer casing of the object, and from there it passes on to a consciousness of the object which claims to hold within itself the law or secret of that object, and which for this reason deprives the development of the experience of its contingency and the object of its distinctive perceptual style [*son style perceptif*]. (*PhP*, 38–9/48–9)

So, again, the concept of style is to be opposed to the concept of 'law' that is employed in the sensorimotor and ecological accounts of perception. And the sensation (as always already stylized in perception) is thus also to be contrasted with the notion of 'information' used in those accounts. This also means that we must rethink, along the lines that we suggested above, the whole question of sensorimotor know-how. In contrast to the information-processing machine metaphors prevalent in much recent cognitive science, Merleau-Ponty repeatedly looks to the art of painting as an exemplary case of sensorimotor know-how.

Painting, for Merleau-Ponty, is not merely an *example* of the sensorimotor know-how involved in perception. Rather painting is itself a kind of prolongation of the sensorimotor dynamics of perception. What Merleau-Ponty particularly emphasizes in his reflections on painting is that perception is inherently a matter, not merely of movement, but of *expressive* movement. We have already seen the reasons for this in considering Merleau-Ponty's claim that the body is an 'expressive unity' that 'interprets itself.' The unity of the body, as we have just said, is neither a fact, nor *simply* an a priori. Rather the body becomes an a priori (constantly *transforming* itself) by virtue of the manner in which it 'makes space' for things to appear. Merleau-Ponty writes, for example, that "it is the expressive operation of the body, begun by the smallest perception, which is amplified into painting and art" (S, 70/112), and, for this reason, he says that there is a little of the painter in every human being (S, 64/104). Through his painting, says Merleau-Ponty, Cézanne "learned that expression is the language of the thing itself and springs from its [the thing's] configuration" (PhP, 322/372). But Merleau-Ponty also says that "expression is everywhere creative, and [that] what is expressed is always inseparable from it" (PhP, 391/448; my italics). Thus the being of the perceived is to be sought in an expressivity that, paradoxically, does not ex-press anything outside of itself. Painting does not reproduce what a perceiver sees, nor does it reproduce the subjective experience of seeing; rather, the act of painting is the language of the thing itself. Now if painting is an amplification of a creative expressivity already at work in perception, an expressivity that is the 'voice' of things, then clearly the painter's know-how is something other than a propositional knowing. But this is not merely because the painter does not explicitly 'know' structures of co-variants governing the relation between what she senses and how her body moves; rather, it is because the activity itself generates the norms that guide it. The know-how arises from within the sensorimotor dynamics of the activity. The color 'red' finds its own expression as a certain 'motor value' that is only established within the dynamic context of the emerging painting.

The painter does not work in a medium of sensorimotor laws but of motor values—each of Cézanne's paintings of La Montagne Sainte-Victoire involve new 'decisions' and 'evaluations,' and each of these allow the familiar greens and blues and yellows to become strange again, to 'speak' in novel ways. But neither does the painter begin completely afresh each time he begins to paint. In a certain sense, we could say that the painter is able to paint only because he also does not know how to paint. As we said earlier, Merleau-Ponty's concept of 'motor value' implies that perception is not a matter of knowledge but of movement discriminatingly allowing 'itself' to be moved. The painter must begin the activity in order to begin to subject himself to the norm that will guide his activity. As Merleau-Ponty writes, "Cézanne is an example of how precariously expression and communication are achieved. Expression is like a step taken in the fog [comme un pas dans la brume]—no one can say where, if anywhere, it will lead" (SNS, 3–4/8). But the painter is also not entirely without resources before he begins: his activity draws on cultural traditions, on the styles of other painters, on events in the painter's personal history, on his patiently developed skills and techniques, on materials like oil paints and brushes. These resources are not laid out before the painter, and he does not draw on them, as it were, 'knowingly.' Rather, it would be better to say that the expressive movement of painting itself makes use of these things. All of these contingent elements are taken up, through the painter's activity, into an expressivity of the things themselves. Merleau-Ponty says in a later work that "the painting relates to nothing at all among experienced things unless it is first of all 'autofigurative'" (EM, 181/69). The point here is that the painter (as a sensorimotor subject) is a kind of point of passage, or translation, where all of the elements of the art of painting can come together. And this is true of the subjectivity of perception in general. As Merleau-Ponty writes, "The *person who* perceives is not spread out before himself as a consciousness must be; he has historical density, he takes up a perceptual tradition [*il reprend une tradition perceptive*] and is faced with a present" (PhP, 238/275). The perceptual tradition (an 'original past') is retroactively determined in the form of a 'motivation' concerning which the subject (including the subject as painter) is the enactment of a 'decision'; the subject is the site where 'evaluation' happens such that sensible being can find its own 'voice.' We cannot say that the painter's know-how is guided by the sense of a task (on the analogy with a missile guidance system) because here the sense (*sens*) of the task is, again, only articulated in the execution of it.

We began, in chapter 1, by saying that scientific approaches to the problem of subjectivity end up occluding the very thing that is in question: the first-person perspective. But I now want to highlight a claim that has been implicit in what we have said about subjectivity here and in chapter 2: the assertion of the primacy of the first-person perspective can occlude aspects of perception that are neither subjective nor objective—including the body with its spatio-temporal and historical density.

In fact, it is not merely because we overlook the first-person perspective that a certain objectivist prejudice (what Merleau-Ponty calls, the "prejudice in favour of determinate being" [PhP, 51n/62n]) determines our thinking about, or scientific investigations of, perceptual experience. Indeed, intellectualism unambiguously asserts the primacy of the first-person; nevertheless, Merleau-Ponty says, empiricism and intellectualism share a common prejudice:

> Both take the objective world as the object of their analysis, when this comes first neither in time nor in virtue of its meaning; and both are incapable of expressing the peculiar way in which perceptual consciousness constitutes its object. Both keep their distance in relation to perception instead of sticking closely to it. (PhP, 26/34)

In either of its forms, Merleau-Ponty says, "Objective thought is unaware of the subject of perception. This is because it presents itself with the world ready made [*le monde tout fait*], as the setting of every possible event, and treats perception as one of these events" (PhP, 207/240). For the ready-made world of naïve realism intellectualism substitutes a 'ready made thinking,' and thus, "it remains true to say that intellectualism too provides itself with a ready-made world. For the constitution of the world, as conceived by it, is a mere requirement that to each term of the empiricist description be added the indication 'consciousness of . . .'" (*PhP*, 208/241). Modern epistemologies oscillate between viewing the subject as a passive subject of sensation (information) and association, or an active subject of judgment and understanding. Even the sensorimotor and ecological accounts of perception seem unable to overcome the opposition between activity and passivity which has characterized the modern metaphysics of the subject. The question is: do we get away from the alternatives of intellectualism and empiricism when we conceive consciousness as, first and foremost, *prereflective* consciousness?

As we saw with Thompson, what the doctrine of prereflective consciousness adds to the sensorimotor account is the assertion that the field of the embodied subject, at any given time, contains features of which the subject is not currently (explicitly) aware and other contents of which it is— the subject is not completely *unconscious* of these background features, but only tacitly conscious of them. (This is, again, in contrast to O'Regan and Noë's contention that attentional shifts are transitions from unconscious appearance, registered by the nervous system, to consciously experienced appearance. Recall that for Thompson, consciousness is an autonomous, or autopoietic, system; nothing enters it as *caused*.) The 'world,' or situation, of the situated subject is thus characterized by first-personal givenness because it is defined as the field of things of which it is, in principle, possible to have explicit conscious awareness. In other words, perceived being is defined in terms of perceptual lived-experience which is in turn determined according to the possibility of knowledge. Merleau-Ponty seems to endorse just such a view when he asserts the doctrine of a teleology of consciousness. This doctrine seems to involve the claim that objective truth is the implicit aim of our prereflective bodily engagement with the world. Let us cite again a passage we looked at in chapter 2 concerning the teleology of consciousness:

> We must contrive to understand how, at a strike, existence projects round itself worlds which hide objectivity from me, at the same time fastening upon it as the aim of the teleology of consciousness, by picking out these 'worlds' against the background of one single natural world. (*PhP*, 294/340)

The 'teleology of consciousness,' Merleau-Ponty says, is a striving toward 'truth'—"such is the primary phenomenon [*phénomène originaire*]" (*PhP*, 296/342). Later, in the "Cogito" chapter, Merleau-Ponty repeats this claim about a teleology of consciousness:

*Habeum ideam veram*, we possess a truth, but this experience of truth would be absolute knowledge only if we could thematize every motive, that is, if we ceased to be in a situation. The actual possession of the true idea does not, therefore, entitle us to predicate an intellectual abode of adequate thought and absolute productivity, it establishes merely a 'teleology' of consciousness which, from this first instrument, will forge more perfect ones, and these in turn more perfect ones still, and so on endlessly. (*PhP*, 395–6/453)

We could only possess 'absolute knowledge' if we could 'thematize every motive,' but we have seen that every thematization of a motive would also be an occlusion of an original past. This original past, then, as the call for a decision concerning the shape of the field of presence, would motivate the thematization while at the same time making an exhaustive thematization impossible in principle. But consciousness, as consciousness of an inexhaustible *reality*, cannot, as we have seen, be indifferent to this impossibility, which is also the impossibility of its teleological movement *toward* objective truth. The experience of reality is also an experience of the impossibility of objective truth, of an exhaustive synthesis. Our 'first instrument,' the one that would set consciousness on its way toward truth, is inevitably a 'repetition without original.' And this is why consciousness, in being a consciousness of an inexhaustible reality, is haunted by the lack of the ground that would render transparent the meanings of its life and its world. The thesis of teleology is in fact introduced, as we noted in chapter 2, right after the discussion of the 'phantom' spaces of the schizophrenic, the 'primitive' man, and the dreamer, when Merleau-Ponty says that these 'spaces' have no less claim to being grounded in perception than does the 'objective' space of the scientist. He then asks this rhetorical (but serious) question: "Is not the origin of precise knowledge being identified with a decision as unwarrantable as the one which shuts up the madman in his madness . . . ?" (*PhP*, 292/338). Insofar as we are alive to an inexhaustible reality, a world-in-depth that motivates and simultaneously resists its own synthesis, this question cannot be avoided.

It is precisely insofar as Merleau-Ponty, in *Phenomenology of Perception*, tends to interpret the meaning of embodiment, of 'the unreflective fund of experience,' from the standpoint of the consciousness of a telos, that he, at times, treats the body as an "intermediary," or as a "means" of communication with the world (*PhP*, 138–9/161; 92/109), and that he also, at times, treats depth, and absence, merely as "variations within a field of primordial presence, a perceptual domain over which my body exercises power [*d'un domaine perceptif sur lesquels mon corps a puissance*]" (*PhP*,

92/108). That is to say, he tends to treat the prereflective merely as the *pre-* of *reflective* consciousness, whereas we have seen that it also indicates a domain of what has never been a present to any consciousness, but that nevertheless haunts consciousness. As Merleau-Ponty says, the essence of consciousness is self-presence (*PhP*, xv/x). 'Consciousness' is the word with which modern metaphysics has designated a domain of self-transparency, truth, and knowledge. The notion of tacit or prereflective consciousness seems to involve a mere modification of the Cartesian notion of consciousness. The modification would appear to say simply that because it is not *pure* self-presence, because it is held back from objectivity and truth by the opacity of its situatedness, *prereflective* consciousness designates a domain of appearance which, as Merleau-Ponty says, merely "foreshadows" the domain of the *in-itself* (*PhP*, 294/340). It is implied in these passages that the 'one single natural world' that is in the background of all our experiences is an objective world that is 'hidden' from me, within the folds of my prereflective life, though it remains the implicit telos of consciousness.

But Merleau-Ponty also says that we must "recognize the indeterminate as a positive phenomenon" (*PhP*, 6/12). If we can understand 'indeterminacy' here in the profound sense, in connection with spectral depth, then this indeterminacy is not merely a foreshadowing, for consciousness, of some knowledge temporarily lacking to it, some indeterminacy waiting to be determined according to the 'essential structures' of the field of presence. Rather it attests to a fundamental ontological dimension that is older than, and *other* than, consciousness. In one of his last working notes, Merleau-Ponty says that it is "inevitable" that consciousness be "mystified, inverted, indirect" because:

> [Consciousness] disregards Being and prefers the object to it, that is, a Being with which it has broken and which it posits beyond this negation, by negating this negation—In it it ignores the non-dissimulation of Being, the *Unverborgenheit*, the non-mediated presence which is not something positive, which is being of the far-offs [*être des lointains*]. (VI, 248/296–7)

Insofar as it *is* conscious, consciousness aims at objectivity. It originally breaks with Being and then negates its negation. This, as we have seen, is the way living movement inaugurates sense. It begins (like Cézanne at his canvas) with a step into the fog, and then recuperates its beginning as the ground of the sense that the movement would inaugurate, as the subjective *source*, or the objective *destination*, at either end of its aim. Reflective thinking *posits* these as grounds. But the anarchic beginning of movement, the radical contingency of its *other* beginning, is, for consciousness, an original past, intimated, in the present, by the spectral presences of the 'far-offs.' It is thus always in relation, precisely through the births and deaths of its sentient flesh, to what Merleau-Ponty, using Heideggerian language, calls the *Unverborgenheit*—the unconcealment, or disclosure. To put this another way, we could say that that the term 'prereflective *consciousness*' designates the manner in which reflective consciousness is determined to view its own past—as the implicit form of its conscious life. But phenomenological description must also attend to what is occluded by this determination; that is to say, it must recognize that the act of reflection introduces a decisive change into the structure of unreflective life precisely by the manner in which it insists on grasping that life *as* its own prereflectively *conscious* life. What reflection thereby occludes are those features of the unreflective fund of experience that we have described as constitutive non-presence, spectral depth, generality, a (pre-personal) past that has never been a present. Phenomenology then must involve a critique of the primacy of presence, including the absolute primacy ascribed to the first-personal givenness of phenomena. We will take this up in greater detail in chapter 4.

This critique of the primacy of presence points to the possibility of another teleology, or a teleology *of* the other. Merleau-Ponty is led to this more profound sense of teleology, which I think we find not only asserted, but attested to in his later writings, by his reflection on the meaning of painting. In "Cézanne's Doubt," he writes,

> The meaning [*sens*] of what the artist is going to say *does not exist* anywhere—not in things, which as yet have no meaning, nor in the artist himself, in his unformulated life. It summons [*Il appelle*] one away from the already constituted reason in which 'cultured men' are content to shut themselves, toward a reason which contains its own origins [*à une raison qui embrasserait ses propres origines*]. (SNS, 19/32)

The telos of a logos 'which contains its own origins' cannot be posited. It would be the telos of a responsive activity not content with positing objective truth by negating the negation of Being, as a consciousness in presumed possession of itself would be. Rather, it seeks precisely to remain *open* to the demands of the sensible, the demands of singularities, to preserve, in the painting, the incompossibility of the 'spaces' of the sensible—which is why Cézanne could teach us what a *scientific* psychology could not: that we do not see either a circle or an ellipse when we view a plate from an oblique angle. The concern with objectivity, with the *in-itself*, would thus only be one way of responding to a more original demand to adhere to the call of singularities (and insofar as objectifying reason occludes its own origins, it would be an inadequate way). This more original demand is the demand of expression; it is not the teleology *of* a consciousness, but rather, it imposes itself on a consciousness, which, then, could not ever quite have its telos in full view.[50] Like a supposed teleology of objectivity, which, as Husserl teaches us, aims toward the truth of an ideal being-for-everyone, this teleology has its source and vectors marked out in the domain of intersubjectivity. But, in this case, I am suggesting, rather than seeking to disclose the truth of a being-for-*everyone*, the demand would be to express a truth that would not cease to adhere to the singularity of the sensible, and the incompossible 'spaces' of sentient bodies; thus, it would concern itself with the truth of a being-for-*each*-one:

> It is not for the painter like Cézanne, an artist, or a philosopher, to create and express an idea, they must also awaken the experiences which will make their idea take root in the consciousness of others [*mais encore réveiller les expériences qui l'enracineront dans les autres consciences*]. A successful work has the strange power to teach its own lesson. The reader or spectator who follows the clues of the book or painting, by setting up stepping stones and rebounding from side to side guided by the obscure clarity of a particular style [*guidé par la clarté confuse d'un style*], will end by discovering what the artist wanted to communicate. The painter can do no more than construct an image; he must wait for his image to come to life for other people. When it does, the work of art will have united these separate lives; it will no longer exist in only one of them like a stubborn dream or a persistent delirium, nor will it exist only in space as a colored piece of canvas. It will dwell undivided in several minds, with a claim on every possible mind like a perennial acquisition. (*SNS*, 19–20/33–4)

The 'truth' of expression then would have nothing to do with the overcoming of time, otherness, singularity, the singularity of the other, other bodies, hands, eyes, skin, the facticity of birth and death; rather it would find in these its sole mode of response to the *Unverborgenheit*. And far from alleviating anxiety concerning a decision 'as unwarrantable as the one which shuts up the madman in his madness,' it would have to be open to this risk. That is to say, it would, each time, have to put its faith in a future in which the expression would be able to unite 'separate lives' and broach the solitude of 'the stubborn dream' or the 'persistent delirium.'

    This other teleology would imply a very different meaning of the unreflective than that suggested by the notion of 'prereflective' consciousness, or a tacit cogito. We have seen that what lets appearance happen for a consciousness is, first of all, self-movement that makes sense (*sens*), movement that is also an evaluation concerning what will count for it as a motivation (and thus, also, what will count for it as a telos). But the logos of movement arises from a dynamic that is in play before there can be any first-personal consciousness of movement, before movement can be *my* movement. The unreflective body, as a unity of style, as the point of passage between the singular and the universal, would not, then, be a tacit cogito—not simply because it is opaque to itself, but because its very mode of being also attests to the impossibility of a cogito. We will develop this claim over the next two chapters (chapters 4 and 5) wherein we will directly confront the arguments of the two chapters of *Phenomenology of Perception* in which Merleau-Ponty seems to explicitly privilege consciousness-as-presence: the "Temporality" chapter and the "Cogito" chapter.

FOUR

# AUTO-AFFECTION AND ALTERITY

But do we know whether plenary objectivity can be conceived? Whether all perspectives are compossible? Whether they can all be thematized together somewhere? Do we know whether tactile and visual experiences can, strictly speaking, be joined without an intersensory experience? Whether my experience and that of another person can be linked in a single system of intersubjective experience? There may well be, either in each sensory experience or in each consciousness, 'phantoms' ['*fantômes*'] which no rational approach can account for.

—Merleau-Ponty

## I. PRESENCE

Perceptual experience is inherently temporal. The subject of perception is *situated* (spatially and temporally) by means of the manner in which experience anticipates its own future unfolding, and retains its past accomplishments both in the temporal thickness of the perceptual field and in the form of 'habits' carried forward from past experience. The subject is situated because it allows its situation to appear as a meaningful context, a field of presence. Thus the subject encounters *its own* possibilities and history *as* the meaning of that situation; it encounters *itself* in a situation's horizons of futurity and pastness. In the "Temporality" chapter of *Phenomenology of Perception*, Merleau-Ponty makes this claim about subjectivity and time:

It is of the essence of time to be not only actual time, or time which flows, but also time which is aware of itself, for the explosion or dehiscence of the present toward the future is the archetype of the *relationship of self to self* [*rapport de soi à soi*], and it traces out an interiority or an ipseity. (*PhP*, 426/487)

113

It is in terms of the investigation of time then that we come to the heart of the problem of subjectivity. In light of the claims that we have been making, over the past three chapters, about the haunting of consciousness (the field of presence) by a 'spectral depth,' by the facticity of sensation, and, thus, about the dependence of consciousness on 'a past which has never been a present,' it may seem somewhat surprising, then, to find Merleau-Ponty, in this context, say the following: "No one of time's dimensions can be deduced from the rest. But the *present* (in the wide sense, along with its horizons of primary past and future) nevertheless enjoys a privilege because *it is the zone in which being and consciousness coincide [la zone où l'être et la conscience coïncident]*" (*PhP*, 424/484–5; my italics). Passages like this one, and a few others like it in the "Temporality" chapter, have led some readers to conclude that, after all, *Phenomenology of Perception* remains firmly rooted within the tradition of what has come to be called a "metaphysics of presence."[1] We have been arguing that, according to the Merleau-Ponty of *Phenomenology of Perception*, perceptual experience is dependent on the emergence of *sense* in movement. Thus, we have argued that experience is temporal not only in the sense that it always presupposes a 'field of presence,' but also in that it is always haunted by its own originary delay (its dependence upon an origin from which it has always already departed, 'a past which has never been a present'). These claims might appear to be in tension with Merleau-Ponty's claim concerning the 'privilege' of the present, and thus we must seek to understand the nature and limits of this 'privilege.' And to do this, we must understand it in the context of the central claim of the "Temporality" chapter: the notion of time as auto-affection.

In chapter 2, we distinguished three ways of talking about depth: 1) there is depth as it is understood in traditional accounts of 'objective,' geometrical, space—depth as a third dimension that cannot actually be perceived, but must be 'inferred'; 2) there is what we have called 'affordance depth,' or depth understood in terms of the 'spatiality of situation,' and; 3) there is 'spectral depth,' which Merleau-Ponty does not thematize as such in *Phenomenology of Perception*, but which is intimated in connection with certain liminal experiences of space, as, for example, in dreams, or in passing moments of intersensory conflict. In the "Temporality" chapter we again see a tripartite scheme—here employed with regard to time. Merleau-Ponty borrows this scheme from Husserl. The three 'levels' are: 1) "objective time" (*PhP*, 420/480); 2) 'lived' time (*PhP*, 413/473)—what we could also call the temporality of 'situation' (*PhP*, 423/484)—and; 3) an "ultimate consciousness" or "primary flow" (*PhP*, 424/485; 426/487). In encountering this deepest 'level' of temporality, Merleau-Ponty tells us, we come to the heart of the problem of subjectivity: auto-affection. With the doctrine of time as auto-affection, or ultimate consciousness, we seem to find, in Merleau-Ponty's philosophy, the very notion of prereflective, or non-transitive, self-consciousness that, according to some recent figures working at the intersection of phenomenology and cognitive science, is lacking in the sensorimotor and ecological accounts of cognition that we discussed in chapters 1 and 3. However, at the end of chapter 3, we claimed that Merleau-Ponty's notion of the 'unreflective' is not simply equivalent to the notion of 'prereflective *consciousness*.' In chapter 5, we will encounter what appears to be Merleau-Ponty's most explicit argument for a notion of pre-reflective (nontransitive) self-awareness, or what in the "Cogito" chapter he calls a 'tacit cogito,' and we will there offer an interpretation of this notion that will make use of what we have learned concerning the emer-gence of sense in movement. But we have already seen that the notion of a prereflective consciousness is rendered problematic by the results of the analysis of sensation. The 'past' of reflective consciousness is not *simply* an implicit consciousness. Reflective consciousness, as presence, determines its past on the basis of the 'essential structures' of the present and thus takes itself to be the explicit form of what was already implicit—but this retroac-tive determination never quite succeeds in overcoming the facticity of the 'unreflective fund of experience.'

In this chapter, I will argue for an interpretation of Merleau-Ponty's notion of auto-affection according to which it refers, at once, to the dehis-cence of an origin—sensation—*and* to the 'decision' of living movement that lets the origin appear on the one hand as a 'motivation,' and on the other hand as 'subjectivity.' Time is subjectivity because it temporalizes itself in movement that lets itself be moved (motivated, affected). Merleau-Ponty employs Husserl's notion of an "ultimate consciousness"—a "coincidence" of "being" and "being for itself"—to designate this auto-affection of time, but he also says that time is "the power which holds [events] together while keeping them apart [*la puissance qui les maintient ensemble en les éloignant l'un de l'autre*]" (PhP, 422/483). Consciousness, as a holding-together, depends upon a keeping-apart that it can never succeed in overcoming. Our reading of the analyses of space and sensation has prepared us to recognize that this keeping-apart, the very 'dehiscence' of time, 'appears' to consciousness as an original past, a haunting of the present by what has never been a pres-ent. Experience begins with a repetition, a movement that generates sense and that, in doing so, generates its own origin and end—but, in doing so, movement dissimulates the facticity of its own beginning. As Merleau-Ponty says, in *The Visible and the Invisible*, "the originating breaks up [*l'originaire éclate*], and philosophy must accompany this break-up . . ." (VI, 124/163). Auto-affection, I will argue here, cannot simply be identified with an 'ulti-mate consciousness'—it must also be understood as a hetero-affection upon which consciousness depends. Merleau-Ponty's use of the term 'ultimate consciousness' is thus perhaps misleading insofar as it seems to occlude this constitutive element of non-presence, a non-presence which thus ceaselessly contests the self-identity of the subject. We should recall, in this connection, that the Husserlian text from which Merleau-Ponty draws his inspiration in identifying the auto-affection of time with 'ultimate consciousness' includes this admission: "For all this, we lack names."[2]

In developing these interpretations of the statement of the 'privilege' of the present and of the doctrine of auto-affection, I will confront Merleau-Ponty's philosophy with a particularly powerful challenge to phenomenology, the challenge of 'deconstruction.' Beginning with his 1967 *Speech and Phenomena*, Jacques Derrida has argued that there is a tension in phenomenology insofar as it seems to rely upon a notion of subjective self-presence that its own phenomenological descriptions of time, intersubjectivity, language, and embodiment, also contest. Derrida develops this appraisal of phenomenology through a number of readings of the texts of Husserl. Most recently, in his 2000 *On Touching—Jean-Luc Nancy* [*Le Toucher—Jean-Luc Nancy*], Derrida has claimed that the notion of the 'lived-body' (*Leib* in Husserl's German, *le corps propre*—"one's own body"—in Derrida's French, as in Merleau-Ponty's) is infected with the same tension. In that work, Derrida directs his attention to the notion of 'intercorporeity' in Merleau-Ponty and criticizes what he considers to be an occlusion of the alterity of the other in Merleau-Ponty's thought. I will argue that Derrida has not sufficiently heeded the sense of alterity in Merleau-Ponty's account of *le corps propre* and thus that he mischaracterizes the latter's account of our embodied relations with others.

According to Derrida, phenomenological treatments of the lived, or own, body have emphasized the continuity and identity of the lived (own) body at the cost of occluding the elements of difference, non-presence, and alterity, that interrupt the self-coincidence of the corporeal subject and that require us to speak, not of 'auto-affection' *simpliciter*, but "auto-affection '*effects*.'"[3] In fact, I do not think that this position is different from that of Merleau-Ponty. I have already suggested that, for Merleau-Ponty, the *autos* of *auto*-affection is always a retroactive determination, and in this chapter I will argue that bodily auto-affection, as such, is another name for a hetero-affection in which a certain making-space is demanded. Before I am, my body is already (as an ensemble of expressive movements) enacting 'tacit decisions,' already articulating itself (becoming itself in differing from itself) in responding to demands for space, and, thus, it is emerging in the movement that articulates the space across which I *affect myself* as subject, consciousness, presence. The body is at once the generality of a schema (enabling it to anticipate the unfolding of the perceived) *and* the 'generativity' of the event of its birth, of sensation, of its original past. The body schema is a generalizing power that stylizes the sensible; sensation is generativity because each sensation is a singular event in which some fragment of sensible being has called upon sentient flesh to begin the work of stylizing in order that something may appear, or find its 'voice.' It is in the coming-together of a schema and sensible being, in a living body, in a dynamic structure (body schema) that is open to singularities, that the self is individuated. Time, as auto-affection, is this coming-together-while-holding-apart.

In the opening sentences of the chapter on temporality in *Phenomenology of Perception*, Merleau-Ponty alerts us to the importance of the topic of this chapter with respect to the problem of subjectivity:

> To analyse time is not to follow out the consequences of a pre-established conception of subjectivity, it is to gain access, through time, to its concrete structure. If we succeed in understanding the subject, it will not be in its pure form, but by seeking it at the intersection of its dimensions. We need, therefore, to consider time itself, and it is by following through its internal dialectic that we shall be led to revise our idea of the subject. (*PhP*, 410–11/469–470)

Here Merleau-Ponty lays down a kind of methodological principle for the investigation of subjectivity—we must first of all bracket our presuppositions concerning subjectivity and allow ourselves to be led to a proper determination of the subject by way of the investigation of time. The phenomenological investigation of time is the key to the problem of subjectivity not merely because time is, as Kant says, the form of inner sense, nor because time (as empiricism holds) characterizes 'psychic facts'; rather, Merleau-Ponty says, "we have already discovered, between time and subjectivity, a much more intimate relationship" (*PhP*, 410/469). Temporality, he argues, is not merely a *characteristic* of the subject but is subjectivity itself. All of the existential dimensions previously explored in *Phenomenology of Perception*—spatiality, sexuality, language, and so on—lead to the problem of time because each of them points to a subject who exists temporally. We have already seen that the subject is not first and foremost a supra-temporal 'I think': it is only thanks to the 'concrete structure' of time that the contingent events of the subject's 'life' are able to acquire enduring dimensions in the formation of bodily habits, culture, language, ideality, and, thus, thought. In short, we do not discover time by directly investigating the subject; we discover the meaning of subjectivity by investigating the temporal dynamics of experience.

*The 'Privilege' of the Present*

Let us begin by recalling the temporal dynamics of perception and the manner in which even the simplest perception already anticipates a certain spatial articulation of the perceived world:

> The act of looking is indivisibly prospective, since the object is the final stage of my process of focusing, and retrospective, since it will present itself as preceding its own appearance, as the 'stimulus,' the motive or the prime mover of every process since its beginning. The spatial synthesis and the synthesis of the object are based on this unfolding of time. In every focusing movement my body unites present, past and future, it secretes time, or rather becomes that location in nature where, for the first time, events, instead of pushing each other into the realm of being, project around the present a double horizon of past and future and acquire a historical orientation. (*PhP*, 239–40/276–7)

In attending to certain objects, or surfaces, my body also lets other things slip into, or remain in, the background. It is for this reason that perception only ever encounters figure-ground structures: perception is temporal. Things are able to present themselves in perception only against a 'double horizon' of pastness and futurity (the spatio-temporal arena of the 'I can'). As Merleau-Ponty writes (highlighting the body-based metaphors of holding and grasping that we often speak of time): "I 'hold,' I 'have' the distant object without any explicit positing of the spatial perspective (apparent size and shape) as I still 'have in hand' [*je 'tiens encore en main'*] the immediate past without any distortion and without any interposed 'recollection' [*le passé prochain sans aucune déformation, sans 'souvenir' interposé*]" (*PhP*, 265/307).

    Here, with the words, 'without any distortion,' 'without any interposed recollection,' Merleau-Ponty alludes to the distinction that is crucial for Husserl's phenomenology of time: the 'opposition' between, on the one hand, *perception* (with its *retentional* modifications) and *recollection*, or re-presentation (*Vergegenwärtigung*).[4] The retention of *Abschattungen* ('profiles,' or 'adumbrations') *within* the field of the living present is, according to Husserl, to be distinguished from the re-presentation of experienced contents in acts of explicit recollection. Husserl's own favored example here is the perception of a melody: there is, in the experience of listening to music, a distinction to be made between a) the manner in which I perceive the unfolding of the melody—by holding the experiential phases corresponding to the notes that have just passed together with the now-phase in which the present note appears—and, b) the manner in which I explicitly recollect (during a break in the performance) some other piece of music that I have heard in the past and that is presently called to mind. Merleau-Ponty insists on this distinction in the "Temporality" chapter:

> Husserl introduced the notion of retention, and held that I still have the immediate past in hand, precisely for the purpose of conveying that I do not posit the past, or construct it from an *Abschattung* really distinct from it and by means of an express act; but I reach it in its recent, yet already elapsed, thisness. (*PhP*, 417/477)

This notion of the field of presence is the basis upon which Merleau-Ponty establishes the 'privilege' of the present. The present is, as we have seen, the 'zone in which being and consciousness coincide.' The *act* which holds, in the protentional fringes of my present consciousness, the 'appearance' of the hidden side of the object in front of me, is present *to itself* as consciousness. Using Gibson's term, we could say that even if an affordance appears, so to speak, as something 'in the future,' over yonder, the act which intends an affordance in the present is immediately present to itself.[5] The protentional consciousness *appears to itself* in the present of consciousness. Again, this is the case even when it is a question of my recalling some experience of an event in my *distant* past—my *act* of recalling a past appearance, an act with its own protentional and retentional fringes, is present to itself in the present. It is intuitively given, tacitly, or prereflectively, to itself.[6] But in this second case, my act of recollecting offers only a mediated appearance of the intentional object—what immediately appears to itself (as conscious experience) in the present is an appearance of an appearance: a re-presentation. The privilege of the present, in Merleau-Ponty, thus relies, in part, on Husserl's delimitation of the living present on the basis of an 'opposition' between retentions and re-presentations. My relation to the past begins from here, from the present in which the field of manifestation (consciousness) appears to itself as a *consciousness of* the past.

While I think that this standard interpretation of Merleau-Ponty's remark about the privilege of the present as a claim about the self-presence of consciousness is, so far as it goes, correct, I also believe that it presents an incomplete picture of the doctrine of auto-affection. Once again, what is missing in the 'metaphysics of presence' interpretation is an appreciation of the constitutive non-presence, or spectrality, at the heart of the present. The very presence of the present (as auto-affection) is dependent upon the spacing, or difference, opened up by the non-presence of the original past. But before we explore the development of this theme in connection with the temporality chapter, I want to further clarify what Merleau-Ponty does and does not say about this privilege of the present.

Although in many passages of the "Temporality" chapter Merleau-Ponty's description of the three-fold structure of the living present is dependent
upon Husserl's description, let us also note that in a number of other passages
his analysis is inflected slightly differently than Husserl's, in a manner that
reveals Merleau-Ponty's concern to overcome the vestiges of intellectualism
and intuitionism that he finds in Husserl's approach to phenomenology.
Where Husserl delimits the field of presence, with its crucial distinction
between originary *intuitive givenness* (in the present) and *re-presentation* (in
the present), from the point of view of time-*consciousness*, Merleau-Ponty
characterizes presence in terms of the sense (*sens*) of environmentality. The
formality of Husserl's 1905 description of the structure of time-consciousness
arguably lays the ground for his egological theory of subjectivity (which
makes its appearance in his writings around 1911) insofar as it envisions a
field organized around a 'now' of intuitive givenness. But rather than emphasize intuitive givenness (of the primal impression) as the centering point
and organizing principle of the field of presence, Merleau-Ponty describes
the field of presence as a spatio-temporal context of the (Heideggerian)
ready-to-hand:

> The present itself, in the narrow sense, is not posited. The paper,
> my fountain pen, are indeed there for me, but I do not explicitly
> perceive them. *I do not so much perceive objects as reckon with an
> environment* [*je compte avec un entourage plutôt que je ne perçois des
> objets*]; I seek support in my tools, and am at my task rather than
> confronting it. Husserl uses the terms protentions and retentions
> for the intentionalities which anchor me to an environment. They
> do not run from a central I, but from my perceptual field itself, so
> to speak, which draws along in its wake its own horizon of reten-
> tions, and bites into the future with its protentions. (*PhP*, 416/476;
> my italics)[7]

While his account of temporality makes use of the terminology (and even
reproduces the schematic diagram [*PhP*, 417/477]) from Husserl's formal (or
'static') description of the structure of time consciousness, Merleau-Ponty's
account stresses the elements of passivity and embodiment, the dynamics
of behavior and absorption in practical concerns. The co-penetration of
protentions and retentions is illustrated here, not primarily by means of a
formal determination of the structure of the *consciousness* of time, the temporal *form* of intuition, but starting from the belonging-together of paper
and fountain pen according to the sense of a task.

The distinction here is analogous to the one that operates in the
Gibsonian critique, which we encountered in chapter 1, of traditional ways

of talking about the problem of depth. Recall that, for Gibson, it is more appropriate to speak of depth perception as affordance perception. Similarly, here, we could say that, for Merleau-Ponty, the temporal present is conceived in terms of the *dynamic structure* of the field of affordance perception.[8] Though, as we have seen, Merleau-Ponty asserts the priority of time over space, lived time is, for him, manifested in the temporality of the situated 'I can': 'I do not so much perceive objects as reckon with an environment.' The *temporal* category of (bodily) 'possibility' explains the phenomena of nearness and farness, of graspable and out-of-reach; but it is also precisely as the principle of the body's *spatial* inherence in its *Umwelt* that we glimpse the phenomenological character of time. When Merleau-Ponty says that we must investigate the subject by first of all investigating time, he means that we reach subjectivity by starting from the spatio-temporal sense of situation. The spatio-temporal *sense* of situation is conditioned by two things: first, as Merleau-Ponty stresses repeatedly in the "Temporality" chapter, it requires a sense of the continuity of time, which is itself rooted in the form of my experience as *presence*. But, second, as we learned in chapter 2, when we considered Lawlor's interpretation of the notion of an 'original past,' it presupposes a sense of the *difference* between the present and the past. Again, I would like to postpone discussion of this second condition for the moment because there is yet more to be said about Merleau-Ponty's argument for the privilege of the present, as well as Derrida's challenge to the phenomenological notion of presence, before can consider the ways in which Merleau-Ponty might respond to this challenge.

The unified field of affordance-time subtends all of our particular acts of recollection, as well as our various ways of dividing up time in terms of before and after, or according to the clock. Thus Merleau-Ponty writes, "The origin of objective time, with its fixed positions lying beneath our gaze, is not to be sought in any eternal synthesis, but in the mutual harmonizing and overlapping of past and future through the present, and in the very passing of time" (*PhP*, 420/480). According to this account, I am able to recall events in my past not because my past already exists for me in some kind of reified form, as a stock of representations, but "because, from the moment in question to my present, the chain of retentions and the overlapping horizons coming one after the other ensure an unbroken continuity" (*PhP*, 418/478). Things in my present experience can, like the madeleines in Proust's *In Search of Lost Time*, awaken recollections of a 'lost time' only because I exist temporally in the present. Of course, the narrator's madeleine does not, in itself, belong to the past, but it can awaken the past for him because, in the unbroken series of retentions of retentions, that past-present overlaps with his present-present. Thus, though I may have to engage in an act of explicit recollection in order to gain access to the details of an event in my distant past, I am able to do so only because the flowing unity of the present affords me a direct link to that past. Thus, the meaning of pastness and futurity here seem to be determined according to the form of presence. Let us explore this a little further.

The sense of temporal continuity, the sense (*sens*) of situation, is indicated by Merleau-Ponty's notion of the "intentional arc":

> Let us say . . . that the life of consciousness—cognitive life, the life of desire or perceptual life—is subtended by an 'intentional arc' ['*arc intentionnel*'] which projects round about us our past, our future, our human setting, our physical, ideological and moral situation, or rather which results in our being situated in all these respects. It is this intentional arc which brings about the unity of the senses, of intelligence, of sensibility and motility. (*PhP*, 136/158)

This sense of the 'continuity' of the intentional arc should not prevent us from recognizing that it is only because we are outside of ourselves, ahead of ourselves, or behind, that we are able to meet with ourselves in the present (*PhP*, 363/417). As Merleau-Ponty writes, "in order to be apparent to itself, and in order to become explicitly what it is implicitly, that is, consciousness, needs to unfold itself into multiplicity" (*PhP*, 424/485). Merleau-Ponty repeatedly invokes Heidegger's concept of the *ek-stase*, of the ecstatic ('outside-of-itself') character of temporality (*PhP*, 421/481; 422/482; 426/487; 427/489; 430/491).[9] It is because the future, as I live it, is not a *real* feature of the objective world, but a function of *my* being-ahead-of-myself, as an 'I can,' that we must say that the subject exists temporally and that time is the mode of being of subjectivity: "[Time] exists only when a subjectivity is there to disrupt the plenitude of being in itself, to adumbrate a perspective, and introduce non-being into it [*y introduire le non-être*]" (*PhP*, 421/481). As we have seen, it is only for a motor subject (an 'I can') that a surface can appear as a certain bit of redness, or that a surface can appear *as* the surface of some thing with other unseen surfaces. It is only for a motor subject that objects have a past and a future, a surface, a texture, and an inside. This is because the embodied subject, as a being outside of itself, as a being circumspectively absorbed in the world, lets the things in its environment show themselves according to possibilities determined in reference to itself as a bodily 'I can.'

We should however, in this connection, take care to notice that Merleau-Ponty's account of ecstatic time differs in at least one important respect from Heidegger's (or, at least, Merleau-Ponty insists upon there being a difference). In *Being and Time*, Heidegger writes, "Temporality is essentially ecstatical. Temporality temporalizes itself primordially out of the future."[10] This is because temporality is originally disclosed as the meaning of 'care'

(*Sorge*), as concernful being-toward-death. If, using Merleau-Ponty's terminology, we must understand time in terms of a sense (*sens*) of the temporal,
then we could say that, for Heidegger, time temporalizes itself out of the
future as the sense of mortal, finite, time—this *sense* of the temporal would
thus depend upon the singular threat of *non-sense* that is my death. But
Merleau-Ponty finds something inconsistent in Heidegger's claim that time
is ecstatic *and* that it temporalizes itself from the future:

> Heidegger's historical time, which flows from the future and which,
> thanks to its resolute decision, *has* its future in advance and rescues
> itself once and for all from disintegration, is impossible within the
> context of Heidegger's thought itself: for, if time is an *ek-stase*, if
> present and past are two results of this *ek-stase*, how could we ever
> cease completely to see time from the point of view of the present
> [*comment cesserions-nous tout à fait de voir le temps du point de vue du
> présent*], and how could we completely escape from the inauthentic?
> It is always in the present that we are centred, and our decision
> starts from there. (*PhP*, 427/489)

This seems to be the clearest statement of Merleau-Ponty's privileging of
the present. In this objection, Merleau-Ponty in fact employs the concept of
'decision' that we encountered in his phenomenological account of depth,
but he does not speak of the corresponding concept of motivation for which,
in this case, he might have found an analogue in Heidegger's notion of the
'call' (*Ruf*). For Heidegger, the 'call' is the call of a certain futurity, my death,
as the possibility of my own impossibility. But just as with Merleau-Ponty,
so with Heidegger, the decision concerning how I am to heed any call happens in, or *as* a present. Heidegger writes, for example: "Resoluteness, by
its ontological essence, is always the resoluteness of some factical Dasein at
a particular time."[11] Decision, for Heidegger, *no less than for Merleau-Ponty*,
involves taking up the factical conditions of a given moment and allowing them to have a certain meaning/direction (*sens*) with respect to our
already-having-been and our futural being-toward. But Heidegger says that
primordial time temporalizes from the future because Dasein's relation to its
futural possibility (of impossibility) is what grants to the present (to what
we could call the decision of presence) its possibility of being meaningful. Only in the phenomenon of the resolute decision are we able to see
what ultimately 'motivates' all decisions (even those inauthentic ones that,
in fact, occlude their own proper [essentially futural] motivation)—a 'call'
emanating from a future that will never be a (living) present.

But we need to be careful not to be too hasty in reading the disagree-
ment with Heidegger, on this point, as further evidence of Merleau-Ponty's putative commitment to a metaphysics of presence. I just said that

Merleau-Ponty might have found, in his own notion of motivation, an analogue for Heidegger's notion of the 'call' and he might thus have said, *with*
Heidegger, that while 'our decision' happens in the present, its motivation
is futural—the decision would be motivated by an intimation of my own
finitude. But, in fact, this would not be the correct analogue. 'Motivation' for
Merleau-Ponty is always the motivation that functions *for* a certain decision
concerning a determination of the present. The motivation, with respect to
the sense of movement, is, as we have said, the aim, or the source, implicitly
referred to by a movement that would make sense, the way my reaching
hand makes sense as an expression of my intention to reach the glass on
the table. But, as we have also noted, every determination of a 'ground'
of sense always leaves behind some residue of the spectral, of the anarchic
beginning of movement, which cannot be absorbed into the order of sense
inaugurated by the movement, and which continues to haunt consciousness
with a sense of its contingency. It is ultimately the sensible, in its singularity,
that 'calls' for a determination of the present, the space in which something
can appear. And recall, in this connection, the claim that Merleau-Ponty
repeats several times, concerning sensation, that it is, each time, the birth
and *the death* of the subject (e.g., "Each sensation, being strictly speaking, the
first, last and only one of its kind, is a birth and a death" [*PhP*, 216/250]).
Decisions that give themselves *grounds* do so only by occluding this event,
this '*call*'—sense *begins* in a movement that is already responding before
there is any sense. Sense (meaning, presence, consciousness) is always a
way of having a relation to the event of sensation (my birth, my death)
by not having a relation to that event as such. And Heidegger would not
disagree: "for the most part," *Dasein* (Heidegger's name for human reality)
is, as Heidegger says, "they."[12] Thus, for the most part, *Dasein does not* live
authentically toward its own future. And this 'for the most part' is not meant
to imply that we are wholly authentic only on exceptional occasions. We
never 'completely escape from the inauthentic.' Decisions give themselves,
so to speak, 'motivations' originating in the present or the past—we have
places to be, obligations to fulfill, roles to adhere to. These decisions may
be various responses to a 'call' originating from a future that will never be
a present (my death), but we would not say that they are 'motivated' by my
death because my death (the possibility of impossibility) is precisely what
these ordinary everyday motivations usually occlude. Thus we never '*completely* escape from the inauthentic' because we never escape the necessity
of enacting some response to the call in the here and now, a response that
must take the form of a decision concerning *meaning*, the meaning of my
own life. So Merleau-Ponty appears to privilege the present insofar as his
analysis is concerned with the conditions of a decision that would give shape

to our existence. But the point is that, for Merleau-Ponty, this privilege is inevitably contested from within, as is clearly brought out in the analyses of sensation and spatiality, and in the ambiguous notion of auto-affection in the "Temporality" chapter. Let us first turn directly to what Merleau-Ponty says about auto-affection.

*Auto-affection*

In the discussion of auto-affection we see, once again, both Heidegger's and Husserl's influence in Merleau-Ponty's thinking about temporality. "Time," says Merleau-Ponty, quoting from Heidegger's book on Kant,

> is 'the affecting of self by self'; what exerts the effect is time as a thrust and a passing towards a future: what is affected is time as an unfolded series of presents: the affecting agent and affected recipient are one, because the thrust of time is nothing but the transition from one present to another. (*PhP*, 426/487)

Here Merleau-Ponty comes to the heart of the problem of subjectivity as he understands it in *Phenomenology of Perception*. The relation between the 'affecting' and the 'affected' is not to be understood on the model of a cause and effect relationship, for there are not two positive entities here but a pure "dehiscence," or bursting open, of time (*PhP*, 426/487). Each of the phases of the temporal flow "issue one from another, and each of these projections is merely one aspect of the total bursting forth or dehiscence [*de l'éclatement ou de la déhiscence totale*]" (*PhP*, 419/480). In this sense, then, there is no privileged phase. Time is the breaking up of origins. So how then does time come to be the affecting of self by self?

Once again we may employ the model of the relationship between a decision and its motivation according to which the decision can be said to reveal a motivation as the 'ground' of its own immanent *sens*. As Merleau-Ponty says, "time and significance [*sens*] are but one thing" (*PhP*, 427/487). The present lets itself be affected by a pure passing-toward, but this affection is also a call for a decision; we could say that the decision, in the form of a project or behavior, validates a certain futurity by which it thus *lets itself be affected* (we could say, it lets itself be 'moved'). In referring to 'decision' here we are, again, not necessarily speaking of what we would call a 'conscious' or 'deliberate' decision (though we do not mean to *exclude* this either) but a broader sense of decision, one that includes the more primordial sense of decision ('tacit decision') that we saw Merleau-Ponty introduce in connection with depth-perception:

I am not the initiator of the process of temporalization; I did not choose to come into the world, yet once I am born, time flows through me, whatever I do. Nevertheless this ceaseless welling up of time [*jaillissement du temps*] is not a simple fact to which I am passively subjected, for I can find a remedy against it in itself, as happens in a decision which binds me or in the act of establishing a concept. It withholds me from what I was about to become, and at the same time provides me with the means of grasping myself at a distance and establishing my own reality as myself. (*PhP*, 427/488)

This 'withholding,' which is also the means of 'grasping myself at a distance,' is precisely what is indicated by the idea of time as a 'transition from one present to another.'[13] It is because time is the breaking up of origins that it allows for a decision concerning a present. The present is not an a priori form, but an event, an enactment. 'Transition' here implies a movement of differentiation (a rhythm) which is neither a movement under the control of a prior identity nor a relation between two terms, but which nevertheless involves the enactment of some determinacy, an identity.

This dehiscence provides me *with the means* of establishing my reality as myself, of enacting my reality in a decision, of being present. Thus Merleau-Ponty's account of the auto-affection of time here reflects the sense of 'self-activation' that we find in Heidegger's discussion of auto-affection in *Kant and the Problem of Metaphysics*.[14] Heidegger writes:

As pure self-affection, time is not an acting affection that strikes a self which is at hand. Instead, as pure it forms the essence of something like self-activating. However, if it belongs to the essence of the finite subject to be able to be activated as a self, then time as pure self-affection forms the essential structure of subjectivity.[15]

Time does not happen to a self; rather, it happens *as* a self because it is a dehiscence that manifests itself only by, as it were, interrupting itself, or doubling-back on itself. We could say that it is the *Unverborgenheit* (unconcealment) that we discussed at the end of chapter 3 and of which Merleau-Ponty later (in *The Visible and the Invisible*) says that *consciousness* prefers objects to it. Consciousness always views its time from the point of view of the present because it sees time from the point of view of its decision, from its momentary congealing, under the form of some intentional object, of the ceaseless welling-up, and it thereby misses the dehiscence and the doubling-back that first permits anything to appear. What Merleau-Ponty calls "primordial temporality" thus has the very structure that we have discovered in connection with bodily motility. The phases of lived time are not external to each other but rather enveloped in a *sens*, just as living movement is retroactively enveloped in the *sens* of a motor *project*. At more than one point in the "Temporality" chapter, Merleau-Ponty explicates this character of time as holding-together-while-holding-apart by using the analogy of the gesture: "I am already at the impending present as my gesture is already at its goal" (*PhP*, 421/481); "Time is one single movement appropriate to itself in all its parts, as a gesture includes all the muscular contractions necessary for its execution" (*PhP*, 419/479). Thus, when Merleau-Ponty writes that "We must understand time as the subject and the subject as time," he adds: "What is perfectly clear, is that this primordial temporality is not a juxtaposition of external events, since it is the power which holds them together while keeping them apart" (*PhP*, 422/483). Time is a synthesis, of a sort, but a synthesis-in-motion, one that is made of pure transitions.[16]

However, having said all this, it must also be said that just as Merleau-Ponty seems, at times, to conceive of the 'unreflective' on the basis of the concept of consciousness, as a consciousness not quite in full possession of itself, he also, borrowing terms from Husserl, tends to speak of this dehiscence and doubling-back, of time as a more original form of consciousness, an "ultimate consciousness." He writes, "we are forced to recognize the existence of a 'consciousness having behind it no consciousness to be conscious of it' which, consequently, is not arrayed out in time, and in which 'being coincides with being for itself'" (*PhP*, 422/483). Thus, it would seem that Merleau-Ponty continues to oscillate between saying, on the one hand, that time is auto-affection because it is first of all the movement of differentiation that then allows me to 'grasp myself at a distance,' and, on the other hand, that time is auto-affection because it is an ultimate *consciousness* (self-presence).

What necessitates the thesis of an ultimate consciousness is, for Merleau-Ponty as it is for Husserl, the threat of an infinite regress. If reflection is ever to be possible, then, both Merleau-Ponty and Husserl argue, it must be the case that I am tacitly self-aware (prereflectively self-*conscious*) before I begin to reflect, and we cannot look to another level of self-consciousness to subtend *that* self-consciousness. But Merleau-Ponty has already alerted us to the many ways in which our experience is haunted, delayed, anonymous, 'out-of-sync' with itself. And he has also alerted us to the fact that the act of reflection is a creative operation. It is a creative operation that generates sense (*sens*). We have already seen that such operations are, according to Merleau-Ponty, ultimately rooted in living movement; and they are creative insofar as they are also responsive. As we argued in chapter 2, movement that generates sense gives itself a past, a motivation that would be its ground—its source, aim, object. But, in generating sense, as we have said, movement also occludes another past, the past of the beginning of

movement which cannot be absorbed into the order of sense that the movement inaugurates. Employing this logic, then, we could say that reflection is
an act that generates sense insofar as it, so to speak, turns back upon itself,
making its subjective source the object of its aim. In doing so, it occludes
its 'other' beginning, a non-presence (a past that has never been a present), a hetero-affection which thus can never be excluded from the sphere
of auto-affection. To explain the possibility of reflection, then, we would
need to account for the possibility of a movement that generates the sense
of interiority, or ipseity. And, in chapter 5, we will see that this requires
an account of the way in which expressive movement becomes language.

   Jacques Derrida argues that phenomenology occludes this dimension of hetero-affection precisely insofar as it understands itself to be an
interrogation of subjective *consciousness*; in his view, phenomenology thus
occludes the manner in which consciousness depends upon language. This
very dependence is, in Derrida's view, also a threat to the notion of subjective self-presence, and thus to the idea of consciousness as such. Derrida,
as we have indicated, turns his attention to Merleau-Ponty's concept of
the lived, or own, body (*le corps propre*) in the recent work On *Touching—
Jean-Luc Nancy*. His challenge to Merleau-Ponty brings out the very issues
that we have been highlighting: the themes of continuity and discontinuity.
Derrida argues that, notwithstanding his critique of intellectualist philosophies of consciousness, Merleau-Ponty, in his deployment of the concept of
the lived body, ultimately privileges continuity, identity, and self-presence
over discontinuity and difference. I want to consider this challenge at some
length here in order to show how I think Merleau-Ponty might respond.
Derrida's critical interpretation of Merleau-Ponty is developed particularly
in reference to the text entitled, "The Philosopher and His Shadow," in
which Merleau-Ponty interprets Husserl's account of the lived-body (*Leib*)
in *Ideas II*. Derrida's interpretation of Merleau-Ponty's text thus relies on
his own (Derrida's) interpretation of Husserl, and so, before we can consider
his challenge to Merleau-Ponty, it will be necessary to give a brief outline
of his interpretation of Husserl.

## II. THE DECONSTRUCTION OF PRESENCE

*Derrida's Appraisal of Husserl's Phenomenology*

As we have indicated, Derrida claims that there is a tension at the heart
of Husserl's phenomenology. The two poles of this tension can be roughly
characterized as follows: 1) Husserl affirms that consciousness is essentially characterized by a power for directing itself toward objects, to be a

consciousness *of* something. Insofar as this power belongs to it essentially, consciousness is to be understood as 'intentional' consciousness. The term "intentionality" designates this mode of being correlated with an object, or directed toward it.[17] The correlation between consciousness and the objects toward which it is thus directed is always mediated by ideal structures, meanings, or "*noemata.*"[18] Consciousness directs itself toward an object by bestowing an ideal sense, or meaning, on the contents of its experience. It is only by means of these ideal structures, then, that consciousness can *mean* a particular object, can concern itself with something that it takes to be transcendent to itself and its particular acts. These noemata, the ideal structures of intentionality that Husserlian phenomenology wants to analyze, neither *belong* to consciousness nor subsist *apart* from consciousness. On the one hand, they function only for a consciousness that, as it were, activates them in concerning itself with particular objects or objective states-of-affairs, but, on the other hand, they transcend any particular consciousness, and any particular act, in the sense that they are ideal and thus constitutively include, in their sense, the sense of being infinitely repeatable across time and for different subjects.[19] It is by virtue of this capacity to direct itself toward objects by means of the ideality (infinite repeatability) of the noema, that consciousness is unified for itself. In other words, it is by means of acts which bestow meaning, and thus in which the sense of repeatability is implicit, that experience is unified as a stream of consciousness. As Husserl writes: "Intentionality is what characterizes *consciousness* in the pregnant sense and which, at the same time, justifies designating the whole stream of lived-experiences as the stream of consciousness and as the unity of *one* consciousness."[20]

According to Husserl, even though the ideality of the noema consists in its being able to be reactivated in an infinity of possible acts, it belongs essentially to the noema (with its sense of infinite repeatability) that it be able to be given in a *present* intuition; he calls such experience "eidetic intuition," and it is thanks to this possibility of making the noematic sense present to consciousness that phenomenology is able to analyze the invariant structures linking consciousness to its world.[21] Now, as Derrida points out, Husserl's analyses also show that, insofar as noematic sense relies on this sense of repeatability, the ideality of the noema presupposes intersubjectivity and language. The possibility of this ideality thus depends upon the empirical reality of historical languages, the worldly contexts of actual speech-acts, and, in particular, the sphere of writing in which meanings can be repeated and reactivated for different subjects at different times (even beyond the death of the individual subject). Ideality thus presupposes the possibility of slippages of meaning, the possibility of a loss, or alteration, of sense. As Derrida writes,

Since the possibility of constituting ideal objects belongs to the essence of consciousness, and since these ideal objects are historical products, only appearing thanks to acts of creation or intending, the element of consciousness and the element of language will be more and more difficult to discern. Will not their indiscernability introduce non-presence and difference (mediation, signs, referral back, etc.) in the heart of self-presence?[22]

If it is the case that the element of consciousness and the element of language are difficult to discern, why should this be a problem for Husserl's phenomenology? This question brings us to the other pole of the tension highlighted in Derrida's interpretation.

2) While Husserl emphasizes the transcendence of the noema to the particular acts of intending by which it is activated, and while he acknowledges the constitutive function of language in the formation of these idealities, he also, according to Derrida, seeks to ground the possibility of repetition (the very ideality of the noema) in the self-presence of a consciousness, and he wants to say that this self-presence (which, Derrida insists, is itself an idea) is *not* dependent on language. Derrida writes:

> In order that the possibility of this repetition [of noematic sense] may be open, *ideally* to infinity, one ideal form must assure this unity of the *indefinite* and the *ideal*: this is the presence of the *living present*. The ultimate form of ideality, the ideality of ideality, that in which in the last instance one may anticipate or recall all repetition, is the *living present*, the self-presence of transcendental life. Presence has always been and will always, forever, be the form in which, we can say apodictically, the infinite diversity of contents is produced.[23]

According to Derrida, Husserl grounds sense in the acts of a self-present consciousness ("transcendental life") because this self-presence is absolutely a priori: it is an ideal form that does not depend on anything empirical, but that, as the very 'ideality of ideality,' is the ground of the possibility of the appearance of anything empirical—including language. Now, as we have said, Husserl affirms that the unity of consciousness is itself dependent on the noema, and he also affirms that the noema is dependent on those particular acts of meaning in which meaning is first instituted. Thus, it would appear that consciousness is dependent on language and thus that the sense of the transcendental can never be rigorously isolated from the empirical realities of languages and signs. But, according to Derrida, Husserl wants to avoid this conclusion.

This, according to Derrida, is why, beginning in *Logical Investigations*, Husserl must concern himself with the problem of language, with the distinction, *within* language, between what is properly *meaningful* in the linguistic sign (what carries a signifying intention) and what is accidental. This is what lies behind Husserl's careful distinction between 'expression' (*Ausdruck*) and 'indication' (*Anzeichen*).[24] He claims that indication (which would cover the whole set of so-called natural signs—the way, for example, smoke visible in the distance indicates a fire) is not, as such, meaningful. What assures the meaningfulness of the sign is a signifying intention, a subject *wanting to say* or meaning to express something.[25] It is thus, according to Husserl, possible, and necessary, to exclude from the essence of *language* that which belongs to indication (e.g., the word's sensible content, its sonority, the empirical determinacies that would allow it to function as a sensible *carrier* of a signifying intention) in order to isolate a stratum of pure expression—of a pure 'meaning to say.' Though, according to Husserl, the expressive function of the sign depends upon the intention or will to signify, it is necessary to exclude even the communicative function if we are to grasp expression in its purity, in abstraction from anything accidental. As Derrida comments, "By a strange paradox, meaning would isolate the concentrated purity of its *ex-pressiveness* just at the moment when the relation to a certain *outside* is suspended."[26] It is, Derrida says, always "from the standpoint of 'interiority,' or rather from a self-proximity, an *ownness* (*Eigenheit*)" that the relation to the outside, as objectivity, is made possible.[27] The investigation into the meaningfulness of language culminates in the exclusion of the sensible, of 'effective speech,' from the essence of meaning. Thus, paradoxically, it is the exclusion of signs, revealing, for Husserl, the interiority of a kind of inward communication that has no need of signs, that finally reveals the principle and ground of all meaning: the silent interiority of mental life. This then is the tension that Derrida claims to find at the heart of Husserl's phenomenology: the latter at once demonstrates the dependence of consciousness on language *and* seeks to occlude that dependency by affirming a primordiality of silent self-presence.

Now, let us note that there is much in this appraisal of Husserl's phenomenology that evidently does not apply to Merleau-Ponty. But Derrida's interpretation of Husserl's philosophy as a "metaphysics of presence"[28] is, as we have said, crucial for understanding his critique of the latter's notion of the lived-body (*Leib*), and it is also in connection with this notion that Derrida claims to find a certain continuity between Husserl's putative metaphysics of presence and Merleau-Ponty's philosophy, particularly in the latter's notion of 'intercorporeity.' We will consider this claim below, but before we do, I want to first point out two ways in which, I think, Merleau-Ponty's philosophy obviously avoids the contradictions that Derrida claims to find in Husserl's philosophy.

First of all, Merleau-Ponty is well aware of the way in which language and signification subtend the sense of interiority, of the 'solitary mental life' that, for the Husserl of *Logical Investigations*, could only be reached in its purity by means of a reduction of language and signification in general. Thus Merleau-Ponty writes:

> No one will deny that here the process of expression brings the meaning into being or makes it effective, and does not merely translate it. It is no different, despite what may appear to be the case, with the expression of thoughts in speech. Thought is no 'internal' thing, and does not exist independently of the world and of words. (*PhP*, 183/213)

The sense of the 'interiority' of thought, of consciousness, is an effect of the relative stability of meanings in a language, meanings that we revivify each time we hear ourselves utter them: "We live in a world where speech is an *institution* (*la parole est* instituée)" (*PhP*, 184/214). Now it should be made clear that, in Merleau-Ponty's account of expression, in *Phenomenology of Perception*, this *instituted* character of signs is a function of what is called "second-order expression," the circulation of available, sedimented meanings, in contradistinction to "authentic speech," the expressive speech in which meanings are inaugurated (*PhP*, 178n.1/207n.2). But even in the case of authentic speech, according to Merleau-Ponty, the thought does not preexist the speech. I am not relieved of the necessity of finding out what I mean by means of an experience of my own expression in its sensible form: "The word and speech must somehow cease to be a way of designating things or thoughts, and become the presence of that thought in the phenomenal world, and, moreover, not its clothing but its token or phenomenal body (*mais son emblème du son corps*)" (*PhP*, 182/212). So, for Merleau-Ponty, there is no insight to be gained by reducing the indicative function of language or by reducing the communicative function of expression to a pure mental operation.

On the contrary, and this is the second point, Merleau-Ponty, in *Phenomenology of Perception*, thinks of language as essentially gestural. We shall examine this further in the chapter 5, but let us note here that there would, for Merleau-Ponty, be no possibility of isolating a stratum of pure expression from indication in language. Expression, as we have seen, is rooted in bodily movement, movement that responds to a 'call' of the sensible, which it thus allows to appear, but always belatedly, always already stylized, always already incarnated in a phenomenal body. And this means that auto-affection is, as we have suggested, a matter of expressive surfaces and space, skin, eyes, mouths, and hands.[29] But, in particular, in a special case that Merleau-Ponty comes back to again and again: it is exemplified in the experience of touching one of my own hands with the other hand. This phenomenon is, for Merleau-Ponty, "a kind of reflection," in which the body "catches itself from the outside" (*PhP*, 93/109).

*Derrida on the Lived-Body ('Leib'; 'le corps propre')*

This phenomenon of double-sensation (of one of my hands touching the other) is central to Husserl's account of the lived-body (as it is developed in *Ideas II*, §§ 36–8), and it is through his interpretation of Husserl's account of this phenomenon that Derrida develops his appraisal of the phenomenology of the body. Husserl's account of the "constitution" of the lived-body (*Leib*) must be understood in the context of his transcendental egology. In *Ideas I*, Husserl introduces the notion of the pure or transcendental ego, and views it as the subjective source, or ground, of the sense-bestowing intentions correlating a consciousness to its objects. 'Pure,' or 'transcendental,' ego, then, is the name in Husserl's philosophy for the active and self-identifying function of consciousness insofar as it posits objects or posits itself as an object (in reflection). The ego constitutes its own lived-body insofar as it is able to recognize, therein, the instrument at its immediate disposal for the free exercising and expression of its will. Unlike other physical objects, which do not move *themselves*, but which can be used as instruments of *my* will, my body answers to my intentions *immediately*. Husserl writes that, "Our bodies [*Leiber*] are immediately ('freely') moveable, and they are so, specifically, by means of the free Ego and its will which belong to them."[30] According to Derrida, then, the analysis of double-sensation must be read in the context of Husserl's argument for egological self-presence, as an affirmation of the *egological* body, a body through which an ego is immediately in touch with itself.

Husserl's account of double-sensation occurs within the context of a wider discussion of tactual sensitivity and its privileged role in the constitution of the egological lived body as such. Whether it is with respect to self-touch or to the touching of some object, what is at stake, in Husserl's account of touch, is the particular *reflexivity* of touch, a putatively *immediate* sensitivity to my own sensation. Derrida writes that "Husserl is very much set on describing the *reflexive* specificity (and therefore more immediately ego-phenomenological quality) of the sensation of the *living* body *proper*, and its 'self-sensing.' "[31] Husserl pointedly contrasts this self-sensitivity of touch with the mediated self-sensitivity involved in *seeing* one's own body: "Obviously, the Body is also to be seen just like other things, but it becomes a

*Body* only by incorporating tactile sensations, pain sensations, etc.—in short, by the localization of the sensations as sensations."[32] This is a crucial point for Husserl: the constitution of my own body as *visible* cannot be rigorously distinguished from the "analogical appresentation" involved in the experience of another person. What does this mean? As Husserl repeatedly insists (e.g., in *Ideas II*, §§ 44–7 and in the fifth of the *Cartesian Meditations*), I have no direct access to the inner life of another. Thus, when I perceive objects, those objects are given to me in "original presence," and this, according to Husserl, is also the case when I am engaged in an act of reflection—in reflecting and, as he also says, in *touching* my own body, I am given to myself in original presence.[33] But I can only have access to the field of another's 'original presence' by means of appresentation, which is to say, indirectly.[34] What makes this indirect access possible is a transfer of sense from my own body, which I experience directly (in original presence), *as my own*, to the body of another subject, whose subjectivity I am now able to discern on the basis of 'analogical appresentation.' The other's body is experienced as analogous to my own, and, as my own body is immediately present to me (in tactual sensitivity) as an egological body, I am able to discern, indirectly, in the other's body, another ego-subject. Thus the constitution of another subject presupposes two things: 1) an experience of my own body as my own, which, according to Husserl, can only happen by means of self-touch, and; 2) an experience of my body as an object. In recognizing the identity of these two things (this body as my own, this same body as object) I acquire the sense of an egological body, which sense can then be transferred to another body. Let us consider this in a little more detail.

Concerning the privilege of touch in the constitution of the lived-body, everything depends, according to Husserl, on the localization of 'sensings,' and on temporal coincidence. Touching one's own body is the unique way in which the body is constituted as one's own lived-body because it is only in self-touch that I am able to make contact with my body directly—according to Husserl, in double-sensation, the sensing and the sensed coincide in the same instant and in the same location. With regard to the case of *seeing* oneself in a mirror, on the other hand, we cannot say that we have an immediate self-sensing for the *self*-sensing, in this case, would presuppose a transfer of sense from my own originally present lived body to the image of the body in the mirror. Further, the 'sensings' are not, in the case of *seeing* my body, immediately localized in the place of the sensible. Thus, the identification of one's own visible body as one's own involves the same kind of 'analogical appresentation' that must be involved in constituting an *other* egological body.

Concerning the localization of tactual sensations, Husserl distinguishes between two orders of space: 1) the spatial character of what he calls immanent 'sensings' (that is, the spatial quality of sensations as I live them) and 2) the spatiality of 'extension' (*Ausdehnung*) characterizing the external object. The spatiality of immanent sensings is characterized by a "spreading out" (*Ausbreitung*) and "spreading into" (*Hindbrietung*).³⁵ It is because the sensings are themselves already spatial—"the sensings do indeed spread out in space, cover in their way, spatial surfaces"—that Husserl is able to say that, in touching my own body, the sensing and the sensed happen in the same place. Husserl writes that "All sensings pertain to my soul; everything extended to the material thing. On this surface of the hand I sense the sensations of touch, etc. And it is precisely thereby that this surface manifests itself immediately as my body."³⁶ In other words, in the experience of the touch, there is here thought to be a kind of coincidence between the location of a contact with a certain surface and the location of a sensation.

It is on this point, concerning the putatively immediate coinciding, in the same place, of the touching and the touched, that Derrida raises an objection to Husserl's argument. This 'On' (as in 'On the surface of the hand') with which is indicated the spatio-temporal immediacy that putatively establishes the privilege of touch, also marks the crossing-over of the two orders of space—that which 'pertains to my soul' and that which pertains to the 'material thing.' According to Derrida's interpretation, in order for there to be an immediate localization (in the same place) of the touching and the touched (the very thing that would distinguish *tactile* self-sensing from the experience of *seeing* one's own body), Husserl must appeal to a spatiality that is external to that of the tactual sensings—the space of an objective surface. In other words, the 'spatiality' of sensings (an immanent, subjectively *lived*, 'spreading out' and 'spreading into' where no real external object would be, as yet, constituted) and the space precisely of a real thing (a surface, a location in the world) come to depend on each other. As Derrida writes:

> No doubt, in the sensible impression or sensing, I—still I—am the touching and the touched, but if some not-I (material thing, real . . . space, extension, as opposed to phenomenological "spreading out and spreading into," and so forth) did not come to insinuate itself between the touching and the touched, I would not be able to posit myself as I and "say" (as Husserl says), This is not I, this is I, I am I. And it is there, precisely because of *extensio*, because of visibility and the possibility at least for the hand to be seen, even if it is not seen (a possibility involved in the phenomenological content of the sensible impression), that manual touching—even just touching my other hand—cannot be reduced to a pure experience of the purely proper body.³⁷

The privilege of touch is also, according to Derrida, contested by a certain dependence on what is external to it, and an ego thus only touches itself by means of a detour through what is not itself.

Finally, there is an important implication of all this with respect to intersubjectivity (which will become particularly important for us in a moment when we turn to Derrida's reading of Merleau-Ponty). I can see my own body, but as we have said, this constitution of my own body as visible is, in Husserl's view, derivative with respect to my ability to sense my own touching, and, in an exemplary way, to sense myself touching my own body. My own body is a visible body proper when I can touch and see that I am touching. The constitution of my own body as visible (which possibility is, as we noted earlier, grounded, according to Husserl, in an analogical appresentation), is dependent on tactual self-sensing in the same way as the constitution of the other is dependent on my tactual self-sensing. As Husserl writes:

> All this [touching, and seeing myself touching] is given to me myself as belonging together in co-presence (*für mich selbst in Kompräsenz zusammengehörig gegeben*) and is then transferred over in empathy: the other's touching hand, which I see, appresents to me his solipsistic view of this hand and then everything that must belong to it in presentified co-presence (*in vergegenwärtiger Kompräsenz*).[38]

Derrida argues that, in light of what he has said concerning the necessity of mediation and exteriority in self-touch, a certain dependence on an appresentation cannot be made to distinguish my experience of another person from an experience of my own lived body—which, according to Husserl, would not require an appresentation.

We have spent some time setting out some of the details of Husserl's account of the lived-body, and Derrida's deconstructive appraisal of that account, because, as we have indicated, it is essential for our being able to understand what Derrida says about Merleau-Ponty. Derrida is critical of Husserl's notion of an immediate self-sensing, by means of tactual sensitivity, because he does not think that there can be any presentation of one's own body that would not also constitutively depend upon a certain appresentation, an identification of the self where the grounds of this identification can never be assured. Derrida acknowledges that Merleau-Ponty's account of the lived-body (*le corps propre*) differs from the one that he finds in Husserl, but he argues that Merleau-Ponty similarly occludes the element of alterity in the experience of one's own body; in the case of Merleau-Ponty, this occlusion putatively becomes evident when Merleau-Ponty (according to Derrida) *denies* the necessity of analogical appresentation when it is a question of perceiving the lived-body of another. Before we turn to this interpretation, let us again note the ways in which Merleau-Ponty's account of double-sensation apparently differs from the account that Derrida finds in Husserl.

First, there is, for Merleau-Ponty, no possibility of sensing, with my right hand, my left hand *at the same time* that the latter is sensing. Thus, there is no possibility of establishing, by means of this putatively privileged form of self-contact (self-touch), the sense of an egological lived-body in the Husserlian sense. The lived-body cannot overcome a certain delay that would always separate it from itself. Merleau-Ponty writes:

> What was meant by talking about 'double sensations' is that, in passing from one rôle to the other, I can identify (*reconnaître*) the hand touched as the same one which will in a moment be touching. In other words, in this bundle of bones and muscles which my right hand presents to my left, I can anticipate for an instant the integument or incarnation (*je devine un instant l'enveloppe ou l'incarnation*) of that other right hand, alive and mobile, which I thrust towards the things in order to explore them. (*PhP*, 93/109)

The 'my-own-ness' of the body is, a according to Merleau-Ponty, a matter of an *identification*, or *anticipation*: 'I can *identify* the hand touched as the same . . . etc.'; 'I can *anticipate* for an instant . . . etc.' It is, in a sense, an ongoing accomplishment. Thus we do not find, in Merleau-Ponty, any kind of immediate spatio-temporal coincidence between the touching and the touched.

Second, the body, for Merleau-Ponty, is a unity insofar as it 'interprets itself,' 'synchronizes' itself, in movement: it is, as we have seen, 'dynamically acquainted with itself.' And, thus, there is no self-contact, or even self-anticipation, that would not presuppose movement, and thus an *exteriorization* and a *temporalization*. Touching oneself takes time and 'real' space. This is why, for Merleau-Ponty, there would be no possibility of a precise *localization* of *immanent* 'sensings.' Far from being able to bracket exteriority in order to discover a more original, immediate, self-relation, my bodily self-awareness is *dependent* upon the appearance of a 'reality' made possible by the movement of the sentient body:

> When one of my hands touches the other, the hand that moves functions as subject and the other as object. There are tactile phenomena, alleged tactile qualities, like roughness or smoothness,

which disappear completely if the exploratory movement is elimi-
nated. Movement and time are not only an objective condition of
knowing touch, but a phenomenal component of the tactile data.
(*PhP*, 315/364)

Thus, I must be moving in order to have a sensation of my own body; the
self-touch, then, is, as we have said of perception in general, a form of
expressive movement. And it is only by means of expression, then, that I
am able to touch my own body.

Finally, the necessity of exteriorization means that, for Merleau-Ponty,
the possible visibility of my own body is not derivative with respect to the
possibility of (self)-touching my own body. Both modes of bodily auto-appa-
rition are affected with the same inevitable delay, the same non-coincidence:

My visual body is certainly an object as far as its parts far removed
from my head are concerned, but as we come nearer to the eyes,
it becomes divorced from objects, and reserves among them a
quasi-space to which they have no access, and when I try to fill in
this void by recourse to the image in the mirror, it refers me back
to an original of the body which is not out there among things,
but in my own province, on this side of all things seen. It is no
different (*Il n'en va pas autrement*), in spite of what may appear to
be the case, with my tactile body, for if I can, with my left hand,
feel my right hand as it touches an object, the right hand as object
is not the right hand as it touches . . . etc. (*PhP*, 92/107–8)

As we have seen, Merleau-Ponty's notion of the anonymity of sensation, and
of the sentient body, provides the basis for his thinking of intersubjectivity.
The hiatus between the touching and touched not only opens up the space
of the visible body but also opens the space in which a certain access to the
subjectivity of the other can insert itself in the midst of my experience. Thus,
it would appear that Merleau-Ponty does indeed anticipate the concerns
brought out in Derrida's reading of Husserl. This theme, in Merleau-Ponty's
philosophy, is particularly developed in the essay entitled "The Philosopher
and his Shadow [*Le philosophe et son ombre*]," in which he 'interprets' the
very passages in Husserl's *Ideas II* that are analyzed by Derrida. But Derrida
has some grave concerns about Merleau-Ponty's deployment of the 'example'
of manual double-sensation in the service of his phenomenology of intersubjectivity. What is at issue in Derrida's interpretation of Merleau-Ponty
is not merely the latter's account of bodily auto-affection, but the way in
which he develops his description of the double-touch into an account of
the way in which the body subtends the experience of other selves.

*Derrida's Deconstruction of 'Intercorporeity'*

Let us first of all cite, in full, the passage from "The Philosopher and His Shadow" to which Derrida directs the objections with which we are particularly concerned here:[39]

> My right hand *was present* [*assistait*] at the advent of my left hand's active sense of touch. *It is in no different fashion* [*Ce n'est pas autrement*] that the other's body becomes animate before me when I shake another man's hand or just look at him [Husserl, *Ideas II*, p. 174]. In learning that my body is a "perceiving thing," that [it][40] is able to be stimulated [*reizbar*]—it, and not just my "consciousness"—I prepared myself for understanding that there are other *animalia* and possibly other men.
>
>    *It is imperative to recognize that we have here neither comparison, nor analogy, nor projection or "introjection"* [ohne Introjektion (ibid., p. 175)]. The reason why I have evidence of the other man's being-there when I shake his hand is that his hand is substituted for my left hand. (*S*, 168/274)[41]

In his reading of this passage, Derrida is, at least initially, concerned with the "liberties" that Merleau-Ponty takes in interpreting Husserl's text.[42] Merleau-Ponty emphatically states that there is 'neither comparison, nor analogy, nor projection or "introjection"' involved when 'I have evidence of the other man's being-there.' But Derrida points out that "The page in question [*Ideas II*, 184, from which we cited the passage above] clearly says that I can *never* have access to the body (*Leib*) of the other *except* in an indirect fashion, through appresentation, comparison, analogy, projection, and introjection. This is a motif to which Husserl remains particularly and fiercely faithful."[43] Husserl's text is indeed, as we indicated above, unambiguous on this point: I have access to my own body "without 'introjection'"[44] but, to the other's body (*Leib*), I have access only by means of analogical appresentation. But I will argue that we need to understand Merleau-Ponty's words in the context of broader themes in his philosophy, and in doing so, we will see that his position is, on this point, sensitive to the very concerns that Derrida raises.

    Derrida's concern is, in particular, with these words of Merleau-Ponty: 'It is in no different fashion that the other's body becomes animate before me when I shake another man's hand or just look at him [*Ce n'est pas autrement que le corps d'autrui s'anime devant moi, quand je serre la main d'un autre homme ou quand seulement je la regarde*].' Derrida says that, with these words, Merleau-Ponty, *contra* Husserl, "assimilates the touching-the-touching

[*le touchant-toucher*] of my own proper body or my two hands with the contact of the other's hand."[45] Derrida's concern is of course not *merely* with
what he says are the liberties taken by Merleau-Ponty in the course of what
purports to be an interpretation of Husserl's text, but, rather, with what he
(Derrida) takes to be the implications of this reading. He writes that the
consequences of this "active 'interpretation'" are, at once, "paradoxical and
typical."[46] They are 'typical,' Derrida says, in that they reflect a certain tendency ("in France notably") to interpret Husserl in such a way as to make
him seem less egological, and thereby to *affirm* (putatively on the basis of
implications of Husserl's texts, implications that Husserl himself, perhaps,
did not recognize) an alterity *within* the interiority of the phenomenological
subject. They are paradoxical in that, in Derrida's view, they tend to have
the opposite result—that is to say, they tend precisely to *lose* the sense of
the alterity of the other. Derrida writes that:

> One runs the risk of reconstituting an intuitionism of immediate
> access to the other, as originary as my access to my own most properly
> proper—and in one blow, doing without appresentation, indirection,
> *Einfühlung*, one runs the risk of *reappropriating* the alterity of the
> other more surely, more blindly, or even more violently than ever.
> In this respect Husserl's cautious approach will always remain *before*
> *us* as a model of vigilance. It is necessary to watch over the other's
> alterity: it will always remain inaccessible to an originally presen-
> tive intuition, an immediate and direct presentation of the *here*.[47]

An experience of the other's lived-body, as an own-body, *his* own body, that
would be accomplished by means of a blurring of the boundaries of *my own*
body, such that the access to the alterity of the other would be included
in, or substitutable for, my access to 'my own most properly proper,' would
undoubtedly risk losing that alterity at the very moment that one sought
to affirm it. Or this, in any case, is what would happen for any phenomenological account of intersubjectivity that would posit such a 'confusion,'
or 'substitutability' (S, 174/284), as the means of an access to the other's
'own most properly proper.'

Before we begin to respond to Derrida's challenge, let us consider
another interpretation, by Emmanuel Levinas, of the same passages from
"The Philosopher and His Shadow" that Derrida is commenting upon. Levinas is concerned to show that Merleau-Ponty's account of sensibility, in
general, and "double touching," in particular, occludes the ethical dimension
in the relation to otherness, an ethical dimension suggested, but apparently
elided, in Merleau-Ponty's figure of the handshake. As Levinas writes,

In the phenomenological theory of intersubjectivity, it is always the *knowledge* of the alter ego that breaks the egological isolation. . . . The idea that a sensibility may reach the other person *otherwise* than by a "gnosis" of touching, seeing, even if the seeing and contact are those of flesh with flesh, seems foreign to the analyses of the phenomenologists. The psychism is consciousness [*conscience*], and in the word "consciousness" the radical science [*science*] remains essential and primordial. Thus the order of consciousness is not broken by sociality any differently from the way it is by knowledge, which, joining the *known* [*su*] immediately coincides with what may have been foreign to it.[48]

Levinas' concern then is not with Merleau-Ponty's apparent violation of a Husserlian epistemological stricture (concerning the necessity of appresentation and indirection in the experience of the other), per se, but with the occlusion of an ethical dimension—an occlusion that is, in his view, the direct *consequence* of this violation.[49] Levinas writes, "One may especially wonder . . . whether such a 'relation,' the ethical relation, is not imposed across a *radical separation* between the two hands, which precisely do not belong to the same body, nor to a hypothetical or only metaphorical intercorporeality."[50]

I have cited these passages because, in them, Levinas mischaracterizes the relationship (which, as I have been arguing, is crucial for understanding Merleau-Ponty) between (anonymous) sensation and (first-personal) consciousness. Nevertheless, he draws the distinction to our attention in a manner that Derrida's interpretation does not. It is crucial that we clarify the nature of this relationship if we are going to understand what Merleau-Ponty is saying about auto-affection and intersubjectivity.

## III. AUTO-HETERO-AFFECTION IN MERLEAU-PONTY

*Intercorporeity and Intersubjectivity*

Levinas, in the passages that we quoted above, conflates consciousness and sensation, as Merleau-Ponty understands them, by immediately identifying the latter with a form of 'gnosis.' In fact, the relationship between the concepts of consciousness and sensation, in Merleau-Ponty, is subtle and difficult to unravel—it is clear, however, that sensation is a responsivity to the demands of the sensible (singularities, each demanding a 'total space') and only as this responsivity does sensation subtend conscious 'knowledge.'

As Merleau-Ponty says, "The senses are distinct from each other *and distinct from intellection* insofar as each one of them brings with it a structure of being which cannot be exactly transposed (*une structure d'être qui n'est jamais exactement transposable*)" (*PhP*, 225/260; my italics). But Levinas' references to the category of 'consciousness' especially draw our attention to the fact that Derrida entirely neglects to note the conceptual distinction between sensibility and consciousness (a distinction that is operative throughout *Phenomenology of Perception* as well as "The Philosopher and His Shadow," and whose importance Levinas seems to recognize, even if he distorts it). In fact we find no mention of the word 'consciousness' in the passages of Derrida's text in which he is reading "The Philosopher and His Shadow." This in spite of the fact that, in the passage of particular concern to Derrida, Merleau-Ponty says: "In learning that my body is a 'perceiving thing,' that it is able to be stimulated (*reizbar*)—it, and not just my 'consciousness'—I prepared myself for understanding (*je me suis préparé à comprendre*) that there are other *animalia* and possibly other men" (*S*, 168/274).

This passage in fact points to a crucial theme in Merleau-Ponty: in learning my body (which, as we saw in chapter 2, is also a matter of *its* achieving a unity by means of the manner in which its sentient organs and surfaces respond, in the form of expressive movement, to multiple demands for ['incompossible'] spaces), I 'prepared myself for understanding that there are other *animalia* and possibly other men.' The 'myself' here is, so to speak, a personal self, a *conscious* self, an *I*. But the *I* did not initiate this work of preparation; rather, the *I* is its result, a result that is only retroactively installed as a source. The preparation begins precisely in sensibility, before there is any *own* body. And as a kind of 'result,' I inherit a past that cannot be encompassed in my present, even if it cannot 'appear' *otherwise* than *in* a present: as we have seen, it haunts the present, but is not a former present, and it is not 'my own most properly proper.' The 'confusion' of self and other is a function of this spectrality; it is precisely a function of the element of contingency that persists in contesting the legitimacy of the 'decisions' that determine both my own identity, and the form of the field of presence over which I preside as an 'I can.' My decisions, including the 'tacit decisions' enacted in the movements of my body, which implicitly or explicitly attest to the presence of 'motivations' in relation to which they make sense, do not thereby overcome the contingency of their beginnings; the meanings of my body's movements do not exhaust the possibilities for responding to the 'call' of the sensible. Thus, my sentient body, in its presence to me, as my own body, attests to what can never be present to me. It prepares me to 'experience' the other because it attests to that which can never be presented *within* any experience. The sense of my own embodiment is also a sense of my own non-self-identity and is thus a kind of opening to the presence of others. The my-own-ness, so to speak, of my body is enacted in the form of an expressive style that is reflective of my being-with-others and subtends my understanding of the behavior of others.

I ultimately cannot say what defines the 'style' of another who has been in my presence—style, as we have said, appears at the intersection of a singularity and a generality. If it is a 'knowing,' as Levinas says, it is a knowing that never ceases to be open to what it does not, and even cannot, know. Thus, the necessity that all ideality, or intelligibility, be ultimately grounded in a stylization of the world, beginning in sensibility, means that knowing never ceases to have an *ethical* meaning. The epiphany of another person is made possible by the expressive style of behaviors—style being the way in which a singularity calls for movement that establishes a horizon of generality without thereby ceasing to bear witness to a singularity. This means that I can never simply subsume the other person to a rule, or reduce the other to a 'case.' This necessity attests to an impossibility of knowledge that would not simply be a failure of understanding, but would be, as Derrida would say, its "threatened chance."[51] Knowledge ('the order of consciousness'), as the knowledge of *reality*, is dependent upon the dynamic structures of living movement and never ceases to be open to the interjection of a singular demand, or the demand of a singularity. The call 'to watch over the other's alterity' is announced in the resistance of bodily behavior to any exhaustive interpretation or identification. This fundamental ethical injunction is rooted in the resistance of flesh to the order of consciousness (as full and transparent presence).

Here is another passage, also cited by Derrida, in which Merleau-Ponty pointedly makes use of the category of 'consciousness,' thus deploying, again, the distinction between the *I*, as self-presence, and the (anonymous) sentient body:

> The reason why I am able to understand the other person's body and existence "beginning with" the body proper, the reason why the compresence of my "consciousness" and my "body" is prolonged into the compresence of my self and the other person, is that the "I am able to" and the "the other person exists" belong here and now to the same world, that the body proper is a premonition of the other person [*que le corps propre est prémonition d'autrui*], the *Einfühlung* and echo of my incarnation, and that a flash of meaning [*qu'un éclair de sens*] makes them substitutable in the absolute presence of origins. (S, 175/285–6)[52]

First of all, let us be clear about the implications of the phrase "absolute presence of origins," which, as Derrida notes, Merleau-Ponty "unhesitatingly" employs here.[53] Let us simply recall that, for Merleau-Ponty, according to the logic of *Fundierung*, which we encountered in chapter 2, an origin is only ever manifested (presented) in an 'originated,' and the latter is not simply reducible to the 'origin' of which it is the manifestation: the absolute presence of an origin would thus be the *appearance* of an origin that is *absolute* in the sense that there would be no *real* origin that could ultimately ground this appearance. It is also notable that Merleau-Ponty speaks here of 'origins' (in the plural). My hand and the other's are substitutable insofar as each is a presence of what has never been a present (singular, non-substitutable, origins): each hand makes its appearance in a movement of repetition. It is, then, precisely *as* repetitions without originals—in 'a flash of meaning'—that they *become* substitutable. But it is important to recognize what this also means: no substitution is legitimate; the possibility of substitution depends on a 'flash of meaning' (*sens*). But, as we have seen, while the emergence of sense (*sens*) makes identities and identifications possible, these identities cannot, so to speak, purify themselves of the contingency of the 'decisions' that necessarily subtend the emergence of *sens*.

Our analysis of the "*Sentir*" chapter has alerted us to the fact that the 'compresence' of 'consciousness' and 'my body' is not accomplished by a prior identity. The body (*Leib*) is not constituted by an ego. This unity of the lived-body is first of all a 'unity of style,' which is to say, the unification involves a passage between singularities accomplished in, and as, stylizing, responsive, movement—thus, *what* is unified never appears in any 'originally presentive intuition' and the unity is never assured. The unity of one's own body is accomplished in the field of what Merleau-Ponty calls, "intercorporeity"—"he and I are like organs of one single intercorporeity (*intercorporéité*)" (S, 168/274). The concept of intercorporeity must be distinguished from the concept of intersubjectivity, which would concern a relation between (conscious) *subjects*. The point here is that my body is already bound up with the other's body before there can be any relation between conscious subjects. But this mutual involvement of bodies does not overcome the *difference* between *conscious* subjects. It simply asserts that this difference must be watched over; it is a matter of responsibilities and decisions, decisions that did not begin as conscious decisions, but that must be assumed by a consciousness.

The position that we find in Merleau-Ponty does not appear to be foreign to the position that Derrida adopts in *criticizing* Merleau-Ponty. Derrida says that he is "tempted to extend rather than reduce the field of appresentation and to recognize its irreducible gap even in the said touching-touched of my 'own proper' hand, my own body proper as a human ego, and so forth. And this would be strictly neither Husserlian nor Merleau-Pontyian."[54] But, in fact, it appears that this is closer to Merleau-Ponty's own position than the "intuitionism of immediate access to the other" that, according to Derrida, Merleau-Ponty's analysis tends toward, or "risks."[55] Now, it must be admitted that Merleau-Ponty *says* that the appearance of the other is *not* a matter of 'comparison,' 'analogy,' 'projection' or 'introjection.' Thus, it appears that, according to Merleau-Ponty, it is not a matter of 'appresentation,' and this might appear to justify Derrida's claim that his own inclination to *extend* the field of appresentation would not be 'Merleau-Pontyian' any more than it would be 'Husserlian.' But I believe that this interpretation would be mistaken.

Merleau-Ponty's point, in the passage in question, is that by virtue of the irreducible gap (which is, as we have seen, explicitly, and repeatedly, asserted by Merleau-Ponty) between the touching and the touched, I would have already had to 'anticipate' the ownness of my body, already had to 'identify' my body as myself.[56] Consequently, the work of constituting the sentient body of another does not need to be performed by a constituting consciousness any more than does the work of constituting my own body. Insofar as this identification *is* carried out by a consciousness (say, when I suddenly recognize my body in a mirror at the edge of a crowded room), the identification *presupposes* a 'communion' of the sentient body, a multiplicity of tacit decisions and stylizings, that have already established the (synaesthetic) unity of a body schema. The 'tacit decisions' of my moving body accomplish an *identity* that is also a *differentiation* between what is my own and what is other. My body has already responded to other bodies, already found itself synchronizing with other rhythms, in the course of its own self-identification, a work of self-identification of which the 'I' is, as we have said, a result rather than an origin—though the 'I' appears to itself *as* the absolute presence of an origin. This is why I (*as a consciousness*) do not need to *constitute* the other's sentient body; my body has already responded, even *participated* in the self-exteriorization of the other's sentient body (which is, after all, sentient only insofar as it moves expressively in responding to otherness, including the otherness of my own moving body). But this does not mean there is no appresentation involved in constituting the other *as* a consciousness:

> I shall never in all strictness be able to think the other person's thought. I can think *that* he thinks; I can construct, behind this mannequin, a presence to self modeled on my own; but it is still my self that I put in it, and it is then that there really is "introjection." On the other hand, I know unquestioningly that that man over there *sees*, that my sensible world is also his, because I *am present at his seeing*, it is *visible* in his eyes' grasp of the scene (j'assiste à sa vision, *elle se voit dans la prise de ses yeux sur la spectacle*). (*S*, 169/276)

The other's sensation, for Merleau-Ponty, is not *fundamentally* the accomplishment of an other *I* any more than my own sensation is the accomplishment of my own ego; rather, the other's sensation is, for him, no less than mine is for me, first of all realized in movement, *expressive* movement, by means of which the sentient body enacts its own unity as a certain response to the call of the sensible. It is thus movement in which my sentient body participates, and to which my body responds, as my body enacts *its* own unity. As to the other's thinking *that* she sees, or thinking about *what* she sees—to this I can never have direct access, as Merleau-Ponty insists. As a consciousness, the other identifies herself *as* this unified body—thus appropriating, for herself, responsibility for meanings enacted in her own behavior—and to the ipseity, the singularity, thus enacted, I can only respond by 'making space.' This 'making space' for the singularity of the other occurs as language, which Merleau-Ponty understands as fundamentally a matter of expressive movement. (We will return to this, and to the ethical implications of this thought, in the next chapter.)

There is then, in Merleau-Ponty's account of intersubjectivity, no need for an analogical transfer in order to be present to another's 'seeing,' because my sentient body is not a self-enclosed identity, but rather, a 'limitless' and 'open-ended' schema. Its identity is accomplished (but never completely accomplished) in relation to others, other bodies, other expressive movements; it is accomplished, in part, by means of an ongoing self-differentiation. This is why we cannot quite agree with M.C. Dillon's understanding of Merleau-Ponty's account of intersubjectivity as involving a "transfer of corporeal schema."[57] Or, to put it more precisely, while we can accept the idea that such a transfer might occur in recognizing another *subject* as another consciousness, this transfer is possible only because, at the level of what Merleau-Ponty calls 'intercorporeity' (which is the level that Dillon is particularly concerned with[58]) no 'transfer' is necessary. Let us consider the difference between the two positions.

According to Dillon, Merleau-Ponty was wrong, at the time of writing *Phenomenology of Perception*, to use the expression 'tacit cogito' to designate the unreflective fund of experience; the unreflective is, in Dillon's view, "the primordial experience of corporeal reflexivity."[59] The confusion, which, in Dillon's view, is produced by the notion of a 'tacit cogito' stems from the apparent contradiction between, on the one hand, a *cogito*, which would involve an act of reflection, or self positing, and, on the other hand, the idea of the *tacit*, or the unreflected. Dillon writes,

> The missing term that resolves the contradiction . . . is the lived
> body. The body is preeminently immanence and transcendence: it
> is the subject of perceptual experience and a possible object of per-

ception. Indeed it is only because it is a worldly object that it can perceive worldly beings: pure consciousness cannot *touch* anything. The body can touch things, but it can touch things only to the extent that it is touched *by* things: to touch something is necessarily to feel the touch of the thing on oneself—an anaesthetized finger does not properly touch, it only bumps up against things, precisely because it cannot feel. Here, then, is the genuine tacit cogito, in the reflexivity intrinsic to bodily perception, but it is misnamed cogito, for it is not thought; it is, rather, our primordial contact with things.[60]

Dillon thus concludes that "The I born of reflection and sedimented in language is an expression of corporeal reflexivity."[61] Explicit self-consciousness, on this interpretation, is the *expression* of the reflexivity of a lived-body, a body in 'touch' *with itself* by means of its 'primordial contact with things.' What the reflective cogito expresses, then, is, in Dillon's view, already a prereflective self. This is why he can find in 'corporeal reflexivity' the true meaning of the unreflective that the doctrine of the 'tacit cogito' was trying to capture. He writes, "The tacit cogito *is* corporeal reflexivity."[62] I am arguing, on the contrary, that a reflective cogito is a creative enactment of an identity. As such, the act of reflection is a *decision* that is, to be sure, *motivated* by, among other things, a certain dynamic acquaintance of my body with itself evident as a style, but the act of reflection cannot overcome the sense of the contingency of the grounds of its decision. It cannot exorcize the phantoms attesting to the non-identity, the anonymity, of (the) body. In short, the unreflective is not simply the unreflective self-presence of my body in its 'primordial contact with things'; rather, the unreflective appears (in my conscious present) as the sense of what has *never* been a present. It is the *sense*, rather than the fact, or the self-evident necessity, of a bodily self-contact. In other words, the act of reflection is an auto-affection effect that at once attests to and occludes a hetero-affection, a primordial intrication of my body with otherness. And it is precisely for this reason that I do not need to 'transfer' corporeal schema in order to witness the advent of another sentient body. While Dillon acknowledges that the unity of the lived body, my own body, is an accomplishment, and that this unity is accomplished by means of a process that inevitably involves a certain confusion of self and other (syncretic sociability), with the notion of a 'transfer' of the corporeal schema, he seems paradoxically to make intercorporeity dependent upon the *results* of this accomplishment.

I have taken the time to discuss the phenomenology of the lived body here because I believe that Merleau-Ponty's account of time, as auto-affection, is fundamentally a claim about the self-temporalizing character of

*Sinngenesis*-in-movement. According to what I have termed the metaphysics-of-presence reading of Merleau-Ponty, the claim in the "Temporality" chapter about the privilege of the present is evidence of Merleau-Ponty's uncritical reliance on the category of consciousness and (according to Derrida) his preference for continuity and unity in his reliance on the notion of the lived-body (*le corps propre*). As we have seen, according to Derrida, the contact of the lived-body with itself—its putatively fundamental sense of livedness, or ownness—is the very formula of immediate self-presence in phenomenology. I am arguing that this interpretation overlooks the very important dimensions of difference, discontinuity, delay and non-self-presence in Merleau-Ponty's descriptions. Needless to say, I interpret these as crucial to understanding what Merleau-Ponty is saying about self-consciousness. The difference between these two interpretations comes out clearly in the different ways in which interpreters of Merleau-Ponty have understood the latter's doctrine of the body schema.

*Body Schema*

Dillon is not the only one to have equated the concepts 'body schema,' 'lived body,' and 'prereflective self-awareness.' But I do not think that 'body schema,' as such, can be equated with prereflective self-awareness—though it certainly subtends the possibility of self-awareness. Let us, then, pause to consider this notion of the body schema. As Shaun Gallagher has pointed out, the classical psychological concept of the body schema has not always been used in a consistent manner and it has often been conflated with what is called "body image."[63] Gallagher insists on the terminological distinction:

> A *body image* consists of a system of perceptions, attitudes, and beliefs pertaining to one's own body. In contrast, a *body schema* is a system of sensory-motor capacities that function without awareness or the necessity of perceptual monitoring. This conceptual distinction between body image and body schema is related respectively to the difference between having a perception of (or belief about) something and having a capacity to move (or an ability to do something). . . . The body schema . . . involves certain motor capacities, abilities, and habits that both enable and constrain movement and the maintenance of posture. It continues to operate, and in many cases operates best, when the intentional object of perception is something other than one's own body.[64]

The body schema, then, is not simply to be equated with proprioception. As a form of behavior, it is a certain dynamic process of figuration,[65] incorporating kinesthetic 'information' about the body, about its movements or its posture, only in terms of its relevance for the organism itself. Here as elsewhere we have a relation, not of stimulus and response, but of motivation and decision. That is to say, the body schema incorporates kinesthetic sensations only "in proportion to their value to the organism's projects" (*PhP*, 100/116). Thus the system of the body schema is at once the ground of the unity-in-difference of the body and of the unity-in-difference of the field of presence. This is because the body is always "polarized by its tasks"— it is unified in the coherence of a being-toward some aim (*PhP*, 101/117).

In fact, as we noted in connection with our discussion of habit in chapter 2, the body has a way of making itself inconspicuous in relation to its tasks. As Merleau-Ponty writes:

> Bodily space can be distinguished from external space and envelop its parts instead of spreading them out, because it is the darkness needed in the theatre to show up the performance, the background of somnolence or reserve of vague power against which the gesture and its aim stand out, the zone of not being *in front of which* precise beings, figures and points can come to light. (*PhP*, 101/117)

In other words, 'body schema' designates the way in which the body 'appears' to itself precisely by not appearing, in letting something else appear.[66] It is the body's dynamic acquaintance with itself. This is what makes it necessary to distinguish between the body schema and the 'body image.' It is certainly the case that my body can appear as a perceptual object and that I can attend to the movements of my body by way of visual monitoring—for example, when I am learning to play a musical instrument—and these kinds of observational relations to my own body can be included under the notion of body image. But, as we have seen, this possibility of visually monitoring *my own* body's movements seems to presuppose a more basic functional directedness and coherence of these movements themselves.

There is in fact considerable evidence that the body schema, as a kind of functional and coordinated directedness-in-movement, is already operative in neonates—well before we see experimental evidence of an *observational* recognition, on the part of the infant, of its body *as* its own body. Philippe Rochat reports the results of studies conducted by himself and others on the tendency of newborn infants to bring their hands into contact with their own mouths.[67] They found that immediately after birth, infants are able to direct their hands to their mouths accurately and to open their mouths in anticipation of the hand entering. The frequency of this complex action increases if a drop of sweet solution is applied to the tongue. Presumably the sucking action motivated by the sensation of sweetness on the tongue is facilitated by the insertion of the hand. This hypothesis seems to be confirmed by the fact that the infant is far less likely to perform the action if a pacifier is placed in its mouth subsequent to the insertion of the drop of sweet solution. It is apparently in order to intensify the sensation of sweetness that the infant puts her hand into her mouth; the sense (*sens*) of the action is not determined in reference to the hand (for the pacifier can serve as a substitute), but in reference to a taste of sweetness. The infant does not need an observational awareness of its own body to perform this task; the action of the hand and mouth seems to be enveloped in a function allowing the sweetness (rather than the hand) to 'appear.' This goal-directed motor action would seem to indicate that infants are born with a basic functional awareness of their bodies' powers of movements and an ability to organize the movements of parts of their bodies in relation to each other.[68] As Rochat observes, "Such observation demonstrates that this behavior is neither accidental nor the product of a chain of simple stimulus-response links, but the expression of an organized action system oriented toward a functional goal. Infants may not be aware of this goal, but the action is organized around it."[69] Thus the body schema, which can legitimately be described as an 'organized action system,' appears to be perfectly capable of functioning independently of the observational, or thematic, awareness of one's own body. But to what extent then would it be appropriate to speak of the body schema as a sense of "one's own" body? In other words, is the body schema sufficient to account for the "lived" (or "own," *propre*) character of the so-called "lived body" (*le corps propre*)?

Gallagher suggests that the equation of lived-ness with "mineness," or, we could say, "one's ownness," may not be appropriate. He is of the view that the 'lived body' is a kind of "absently available performance."[70] As Gallagher suggests, the criterion for saying of some experience that it is "mine" is that it must be directly felt in some way—for example, when I feel a pain, I say it is my pain, but when my neighbor feels a pain, I say the pain is hers (and not mine). But on this basis, Gallagher argues, we cannot equate the lived character of the lived body with a sense of mineness:

> Most processes or happenings in the body described by neurophysiology are unfelt and these events do not seem "to me" to be happening in "my" body. Yet it cannot be denied that they are happening in a lived body, that they are being lived-through in a non-conscious experiential way, and that some of these processes become present in the form of pain, hunger, or tension, they become present as phenomena of "my" body. Most performances of the lived body remain absently available as a lived physiology.[71]

Thus Gallagher wants to shift the terms of the problem of bodily self-consciousness by identifying, at least in part, the "lived" character of the lived body with the body schema as a non-conscious, anonymous, performance of the body (organizing *itself* in relation to, or *as* a certain relation to, its environment[72]). Physiological processes are 'lived' in the sense that they structure the field of presence—they structure the body-environment circuit. But only under special conditions do these absently available performances become conscious—that it to say, *my* lived experiences.

Dan Zahavi objects that Gallagher too narrowly defines consciousness as object-consciousness and then, on the basis of this narrow definition of consciousness, sees in the body schema only an unconscious performance. That is to say, according to Zahavi, Gallagher seems to exclude the possibility of defining the body schema in terms of prereflective consciousness. Further, Zahavi objects that Gallagher's notion of the body schema is plagued by a fundamental ambiguity because it tries to include too much:

It encompasses both the unthematic control and coordination of movement which occurs outside of conscious *attention*, that is, a kind of prereflective body-awareness, and the unconscious, or rather nonconscious, physiological processes that take place completely outside of consciousness. . . . I think it would have been better to distinguish the two rather than combine them under the concept of the body schema.[73]

Indeed it may seem somewhat surprising, given Merleau-Ponty's and Gallagher's own careful distinctions between the physiological body and the lived body, to see Gallagher speaking of a 'lived physiology' or speaking of 'neurophysiological' processes as 'lived.' How exactly can we be said to 'live' physiological processes that we do not directly experience, even tacitly? For Zahavi, as we have seen, to be conscious of something, to 'live' something, is to experience it in terms of "first-personal givenness."

I do not think that either of these interpretations of the body schema is quite right. I agree with Zahavi that Gallagher's notion is too broad. But identifying the body-schema with a first-personal, bodily, lived self-presence is also problematic. Let us pause for a moment to consider the implications of Zahavi's interpretation in terms of what we have been saying about consciousness and presence.

Zahavi's account of prereflective self-awareness is inspired by his reading of Husserl, and is developed partly as a defense of the egological theory of consciousness that the latter introduced in the period after the publication of his *Logical Investigations*. According to Zahavi's reconstruction of this development, it was Husserl's confrontations with the problem of intersubjectivity that led him to the transcendental egological theory that is first fully articulated in *Ideas I*. The nonegological theory of consciousness, which appears in *Logical Investigations*, cannot avoid treating experiences as fundamentally anonymous. But such a theory, according to Zahavi, is faced with a problem: "If I encounter a crying child, we would say that I experience not my own sorrow, but the sorrow of somebody else. But it is exactly this distinction which will evade me as long as I opt for a nonego-logical theory."[74] Without a clear account of the first-personal character of our experiences, I cannot account for the immediate awareness of the distinction between my own lived experience and another's. Husserl's egology enables him to account for this difference. According to Zahavi, Husserl's egology does not postulate a substantial subject (a thinking thing), and it is not meant to explain self-consciousness by claiming that we are somehow always *reflectively* self-aware (which would lead to an infinite regress). On the contrary, according to Zahavi, it refers to a prereflective manifestation of the subjectivity of each of our experiences:

> Whether a certain experience is experienced as mine or not does not depend on something apart from the experience, but on the givenness of the experience. If the experience is given originarily to me, in a first-personal mode of presentation, it is experienced as my experience, otherwise not. . . . We are not (yet) confronted with a thematic awareness of the experience as being owned by or belonging to ourselves. It is the particular primary presence of the experience rather than some specific content which makes it mine, and distinguishes it from whatever experiences Others might have.[75]

Thus, for Zahavi, it makes no more sense to speak of something as 'lived' but not consciously (prereflectively) experienced than it does to speak of an experience as conscious but not first-personally given (i.e., to speak of an anonymous consciousness). For Zahavi, the lived is what is given in 'primary presence.' Thus, again, in Zahavi's view, it is misleading to conflate anonymous physiological functions with bodily self-awareness (which, if we are to equate self-awareness with the 'lived' character of the lived body, must involve the appearance of the body to itself in the mode of first-personal givenness) by placing both of these under the same heading: body schema. We may say that, as a matter of fact, the life of the body involves many non-conscious, anonymous processes, and thus we might say that anonymous physiological processes *subtend* the self-consciousness of the lived body, but they are not, as such, 'lived.' This *subtending* is only of concern to a consciousness insofar as it appears in the first-person. That is to say, these processes are not originarily given.

And yet, if appearances are necessarily 'lived,' then Zahavi's identification of the lived with what is 'originarily given to me, in a first-personal mode of presentation,' seems to imply a more restricted notion of appearance than what we have found in Merleau-Ponty. It would equate the being of phenomena with originary appearance to a consciousness and this would seem to exclude the sense in which the past of the sentient body haunts the present. The phenomenon of the body schema implies a broader sense of 'appearance.'

The unity of the body is, as we have noted, an *expressive* unity—it is accomplished *as* a sense in movement attesting to the unity of my body, but it bears an attestation of the unreflective, anonymous prehistory of this unity. The openness of the body to self-transformation (learning, prostheses) is a function of the open-endedness of the body-schema, its endless striving to accomplish itself, but also its resistance to any final determination. My body is enacted in, and as, the unending process of translation of non-sense (*non-sens*) into sense (*sens*). And, as we have been arguing, this process of translation is originally accomplished in living movement. We have interpreted Merleau-Ponty's notions of motivation and decision in connection with his idea of perception as the motor grasping of a motor *sens*; this has led us to conclude that perception must be understood as movement discriminatingly allowing 'itself' to be moved. And, as we have also seen, movement must already be underway in order to be able to articulate its own direction/meaning (*sens*). If this interpretation of Merleau-Ponty's account of perception is correct then we must say that, for Merleau-Ponty, appearance begins in a dynamic that is older than itself, older than the subject or the object of perception. And this would also mean that it is older than consciousness, and, indeed, older than any 'mineness' or 'first-personal givenness.' The *sens* of appearance relies, as we have said, on its relation (precisely within the living present) to a motivation that cannot be made to exhaustively appear *in the original*. This is because, as movement, perception only happens as the *sens* of what must have begun as non-*sens*. Appearance happens as belated appearance—which is why it does not happen according to laws governing the relations between entities or objective properties. It is also why it ceaselessly motivates further movement, in order to disclose a reality that is 'full of reserves.' And if the motor dynamics of appearance are precisely what allow us to distinguish the subjectivity and the object of appearance then we would have to say that this irremediable belatedness also affects any *self*-appearance. Appearance happens by means of the difference between presence and its (absent) ground—a difference that is articulated, and overcome (though never completely), within the present understood here as decision.[76] This belatedness is a crucial feature of the self-appearance of the lived-body, which is why we must go beyond the alternatives either of including, in the notion of body schema, physiological processes subtending conscious appearance (Gallagher), or of identifying it with an originary first-personal givenness of bodily self-experience (Zahavi).

According to Merleau-Ponty, each of us manifests in our present behavior a certain relation to the "specific past" of our bodies:

> Just as we speak of repression in the limited sense when I retain through time one of the momentary worlds through which I have lived, and make it the formative element of my whole life—so it can be said that my organism, as a prepersonal cleaving to the general form of the world, as an anonymous and general existence, plays, beneath my personal life, the part of an inborn *complex* (*le rôle d'un* complexe *inné*). (*PhP*, 84/99)

Our bodies incarnate a 'prepersonal' past (this incarnation is at the same time a 'repression') which thus constitutes a 'formative element' in the field of presence even though, or, rather, precisely *because*, this 'repressed' element does not itself appear originarily in any present or in any explicit re-presentation in the present. This past "can be recaptured and taken up by an individual life only because that life has never transcended it, but secretly nourishes it, devoting thereto part of its strength, because its present is still that past" (*PhP*, 85/101). Thus we cannot simply equate appearance and originary givenness because appearance is subtended by what cannot be given in the present. And yet, as we have seen, it is also crucial that we not think of this non-presence as external to the appearance—as a thing in itself, a physiological, third-person, fact. It is precisely the non-presence *of* presence. The difference between appearance and non-appearance is articulated *within* the field of appearance. This refers us, again, to the originary past of which Merleau-Ponty speaks in the "*Sentir*" chapter, or the spectral depth that we found intimated in Merleau-Ponty's arguments against traditional epistemological treatments of depth. Insofar as we conceive of this specific past as "a former present (*ancien présent*)" it shuts itself up "in its own autonomous self evidence (*son évidence autistique*)" (*PhP*, 85/100). To experience the past and the future in their fecundity, as the inexhaustible reality toward which we are projected, or the 'anonymous' past in its functioning as a 'formative principle' in our present, we must let it appear in a decision, as the decision's prehistory and its motivation. It is this discontinuity between the original past and the present (which is also a discontinuity between my natural, sentient, being and my consciousness) that subtends the sense of the temporal. My body is a trace of a past that has never been assuredly my own, even though I cannot be a conscious self but by assuming it *as* my own. Thus, Merleau-Ponty concludes: "What enables us to centre our existence is also what prevents us from centring it completely, and the anonymity of our body is inseparably both freedom and servitude" (*PhP*, 85/101).

*Auto-hetero-affection as the Advent of the Intercorporeal Body*

Our analysis of the concept of body-schema has led us to conclude that the presence of the body is also the presence of a non-presence, and that the auto-affection of the body (of the body as temporal, as a dynamic unity) begins in affections that are not the affections of an *autos*: bodily auto-affection is equally a *hetero*-affection. But as this is not exactly what Merleau-Ponty *explicitly* says, we must continue to put this reading to the test. Derrida's deconstruction of the 'metaphysics of presence' has given us a guide for interpreting Merleau-Ponty's statements concerning the 'privilege' of the present. This privilege would be evidence of a metaphysics of presence if it amounted to the following claim: I am able to anticipate the unfolding of the manifestation of being, and this power is grounded in the form ('essential structures') of the present where I coincide with myself in coinciding with being. When Merleau-Ponty writes, quoting Husserl, concerning time as auto-affection, that the flow of time is an "ultimate consciousness" wherein "being coincides with being for itself," he seems to be endorsing just such a claim (*PhP*, 422/483). And when he says that my sense of the past is grounded in the present, and is subtended by "the chain of retentions and the overlapping horizons coming one after the other [ensuring] an unbroken continuity," he, again, seems to be saying that the present, the field of the 'I can,' is the unchanging form of possible appearance (*PhP*, 418/478). My relation to the future and the past is ultimately grounded by the structures of the here and now. This metaphysical commitment to the privilege of the present would be, according the metaphysics-of-presence reading of Merleau-Ponty, manifested in a concept of the lived-body that is "always present for me" (*PhP*, 92/108). The *generality* of the body schema would, on this reading, be the (present) framework in terms of which I comport myself in relation to a past and a future. As Merleau-Ponty says, "The presence and absence of external objects are only variations within a field of primordial presence, a perceptual domain over which my body exercises power" (*PhP*, 92/108).

Now, one way to challenge this metaphysics-of-presence reading would be to point out that this bodily self-presence, as Merleau-Ponty understands it, is never free of a certain fundamental opacity precisely insofar as it is a *bodily* self-presence. The presence of the body is thus not to be equated with the self-presence of a transcendental consciousness, nor is the presence of the lived-body a matter of its being constituted by a pure ego who assures itself of its absolute self-coinciding by means of a self-touch. But this, from a Derridean perspective, is arguably not the point. If my relation to the future and the past is grounded in the presence of my body, and if my body is, as Merleau-Ponty in fact says, a "knowing-body," then my orientation toward the future, my anticipation of it, is always ultimately grounded in structures that are, as it were, incarnated in the form of a presence to self (*PhP*, 408/467). The body would thus be a kind of opaque signifier referring me to myself, to my future and my past, but its opacity would not thereby give me reason to doubt what it teaches me; rather its opacity would only announce a demand to know more, to coincide more adequately with its message. I would always be being-toward the future in terms of the form of the present. We have highlighted (in chapter 2) Merleau-Ponty's use of terms like 'communion' (explicitly connected with the imagery of eucharist, transubstantiation, consecration, inspiration, the infusion of Grace) to describe the unity, the presence to itself of the sentient body. The unity of the body is, as we have said, for Merleau-Ponty, an expressive unity, but since he also speaks of expression as a "miracle," we can think of this unity of expression as a kind of transubstantiation, a miracle that can never fail because I am first of all a *consciousness* (*PhP*, 320/370). In this connection, it should be noted that Merleau-Ponty often speaks of the relation to the future as a matter of "pinning one's faith, at a stroke, in a whole future of experiences," of "placing one's belief in a world" (*PhP*, 297/323). The idea of perceptual faith is perfectly consistent with the idea of the primacy of presence. To challenge the metaphysics-of-presence reading, the question we really need to ask is this: does consciousness's relation to the future (which would also be constitutive of its field of presence), its faith, also necessarily involve, for it, a dependence upon an event that it cannot manage to anticipate? Is auto-affection simply "a pure feeling of the self (*pur sentiment de soi*)" (*PhP*, 404/462), or is it also at the same time a premonition of what dispossesses the self? Or is it the former only as one of the possible (or impossible) effects of the latter—an auto-affection *effect*, as Derrida says?

At the beginning of the chapter of *On Touching* in which he directly confronts Merleau-Ponty's phenomenology of the body and 'flesh,' Derrida cites several passages from Jean-Luc Nancy. These passages mark out the direction and the range of concerns that guide Derrida's reading of Merleau-Ponty, and it is clear that the concern here is with a certain onto-theological concept of *the* body. Here is one of the passages cited by Derrida (and, according to Derrida, one of the few in which Nancy directly refers to Merleau-Ponty):

> The body, therefore, is nothing other than the *auto-symbolization of the absolute organ*. It is unnamable like God, it exposes nothing to the outside of an extension, it is the organ of self-organization,

unnamable like the rot of its self-digestion (Death in Person)—
unnamable, as well, as this self-texture toward which strains a
philosophy of the "body proper" ("What we are calling flesh, this
interiorly worked over mass, has no name in any philosophy," says
Merleau-Ponty). God, Death, Flesh—the triple name of the body
in all onto-theology. The body is the exhaustive combination and
common assumption of these three impossible names, where all
meaning wears itself out.[77]

We are not in a position to engage with all of the themes that this passage
introduces, but the issue for us here is Nancy's suggestion that, in the terms
of a certain onto-theological concept of *the* body, 'all meaning wears itself
out' in the 'auto-symbolization of [an] absolute organ.' To put this another
way, in terms of an ontotheological, or a metaphysics-of-presence, conception of the body, there would be no meaning but the meaning that is, as it
were, auto-inscribed in the self-organization of the body; there is no *other*
meaning, or, what would amount to the same thing, *non-*meaning, that
would come to inscribe *itself* (from outside the system of the self-touching/
tactile body) *in* this system of the body and thereby dispossess the body of
itself. Even its mortality (the threat of non-sense) is, in a sense, its own
*proper* mortality. Again, nothing would enter the onto-theological body from
outside—it is a pure auto-poiesis. But I do not think that this captures the
sense of embodiment that we have discovered in Merleau-Ponty.

I remarked earlier that what Merleau-Ponty takes to be the difference
between his own account of ecstatic temporality and that of Heidegger is
that, while the latter says that time temporalizes from the future (at least
when it is lived 'authentically'), Merleau-Ponty insists that it temporalizes from the present, the place-time from which our 'decision' begins. But
Merleau-Ponty also says this:

> Ahead of what I see and perceive, there is, it is true, nothing
> more actually visible, but my world is carried forward by lines of
> intentionality which trace out in advance at least the style of what
> is to come (although we are always on the watch, perhaps to the
> day of our death, for the appearance of *something else* [*autre chose*]).
> (*PhP*, 416/476; italics in the original)

This being on the watch for *something else* is, as we have suggested in chapters 2 and 3, implicit in the very meaning of the concept of style. Style
is fundamentally rooted in movement that allows things (including the
body itself) to appear within a certain horizon of generality, but it is also
always the generalizing of what cannot be generalized—the singularity of the

sensible. Once again, we find that the concept of style, as that which realizes a passage between a singularity and generality and as that characteristic of expressive movement enabling it to function as the institution of an identity, is a fundamental concept in Merleau-Ponty. Style is not a law, principle, or form of generality already laid down in the self-organization of the body proper—it responds to an event that is a certain demand for *sens* (direction, meaning), but that offers no clear direction for how that meaning is to be actualized. In fact, we could go further and say that the sensible is also a certain resistance to sense-making—as we have seen, the call of the sensible is, each time, a call for a 'total space.' And this is why perception, for Merleau-Ponty, must always be "a violent act" (*PhP*, 361/415). It responds, *must* respond, is *always already* responding, to irreconcilable demands. But as we have also seen, the sense of reality, of transcendence and otherness, is subtended by what we could call, speaking loosely, the *memory* of this violence—the sense of the contingency of our body's 'decisions,' and the (non)-sense of the contingency of our bodies. Perception stylizes precisely because, and insofar as, it is always on the watch for *something else*. And, in this sense, Merleau-Ponty's understanding of subjectivity coincides with Heidegger's: the subjectivity of the subject is accomplished as a relation to its own finitude.

This 'memory' is the facticity of our birth, which has no place within our present (it has never been a present), which, thus, interposes itself into the 'essential structures' of the present. And yet it also subtends the structures of the present by interrupting the flow of time, and by letting us come back to ourselves across a distance. Sensation, as Merleau-Ponty understands it, is this interruption. And the 'privilege' of the present depends on it:

> In the present and in perception, my being and my consciousness are one, not that my being is reducible to the knowledge I have of it or that is clearly set out before me—on the contrary perception is opaque, for it brings into play, beneath what I know [*au-dessous de ce que je connais*], my sensory fields which are my primitive alliance with the world [*mes complicités primitives avec le monde*]—but 'to be conscious' is here nothing but 'to be at . . .' ('être à . . .'), and because my consciousness of existing merges into the actual gesture [*le geste effectif*] of 'ex-sistence.' (*PhP*, 424/485)

As a conscious, sentient, body, what I know (my consciousness of . . . ) depends on what I cannot *know*. My presence is a dependence on what has never been a present. And to be conscious is to merge with the sense (*sens*) of the gesture of ex-sistence. Sensation is a 'continuous birth' of the subject and the fund from which any consciousness draws its vital breath.

But this means that I am constitutively open to unforeseeable transformations. As a sentient body, I am, in a certain sense, open to my own continuous birth. As Merleau-Ponty writes: "In the home into which a child is
born, all objects change their significance; they begin to await some as yet
indeterminate treatment at his hands; another and different person is there"
(PhP, 407/466). This natal event, the event of the emergence of meaning,
is renewed with each sensation. As Merleau-Ponty says, "Consciousness discovers in itself, along with the sensory fields and with the world as the field
of all fields, the opacity of a primary past (l'opacité d'un passé originaire)"
(PhP, 351/403). It is precisely this primary past, the event of my birth, and
the discontinuity between this primary past and any present, that subtends
the sense of the temporal and that allows me to see, in the carvings on the
table, a "trace" of my own past (PhP, 413/472). The trace of the original
past paradoxically withholds my past from me and affords me the chance to
enact ('decide') my identity as this personal history, just as time also 'withholds me from what I was about to become and enables me to grasp myself
at a distance.' It is precisely insofar as my past is not immediately my own
that I can read myself, as a certain depth, in the present evidence. And
this, as we have seen, is part of the meaning of body-schema. As a body
schema, the body is fundamentally open to otherness because its unity is
a continuous enactment and a continuous concealment; the body schema
is constitutively intercorporeal and as such, it is not a simple self-identity.
The body schema subtends a proper body insofar as it also dis-appropriates
it. The body schema makes space for a body proper insofar as it has already
made space for otherness.

    We are open to otherness in being open to our birth and our death.
Each sensation, as an arrival of 'another and different person' within the
field of what is proper to me, is thereby also my death. As Merleau-Ponty
says, "my life has a social atmosphere just as it has a flavour of mortality"
(PhP, 364/418). The 'just as' is crucial here. My death is, for Merleau-Ponty,
not initially mine (and thus, we could add, the term 'my death' is a meaning that presupposes a culture) (PhP, 215/250). A death, the death that I
inherit along with the primordial past that subtends my conscious life, is
attested to by the anonymous singularity of the sensible, which does not
originarily appear to an 'I.' Merleau-Ponty says that I would have to "be
assuming myself to be pre-existent to, or outliving, myself, in order to be
able to experience" my birth and my death—but he says this in the course
of explaining that sensation is precisely a birth and a death of the subject
(PhP, 215/250). Being a conscious, sentient body requires that I outlive
myself in order that I might be a self and in order that I might be able
to let a world appear. And, for the same reason, I would need to outlive
myself in order for there to be a 'my death.' And I am only able to do this

insofar as I am *not able* to do this; in other words, it is the advent of the other that can alone subtend this possibility. Only the other can bestow 'my death' upon me; and only the other can anticipate the other in me. The relation to the other is at once my relation to my birth and my death and precisely my 'threatened chance' for outliving my death, at least for long enough to let there be a world, or for there to ever be a 'my own (proper) body.' This means that the origin of time, the time that is my present, can-not itself be a consciousness of time—or if it is, for me, a consciousness of time, my experience must include an attestation of what cannot be grounded in any consciousness of time. And this *sense* of the temporal, of the pure difference, or dehiscence, that is time, must appear to me, 'beneath what I know,' as a constitutive emptiness. My present must be the memory, and the advent, of *something else.*

In the passage from "The Philosopher and His Shadow" that we cited earlier, and to which Derrida particularly objects, Merleau-Ponty says this about so-called double-sensation: "My right hand was present at the advent (*l'avénement*) of my left hand's active sense of touch. It is in no different fashion that the other's body becomes animate before me" (S, 168/274). We have already noted that Derrida seems to disregard Merleau-Ponty's many careful distinctions between the sentient body (the body of intercorporeity) and the body of a conscious self (the body of the subject and of intersub-jectivity). But he also neglects to highlight this concept of 'advent.' Given the numerous deployments of the concept of 'advent' throughout the essays collected in *Signes*, it would seem to be of no small importance to understand how this concept might serve to qualify the claim that comes after: 'It is in no different fashion that the other's body becomes animate before me.' In *Phenomenology of Perception*, Merleau-Ponty defines advent, in the context of the discussion of the "event" of the birth of the subject, as a "transcen-dental event" (*PhP*, 407/466).[78] "Advent," Merleau-Ponty says in "Indirect Language and the Voices of Silence," is "a promise of events" (S, 70/112). In this sense, advent is connected with the concept of style as a kind of passage effected between incomparables. It is a happening of the impossible, which cannot occur without a certain violence. My body can be the enact-ment of a self only insofar as, in each of the movements of my hands, eyes, feet, there is an anticipation of events, of impossible presences—the unity of my body happens as an event that does not begin by being possible, and yet it is the completion that each of the movements of my sentient flesh are looking for. And 'it is in no different fashion' that the sentient body of another appears to me as a sentient body. My body anticipates the other, but is not the condition of the possibility of the appearance of the other—my body is the 'promise of events,' and the other is the answer that my body was looking for. As a self-conscious body, the body 'pins its faith' on what it cannot anticipate. This is the meaning of advent, and of time as an order (a meaning/direction [*sens*]) of advent.

As we have seen, Merleau-Ponty says that time is auto-affection—"the archetype of the *relationship of self to self*, [that] traces out an interiority or an ipseity" (*PhP*, 426/487). In this sense, time would be the life of the lived-body; it would be understood on the model of the unity of the gesture that is equal to itself in each of its parts. But Merleau-Ponty also says this about time:

> Our birth, or, as Husserl has it in his unpublished writings, our generativity is the basis both of our activity or individuality, and our passivity or generality—that inner weakness which prevents us from ever achieving the density of an absolute individual. We are not in some incomprehensible way an activity joined to a passivity, an automatism surmounted by a will, but wholly active and wholly passive, because we are the upsurge of time (*le surgissement du temps*). (*PhP*, 428/489)

If this 'upsurge of time' is to be understood in connection with generativity, with birth, then it is, for me, always conditioned by an original past. It is like the gesture that succeeds in being equal to itself only by not quite succeeding—it succeeds only by making space for otherness. The generativity of time is the dependence of the present on the constant irruption of singularities into the time of my life. Only on this basis then would time be the "dehiscence of the present toward the future"; it is such only because it is the 'promise of events.' It is, then, perhaps misleading to speak of time in terms of an ultimate consciousness, because time also names this *dependence* of consciousness on what it cannot anticipate or make apparent to itself.

But time only happens for a subject who enacts its reality, a subjectivity that anticipates itself. And this is the meaning of the claim that time is an ultimate consciousness, that the present is the privileged zone in which being and consciousness coincide. As a consciousness, I am not simply passively subjected to 'the ceaseless welling up of time.' As Merleau-Ponty says, "I can find a remedy against it in itself, as happens in a decision which binds me or in the act of establishing a concept" (*PhP*, 427/488). In positing a concept, and in thereby positing myself as an 'I think,' I enact my reality by assuming a responsibility for what I did not initiate. It is from the standpoint of consciousness, then, that we can speak of time as *auto*-affection. This is also the standpoint from which I am able to recognize the other person as another interiority, another ipseity. But when philosophy speaks from the standpoint of consciousness, without attending sufficiently to the constitutive emptiness that is both the condition and the ruin of the essential structures of the present, it can end up occluding the manner in which I depend on otherness in order to be able to achieve this standpoint of responsibility, of presence to myself. I, after all, do not establish concepts on my own. It is because consciousness, as presence, is a decision, a decision for which I may assume responsibility, but whose grounds I cannot ultimately locate *within myself*, that I live my time as an order of advent. *I did not interrupt the flow of time in order to posit myself and thereby to anticipate my own future.*

For as long as I live, in each present moment of my experience, I am on the watch for *something else*. This is what it is to be a consciousness (where consciousness is understood to be a developed form of sentient, bodily, life). This 'something else' is not merely something that would happen *to* me, but would happen, each time, *as* the happening of myself, or *as* the dissolution of myself—but in any case, insofar as I am conscious, the order of advent, the 'promise of events,' is my domain. As a sentient body, I am open to the advent of things, of tools and prosthetics that would "play a part in the original structure of my own body (*la structure originale du corps propre*)" (*PhP*, 91/107). Such things would, as it were, let the *origin* that is my sentient body appear *otherwise*, because the 'original structure of my body' is an origin only in being repeated, and in appearing otherwise, outside of *itself*. The 'something else' can, as we have seen, also be my death; it is, each time, my death, each sensation is a death of the subject. My body, as a sentient body, a body constitutively open to otherness, is a certain openness to an event that is also a death of the 'I.' But insofar as the event of sensation is also the opening of an order of advent, consciousness, we could say, happens *as* a body surviving itself, outliving its situation—it survives thanks to the order of meaning by which it transcends the punctual 'now.' To be sure, it depends on the event of an encounter with otherness in a medium of ideality, or intelligibility, in order to be able to accomplish this survival. To be a 'consciousness,' I must be embodied in such a way as to find, in my present, a 'constitutive emptiness,' an anticipation of a special order of sensible being (gesturing, expressive, perceptive bodies) that would somehow also motivate the inscription of *my* body in a culture and a history. It would have to be the case that, in being haunted by the phantoms of an original past, I am also thrust forward, beyond myself, into the order of advent, toward a certain survival in the orders of culture and truth. In short, my body, to be a conscious body, must be enabled to make the space across which it can meet up with itself as a recognizable 'I,' recognizable for itself, as for others. But the power for making this space is not among the *natural* powers it would find within its silent being and, thus, the body attests to a power that is not natural, a power for transforming its nature.

To begin to understand this, to understand how I can be a consciousness of time, of my future, and of my past, as my own, we must see how time is also, necessarily, a certain kind of hetero-affection, the promise of a certain otherness that would supplement my natural bodily life. It is because the ceaseless welling up of time is a transcendental event that is also a fundamental intrication of my body with otherness, the otherness of persons with whom I speak, and who can allow my body be legible to itself, that I am a conscious subject. What alone makes it possible for me to be a consciousness is the manner in which the non-presence within the presence of my body is, at the same time, the "the advent of another person *who also speaks and listens*" (S, 169/275; my italics). In chapter 5, then, we will turn directly to the question of language in order to understand the emergence of explicit self-consciousness.

FIVE

# IPSEITY AND LANGUAGE

Speech is not a means in the service of an external end. It contains its own rule of usage, ethics, and view of the world, as a gesture sometimes bears the whole truth about a man.

—Merleau-Ponty

## I. LANGUAGE AND GESTURE

In each of the previous chapters we have come up against what some readers have identified as a certain tension in Merleau-Ponty's thinking about subjectivity in *Phenomenology of Perception*. On the one hand Merleau-Ponty seems to suggest that, beneath the explicit self-consciousness of the reflecting subject, there is a more fundamental "primary consciousness (*conscience originaire*)" (*PhP*, xv/X), or, as we have seen in the "Temporality" chapter, an 'ultimate consciousness.' The task of philosophical reflection would thus appear to be to make manifest this prior consciousness, an ultimate presence of the self to itself, through an interrogation of perceptual life, an interrogation concerned with disclosing the 'I can' in reference to which the world appears. Thus, when Merleau-Ponty speaks of a "transcendental *field*" we might be inclined to think that he refers to a transcendental subjectivity that has not yet, as it were, found its voice. And when he says that phenomenology is "a study of the appearance of being to consciousness" (*PhP*, 61/74), we might be inclined to put the emphasis on '*consciousness*' as the ultimate ground of the 'appearance of being.' Thus, as we saw in chapter 4, some readers have suggested that *Phenomenology of Perception* is limited by its reliance on the categories of a philosophy of consciousness, that it is preoccupied with epistemological problems concerning the subjective grounds of knowledge and that it is thus insufficiently attentive to the problems that its own analyses raise with respect to the category of 'consciousness.' In this connection, as we saw in chapter 4, some, like M.C. Dillon, have objected to the use of the term 'tacit cogito' precisely because it seems to suggest that we are already conscious before being *explicitly* conscious and that the act of reflection merely brings this primary consciousness to light. According to these readers, what Merleau-Ponty has in mind with this notion of a primary consciousness is far from clear. Renaud Barbaras, to take another example, argues that the notion of the tacit cogito is arrived at by way of a negation of the intellectualist cogito and that,

> The distance [Merleau-Ponty] takes in relation to intellectualism when he defines this *cogito* as tacit takes the shape of a negation that is devoid of sense. We have to wonder, in fact, what could be meant by a *cogito* not defined by self-presence, a *cogito* that nevertheless makes the world spring forth without knowing it, a *cogito* that divines the world instead of constituting it. Merleau-Ponty cannot maintain the *cogito* and *simultaneously* dismiss the intellectualist interpretation: the negations by which Merleau-Ponty characterizes the tacit *cogito* in order to distance himself from intellectualism would be consistent only if they led to a negation of the *cogito* itself.[1]

According to Barbaras's interpretation, *Phenomenology of Perception* remains caught up in a certain intellectualism insofar as it does not sufficiently criticize the notion of consciousness. It works backward from reflective consciousness toward the world of perception (which it takes to be the objective correlate of a tacit consciousness) instead of grasping the phenomena of perception in their ontological originality.

On the other hand, in our previous chapters, we have heard Merleau-Ponty speak of an original past, a sense of a past that has never been present to a consciousness, but that nonetheless haunts a consciousness. As a conscious subject who is also, fundamentally, a sentient subject, I inherit "another self which has already sided with the world"; I find myself already responding to a 'vague beckoning,' a responsive activity that is my own, but whose origin "is anterior to myself" (*PhP*, 215–16/249–50). We have argued that all of this indeed attests to an ontological dimension *within* which a subject is situated, but that exceeds the scope of the 'I can.' To say that subjectivity is necessarily situated, in the sense that we have been advocating, would not simply entail that it is my 'knowing-body' (precisely an 'I can,' rather than an 'I think') that anticipates the world, and that, for this reason, my consciousness is not able to overcome the world's, and my own, opacity. Rather, it involves the more radical claim that, in a certain sense, Being is not anticipated, that, in a certain sense, Being retains the initiative in its self-disclosure, and a certain 'constitutive emptiness' holds the present of experience open to what it cannot encompass. In this sense, the ultimate concern of Merleau-Ponty's phenomenology is not consciousness, but the emergence of sense in movement and thus the dependence of consciousness on the pre-history of the event of expression.

Thus our interpretation of the concepts of reflection and the unreflective in *Phenomenology of Perception* differs from that of Barbaras. Reflection, on our interpretation, opens up an 'unreflective fund of experience' that is not simply another consciousness, another 'knowing' or opaque thinking. The unreflective fund of experience is not simply a consciousness waiting to be converted to reflective thought. This means that, in order to understand the task of Merleau-Ponty's phenomenology, as the 'study of the *appearance* of being to consciousness,' we must put the accent on 'appearance of being.' We insist that Merleau-Ponty is well aware that reflective consciousness, working with repetitions, echoes, and phantoms, would always be anticipating what it cannot quite succeed in anticipating, or in coinciding with. It must, in a sense, be open to the self-disclosure of Being in order to be able to encounter itself. Reflective consciousness strives to overcome, but never fully succeeds in overcoming, a discontinuity and non-self-identity that are constitutive features of its bodily life. This impossibility of overcoming a certain discontinuity, or non-identity, at the heart of the subject reflects the dependence of consciousness on the movement of expression and thus, as we shall argue in this chapter, language. But how, then, are we to interpret what Merleau-Ponty says about the difference, and the relation, between reflective, or explicit consciousness, and the prereflective, or tacit, cogito?

To explain this, we need to think of the act of reflection in terms of the retroactive character of *Sinngenesis* that we have encountered in previous chapters. As we have seen, according to Merleau-Ponty, all sense is rooted in expressive movement. Expressive movement articulates a sense only by manifesting itself as oriented toward an end. But movement must already be underway before it can make sense and thus the sense of movement can never be free of a residue of non-sense. And it is this other past (an original past) of movement that haunts the present, haunts any consciousness with a sense of its own contingency. We have said that consciousness is haunted by the facticity of the sensible insofar as the sense of movement, in terms of which a consciousness would alone be able to recognize itself and thus be an explicit self-consciousness, can never succeed in absorbing its beginning into the order of sense that it inaugurates. Consciousness is thus also haunted by an anonymous life that is the life of the sensorimotor body. The act of reflection is itself a form of expressive movement that takes its own subjectivity for its object—in chapter 4, we noted that, according to Merleau-Ponty, the possibility of reflection is grounded in movement wherein the body 'anticipates' itself. Reflection is, in this sense, a creative act and so we must say that the unreflective is an implicit *consciousness* only *for* the act of reflection. As with any expressive act, the act of reflection does not fully absorb, into the sense that it enacts, the facticity of its own beginning—its sense is thus never free of opacity and contingency. The 'unreflective fund of experience' is thus not to be *simply* equated with the 'tacit cogito' for it also designates this other past, a past that has never been a present, the movement of a life that was underway before being conscious of itself and that can thus never be brought before any explicit consciousness as a more original consciousness.

In this chapter, I will argue that reflection is a very particular kind of expressive movement in that it constitutes (by means of a creative act) a subjective source of its directedness by making it the explicit object of its aim. If the sense of movement, a sense which consists in an object-directedness, only emerges *in* the movement itself, and if, for this reason, we cannot assume a subjective source as the ground of its meaning, how is it that an expressive movement establishes the sense of a subjective ground precisely in making that ground its own object? Reflection is possible only on the basis of a movement whose sense concerns the grounds of its own sense. This means that, in order to account for the possibility of reflection, we must account for the possibility of movement that, in responding to the demands of the sensible, also responds to the demand to be a recognizably meaningful expression. For Merleau-Ponty, this means that an investigation into the possibility of reflection must begin with an investigation into the way in which movement becomes language and thus becomes legible *in the terms of a language*. To be capable of reflection, I must perceive my body's movement as the expression of *my own* meaning. It is only movement that responds to the *meaning* of movement, as such, that can turn back upon itself, upon its own sense, and can thereby become a movement of reflection. And it is only insofar as living movement, in becoming language, conceals 'itself' as the source of meaning, that it is able to appear as the expressed meaning *of* a subject.

Thus it is only as inscribed within a system of language that expressive movement can enable a subject to be legible for itself, that is, to be a consciousness. In 1959, in his 'working notes,' Merleau-Ponty says, "Self-presence *is* presence to a differentiated world," and then adds, "enclosing being for itself by means of language as differentiation" (VI, 191/242). Some of Merleau-Ponty's readers take this addition as an indication of an important shift in his thinking in the period after *Phenomenology of Perception*. They note that, in the earlier work, Merleau-Ponty refers to the tacit cogito as a "silent" consciousness and they accordingly suggest that the recognition of the dependence of consciousness on language is a later development in his thinking. There is no question that Merleau-Ponty pays greater attention to the systematic, or structural, character of language in the years following *Phenomenology of Perception*, and in this development we may discern the influence of Saussure in his thinking about language (particularly with regard to the diacritical character of signs, which we shall discuss below). But, in keeping with what I have suggested about the logic of retroactive determination in Merleau-Ponty, I will argue that this 'silence' of prereflective consciousness must be understood as the silence of the sentient life that haunts perceptual consciousness—this silence then would characterize spectral depth, the singularity of the sensible, the past that has never been a present. We must characterize these as silent because they impose upon consciousness the demand for expression without determining the manner in which they are to be expressed. This original past of consciousness 'appears' as a silent consciousness only *for* a consciousness that first emerges in the movement of expression; consciousness emerges on the basis of movement that generates sense insofar as it articulates a difference between the act of expression and what calls for expression. There is, for consciousness, an *original* silence insofar as it is referred to retroactively by a consciousness that is already a certain saying. We will begin with this question of silence.

*The Tacit Cogito*

In the "Cogito" chapter of *Phenomenology of Perception*, Merleau-Ponty explains that the act of reflection, the positing of *oneself* as an explicit object of thought, presupposes an act of expression. The 'I' is not simply something that can be discovered alongside other objects of experience; I must, as it were, *enact* myself in order to coincide with myself in reflection. And this of course entails that this self-coinciding is never immediate. Reflection could not take place in the interiority of a self-enclosed subject for it could only occur as an act that would already be the broaching of an outside. He writes, "All inner perception is inadequate because I am not an object that can be perceived, because I make my reality and find myself only in the act" (*PhP*, 383/439). It is only as expression that the passing moments of my life are able to come together in an act which "stabilizes" their meanings and places them under the sway of an 'I think.' The 'I think' thus presupposes an 'I speak' (*PhP*, 402/460). Merleau-Ponty therefore insists that "transcendental subjectivity is a revealed subjectivity" (*PhP*, 361/415). But, according to the Merleau-Ponty of *Phenomenology of Perception*, there is another equally necessary condition of the act of reflection, of explicit self-positing. As we have seen, he says that beneath the "spoken *cogito*" there must be a "tacit *cogito*" which he also calls the "silent" or "unspoken *cogito*" (*PhP*, 402/469). The tacit cogito is, Merleau-Ponty says, simply, "myself experienced by myself"

(*PhP*, 402/461). He calls it an unspoken cogito, a "silent consciousness," because it is "not a product of language" (*PhP*, 402/461); rather, it is "a consciousness *of* language, a silence of consciousness embracing the world of speech in which words first receive a form and meaning (*configuration et sens*)" (*PhP*, 403/462; italics mine).

It is, as we have indicated, precisely this claim, concerning the silence of the tacit cogito, that has motivated a number of criticisms of the notion of prereflective consciousness in *Phenomenology of Perception*. Robert Vallier, for example, argues that, with this notion, Merleau-Ponty seems to want to establish the priority of perception over expression. Vallier suggests that, in *Phenomenology of Perception*, Merleau-Ponty seems to think of the body as a kind of natural subject that, being tacitly self-conscious, makes the world appear *prior* to the mediations of language. He cites the passage in which Merleau-Ponty writes:

> We shall need to reawaken our experience of the world as it appears to us in so far as we are in the world through our body, and in so far as we perceive the world with our body . . . perceiving as we do with our body, the body is a natural self and, as it were, the subject of perception. (*PhP*, 206/239)[2]

The notion of the tacit cogito, according to Vallier, is bound up with this notion of the body as a 'natural self.' He writes:

> The body as a natural self is mute and must, through its expressive gestures, bring itself to language: a tacit cogito tries to bring itself to expression. The problem of the tacit cogito, as we know well, is later submitted to serious criticism. In a nutshell, the problem in Merleau-Ponty's eyes is that his conception of the tacit cogito explains only "how language is not impossible, but not how it is possible" (*VI*, 175–6/229), and consequently does not explain how to pass from the order of perceptual meaning (the Real) to the order of language (the Symbolic). Indeed, it cannot offer such explanations, because to do so would mean that it is already caught up in language, already objectified, and hence neither tacit nor a cogito.[3]

Vallier's interpretation of the tacit cogito is here guided by a number of remarks that can be found in Merleau-Ponty's 'working notes' dating from the period in which the latter was writing the text that was posthumously published as *The Visible and the Invisible*. Let us quote a little more of the passage to which Vallier refers:

The tacit Cogito should make understood how language is not impossible, but cannot make understood how it is possible—There remains the problem of the passage from the perceptual meaning to the language meaning, from behavior to thematization. Moreover the thematization itself must be understood as a behavior of a higher degree. (VI, 176/229)

According to the interpretations of some of his readers, this is the problem that the later Merleau-Ponty finds with the notion of the tacit cogito: it is invoked precisely to explain the possibility of the act of reflection, but it does not explain the passage from perceptual meaning to language meaning upon which the act of reflection would depend. It is, after all, only as a speaking subject that one is able to be a reflecting subject. In fact, according to these interpretations, the problem is not simply that the tacit cogito is inadequate to the problems of language and reflection but rather that it stands in the way of a solution to these problems in that it suggests a reliance of reflection on a form of (mute) consciousness that does not need language in order to be self-conscious. It is perhaps for this reason that Merleau-Ponty writes, in another working note, that "what I call the tacit cogito is impossible," and decries the "Mythology of a self-consciousness to which the word 'consciousness' would refer. . . . There are only *differences* between significations" (VI, 171/222). Thus, there is no such thing as a purely silent consciousness.

The suggestion that Merleau-Ponty, in the later notes, is subjecting his earlier notion of the tacit cogito to, in Vallier's words, a 'serious criticism' is perhaps also supported by a further remark in which Merleau-Ponty begins by repeating his critique of the intellectualist cogito in referring to the "Naïveté of Descartes who does not see a tacit cogito under the cogito of *Wesen*, of significations—," but then adds:

But naïveté also of a silent cogito that would deem itself to be an adequation with the silent consciousness, whereas its very description of silence rests entirely on the virtues of language. . . . This silence will *not be the contrary of language*. (VI, 179/230)

The question we need to ask, concerning the meaning of this passage and the ones we have already cited, is this: is Merleau-Ponty really *criticizing* his own earlier position (the position that he takes, with respect to the tacit cogito, in *Phenomenology of Perception*) with these remarks? When Merleau-Ponty says that the tacit cogito 'should make understood how language is not impossible, but cannot make understood how it is possible,' are we to take this as a repudiation of the tacit cogito, or merely as a claim that the notion of the tacit cogito is not a sufficient explanation of the emergence of language? In the case of the latter explanation, we would need to ask if it was ever really intended as a sufficient explanation of how language is possible. If, as we have suggested, the tacit cogito is only a tacit cogito *for* a reflective consciousness, then we should not be surprised to find Merleau-Ponty later saying that the 'tacit cogito is impossible.' For there to be a cogito, there must be expression. As Merleau-Ponty says, in *Phenomenology of Perception*, "The tacit cogito is a cogito only when it has found expression for itself" (*PhP*, 404/463). Thus the term 'tacit cogito' expresses the paradoxical character of subjectivity: self-consciousness pre-supposes expression, but, in reflecting, consciousness retroactively installs itself as the source of expression and thereby determines the unreflective life of the body as that of a tacit cogito. The tacit cogito is impossible in the sense that, as tacit, it would not meet the conditions for being a cogito. Because the tacit cogito *is* a cogito only for the act of reflection, the expressive act by which an explicit self-consciousness is enacted, its silence (again, Merleau-Ponty calls it a 'silent consciousness') would not be 'the contrary of language'—its silence would depend on expression as language. Thus the doctrine of the tacit cogito, which appears paradoxical, is simply reflective of the paradoxical character of expression (to which we shall return below).

According to our interpretation, the development of Merleau-Ponty's account of expression and language in the works written in the period sub-sequent to *Phenomenology of Perception* would not so much be an overcoming of the position that he takes in the earlier work, but a development and refinement of it. Before we can decide between these two interpretations we need to further consider what has led some readers to criticize the notion of the tacit cogito, or a 'silent consciousness.' I want to proceed, as I have done in previous chapters, by first setting out what we might call the stan-dard interpretation (the metaphysics-of-presence reading) of *Phenomenology of Perception*. I will then present my own alternative interpretation.

*Perceptual Meaning and Natural Expression*

As we have seen, Merleau-Ponty, in the later working notes, makes a distinc-tion between what he calls 'perceptual meaning' and 'language meaning' and he stresses the importance of accounting for the passage from the former to the latter. This also reflects a central concern of *Phenomenology of Perception*. The movements of the perceiving body are inherently expressive and this leads Merleau-Ponty to say that "the body is a power of natural expression" (*PhP*, 181/211). Behavior is inherently meaningful in that it manifests an order of "vital significance (*la signification vitale*)" with respect to situations or projects (*PhP*, 211/244). For example, Merleau-Ponty writes:

> In the action of the hand which is raised towards an object is contained a reference to the object, not as an object represented, but as that highly specific thing towards which we project ourselves, near which we are, in anticipation, and which we haunt. (*PhP*, 138/161)

It is because the body's movements and actions are at the same time revelations of the significance of things with respect to my own projects and concerns that Merleau-Ponty calls the body 'a power of natural expression' and links this expressivity directly to "natural perception" (*PhP*, 186/217). It is apparently on the basis of this natural expressivity of the body, which is to be associated with the notion of perceptual meaning, that language becomes possible. As Merleau-Ponty says, language arises from "the silent language whereby perception communicates with us" (*PhP*, 48/60). This silence of perception is already a meaning, and it is in this meaningfulness of behavior that language is founded—as Merleau-Ponty says, "'mental' or cultural life borrows its structures from natural life" (*PhP*, 193/225).

This grounding of language in perceptual meanings enacted in the field of perception is evident, Merleau-Ponty claims, if we take account of the role played by "the emotional essence," "gestural sense" (*PhP*, 187/218), or "figurative significance (*sens figuré*)" (*PhP*, 194/226) of the spoken word: "words, vowels and phonemes are so many ways of 'singing' the world" (*PhP*, 187/218). There is, Merleau-Ponty says, no problem in explaining how this "figurative significance" is understandable to others because, at the level of perceptual consciousness, we all inhabit the same world, a "perceived world common to all" (*PhP*, 194/226). The common world is here understood as the shared world of naturally expressive living bodies that are constantly open to the meanings implicitly revealed by each other's behavior. Because the body, as a natural self, is not a discrete subject (the explicit consciousness of a discrete ego), but a bodily 'I can,' my own perspective on the perceived world has no definite limits: "it slips spontaneously into the other's . . . because both are brought together in the one single world in which we all participate as anonymous subjects of perception" (*PhP*, 353/406). We understand the behavior of others because it ceaselessly discloses for us new layers of significance determining the situation in relation to which, as 'I can's,' we also anticipate the forms of our future experience (*PhP*, 353/406). The silent language of perception is thus already a form of communication, just not yet a communication between *reflectively* self-conscious subjects. In order for a subject to achieve reflective self-consciousness, it must first of all break through the silence of natural expression:

> Silent consciousness grasps itself only as a generalized 'I think' in the face of a confused world 'to be thought about.' Any particular seizure . . . demands that the subject bring into action powers which are a closed book to him and, in particular, that he should become a speaking subject. The tacit cogito is a cogito only when it has found expression for itself. (*PhP*, 404/463)

To accomplish this, it appears that the subject must break through the 'silent language' of perception into an order of language which is capable of supporting ideality, thought, mental life—that is to say, it must break forth into an order of expression that appears to enjoy a kind of autonomy with respect to the natural expressivity of the body.

Renaud Barbaras argues that Merleau-Ponty's account of expression in *Phenomenology of Perception* does not really permit us to see how the perceptual meanings on which he makes symbolic language depend could ever in fact give rise to a system of ideal, universal, cultural meanings.[4] Merleau-Ponty attempts to connect the orders of nature and culture with his notion of the 'gestural sense' of words, but Barbaras argues that this solution is ultimately unsatisfying: "We can certainly describe speech as 'gesture,' but we still have to understand how speech can actually be a gesture, that is, how a gesture can become something that speaks."[5] The words deployed in a spoken language function as signifiers of ideal meanings precisely by *concealing* their contingency, their indebtedness to the act of expression. The spoken word announces an order of ideality and timeless truth that appears to be independent of any particular situation. An act of expression that would make possible an explicit, reflective self-consciousness, would have to be one that inscribes its meaning *in* this order of ideal sense. Expression is thus a problem for a phenomenology of perception because it imposes the requirement that it be able to show how the world of perception always already contains within itself the germ of ideality, i.e., of its own surpassing. According to Barbaras, Merleau-Ponty's account of gestural language as a singing of the world, or as figurative significance, does not go far enough in this direction. The task would be to show how the world of perception is simultaneously constituted *and dissimulated* in the event of expression itself.[6] The act of expression that subtends *explicit* self-consciousness must involve the "sublimation" of our natural life in an act that would reveal a *recogniz-able* agency. An act of "authentic speech" must involve, as Merleau-Ponty will come to say, a "'coherent deformation' . . . of available significations" (*S*, 91/149). The act whereby a silent cogito becomes a spoken cogito would have to be an act that outlives its momentary phases and, indeed, outlives its context as an act of this particular body in this particular situation, thereby establishing itself in a culture and a history. In other words, it would have to establish itself as a durable truth. According to Barbaras, the doctrine of a silent pre-linguistic cogito which is supposed to subtend the spoken cogito does not help us to see how such a self-instituting act could ever occur.

According to Barbaras, this problem reflects a more fundamental and widespread problem with the analyses of *Phenomenology of Perception*. We have already indicated, in chapter 2, Barbaras's concerns with the notion of a 'teleology of consciousness,' and here we can see how this objection links up with his critique of the tacit cogito:

> The affirmation of the *cogito* . . . weighs heavily on the description of the lived world, which is in the end always already understood as a nature. Because he determines teleology on the basis of consciousness and not consciousness as teleology, because he therefore does not conceive teleology as such, Merleau-Ponty remains somehow caught up in teleology, dependent on its objectifying direction: the phenomenon is always already subordinated to consciousness, the world is always already identified with nature, and finally perception is always already identified with reason, instead of explicating the inscription of reason in the world—that is, instead of explicating teleology itself.[7]

Because Merleau-Ponty allegedly does not sufficiently explicate 'the inscription of reason in the world,' because, in other words, he allegedly does not adequately explicate the passage from natural, perceptual, meaning, to an order of linguistic, or ideal, meaning, we are left with the incoherent notion of a cogito that is somehow both a mute, natural, incarnate subject, and an 'I think.'

As I have indicated, I do not find this interpretation compelling. It is true, as we have seen, that Merleau-Ponty links the concepts of 'silence' and 'nature' with his idea of the tacit cogito. But it seems to me that the whole task of *Phenomenology of Perception* is to show that each of these terms characterizes a pre-history to which consciousness implicitly refers, but which has in fact always already been overcome and transformed. Since he says that a cogito only becomes a cogito by means of an act of expression, it is crucial that we understand what he says about nature and silence in connection with what he says about expression. In the chapter on speech Merleau-Ponty says that in order to understand language we must find "beneath the chatter of words, the primordial silence," and we must then "describe the action which breaks this silence" (*PhP*, 184/214). If this silence characterizes the body as a 'natural self' then we must note Merleau-Ponty's further assertion that "the human body is defined in terms of its property of appropriating, in a series of discontinuous acts, significant cores which transcend and transfigure its natural powers" (*PhP*, 193/226). I am a 'natural' subject insofar as I am a sentient body, but my sentient life is an anonymous life that is only present *to me* by virtue of the meaning of my stylized behavior, which is to say, my access to the natural is always in the mode of a 'repetition without original'—nature is there for me only insofar as I am already in a culture. And, as we saw in chapter 2, the body is thus always already a cultural object, a kind of work of art. We must understand silence and nature starting from the paradoxical character of a creative act that generates the sense of its own origins, but, in doing so, never quite successfully dissimulates the facticity of its own beginning.

## The Paradox of Expression

Merleau-Ponty speaks of expression as a "paradox" (*VI*, 189/184). He also repeatedly invokes, as a sort of motto, the following remark of Husserl's concerning the task of phenomenology: " 'It is that as yet mute experience . . . which we are concerned to lead to the pure expression of its own meaning [*de son proper sens*]' " (*PhP*, xv/X; translation slightly modified). As Bernard Waldenfels points out, this formulation expresses the paradoxical character of expression. On the one hand, experience demands to be brought to expression because it is in some sense silent. But, on the other hand, if experience were ever truly mute it could never be led to the expression of *its own* meaning—there could only ever be talk *about* the experience and this would have the consequence of rendering the expression *impure*: "With the first word that violates the innocence of experience, [the experience] would already be defiled, since it would have an alien sense imputed or inserted into it."[8] The experience only requires itself to be led to its own expression to the extent that there remains something in it that is yet to be said. But this yet-to-be-said cannot be alien to the expression. Thus the experience can be led to the expression of *its own* meaning only on condition that the experience is somehow itself *already* the expression of its own meaning—in which case we would have to understand the difference between the experience and its expression as a function of expression itself. Waldenfels thus observes that,

> The paradox of expression lies first of all in the act of expression and in the event of expression itself; therefore, the paradox lies in the relation between the actual expression and *what is yet to be expressed*, in other words, between what is yet to be expressed and its means, ways, forms, in short, the 'ready-made expressions,' in which something *is already expressed*.[9]

The paradox thus calls for an account of expression that can show how it articulates *within itself* both something yet to be expressed and the means of its own expression. If this difference were to be collapsed, if the yet-to-be-said were somehow reducible to an already-said, or to an already-thought, then experience itself would lapse into total silence, for it would follow that nothing ever *happens* in experience that would call for some novel form of expression. Conversely, if the *means* of expression were somehow lacking— that is, if they were external to the experience—then the experience would again be rendered mute since it could not admit of being expressed without being transformed into something else. As Waldenfels writes,

> Two extremes become impossible here, namely to regard an event of expression either as pure action and pure creation of newness or, in contrast, as pure passion and pure reproduction. The event of expression can to a greater or lesser extent approach either of these extremes of pure innovation or pure repetition, but cannot reach either of them. . . . Purely creative discourse would say *nothing*; purely repetitive discourse would have nothing *to say*.[10]

Thus the action which breaks the 'primordial silence' cannot, in fact, have emerged from out of a pure silence. It is only insofar as the subject already responds to the demands of language, and in the terms of a language, that it can find expression for itself.

In the expression chapter of *Phenomenology of Perception*, Merleau-Ponty means to offer an account of expression that would avoid these two alternatives (pure innovation and pure repetition). He argues against the intellectualist tendency to reduce the meaning of the word to a thought of which the subject would already be in possession. In fact, he observes, "the thinking subject is in a kind of ignorance of his thoughts so long as he has not formulated them for himself, or even spoken and written them" (*PhP*, 177/206). The act of expression "brings the meaning into being"; it is not simply a reproduction or a translation of a thought into a sign (*PhP*, 183/213).[11] And, indeed, as we have seen, in connection with the cogito, the subject is only able to reflect on her own subjectivity in an act which would also give expression to that subjectivity—the cogito must itself be a *saying*. Thus we cannot invoke a transcendental ego to account for the possibility of expression since the unity of the 'I think' is itself dependent upon the *event* of expression. But the event of expression also cannot be a matter of pure spontaneity, or novelty, since, as Merleau-Ponty says, "the new sense-giving intention knows itself only by donning already available meanings" (*PhP*, 183/213). I encounter myself, *my* meaning, in the act of expression because the expression is at once *my* act *and* a certain significance discernable in the terms of a field of available meanings.

Merleau-Ponty's insistence that the subject only discovers its own thinking by means of expression, by means of an inscription of the sense of its own behavior into a field of available meanings, entails that the 'silence' of which he speaks, in connection with the tacit cogito, is, as we have indicated, not the contrary of language. This silence is neither the silence of a consciousness in pre-predicative contact with itself nor is it the silence of natural behaviors. It inheres in the lateral relations between signs and other signs that require us to keep saying the world anew, that prevent the world from ever resolving into a *depthless* totality of present objects. The silence of language, like the spectral depth of which we have spoken in previous chapters, is thus a "fecund negative" (VI, 263/311), a silence that haunts our expressive bodies and insistently "pulls significations from us" (PW, 146/203).

The sense of incarnate ipseity that is implied by this account of expression and silence is characterized by a demand that imposes itself upon us *already at the level of bodily life*, at the level of motility and gesture. This demand is articulated *within* the event of expression itself, as the expression's own 'pre-history,' older than any consciousness or signifying intention. We have already seen this logic at work in our analyses of sensation and spatiality. But what we come to see more clearly in the context of those writings in which Merleau-Ponty directly concerns himself with the problems of expression is that this prehistory of the event of expression also implicates subjectivity in a language. The subject is the embodiment of an instituted, and, in principle, inexhaustible, system of expressive possibilities into which the expression inscribes itself.[12] The body is a subject because it is the embodiment of a logos and is thus legible to itself; indeed, in a manner that we shall elaborate, Merleau-Ponty comes to think the body and the significance of its behavior in terms of Saussure's conception of language as a diacritical system enabling words or gestures to *mean* precisely by organizing their differences from each other. But this does not imply a subordination of bodily ipseity to an impersonal system; unlike Saussure, who is particularly concerned with the synchronic systematicity of language, Merleau-Ponty offers an account of language that retains an emphasis on the spontaneity and generativity of the act of expression. The inscription of the body within the system of expression is also the disruption of that system, the irruption of an irreducible element of non-sense within the order of linguistic sense. The act of expression inscribes the expressive body within a system of expression and, at the same time, resists its complete enclosure within that system.[13] This resistance is also a condition of the emergence of sense within that system—the inscription of the body establishes the context of sense in terms of which there can be a difference between sense and non-sense. The body can be a self only as an expressive body; as an expressive body, the subject is constitutively intertwined, by means of language, with otherness.

*Institution*

In a 'working note,' Merleau-Ponty says that signification is "absolutely distinct from the In Itself and the 'pure consciousness . . .'" (VI, 253/301). Consciousness, as we have said, emerges in expressive movement and thus the relation of the self to itself is mediated by an order of signification, by meanings of which the subject is not itself the origin. This is why Merleau-Ponty also says that "the for itself [is] an incontestable, but derived, characteristic" (VI, 191/242). Expression is not something a *subject* does. That is to say, the unity of the expressive gesture does not need to be subtended by a consciousness who would thus be able to recognize its expressive act as its own; rather the unity of the subject itself depends on the sense that is articulated within the expressive gesture, and this articulation of sense already inscribes itself within a linguistic system in terms of which it is to be understood. Language is rooted in the body only to the extent that the latter's expressivity "continues an effort of articulation which is the Being of every being" (VI, 127/166). As we have seen, Merleau-Ponty, in *Phenomenology of Perception*, says that the subject, as an embodied subject, inherits 'tacit decisions' which have always already established for it a 'field of possibilities'; in his subsequent writings he expresses this idea with the concept of *institution*:

> All perception, all action which presupposes it, and in short every human use of the body is already *primordial expression* . . . the primary operation which first constitutes signs as signs, makes that which is expressed dwell in them *through the eloquence of their arrangement and configuration alone*, implants a meaning in that which did not have one, and thus—far from exhausting itself in the instant at which it occurs—inaugurates an order and founds an institution or a tradition. (S, 67/108; emphasis mine)

Expression is the 'primary operation' which articulates the world of experience in the terms of a culture and a history. To speak of expression as an institution is to affirm its primordiality *and* its historico-cultural fecundity: the event of expression inscribes itself within, and thereby creatively renews, an open horizon of expressive possibilities. And it is within this horizon that the gesture also acquires its own sense; that is to say, the sense of the expression is not to be measured against a silent, implicit meaning of which a consciousness would already be in possession—rather, sense first emerges *in* the expression. But the sense of the expressive gesture thus always remains partly outstanding because its meaning depends entirely upon its fecundity—sense emerges in the articulation, accomplished through the gesture, of the difference between what has been said and what is yet to be said. The expressive gesture, as an institution, belongs to "the order of advent" (*S*, 68/109), and, as we noted in chapter 4, Merleau-Ponty understands advent as "the promise of events" (*S*, 70/112):

> Thus what we understand by the concept of institution are those events in experience which endow it with durable dimensions, in relation to which a whole series of other experiences will acquire meaning, will form an intelligible series or a history—or again those events which sediment in me a meaning, not just as survivals or residues, but as the invitation to a sequel, the necessity of a future. (*PPOE*, 109/61)

Merleau-Ponty thus suggests that we consider the subject not as a "constituting subject" but rather as an "instituting subject."[14] The instituting subject is only able to encounter itself as instituted, or inscribed, within an 'intelligible series or a history.' Reflective self-consciousness is thus, first of all, a *reading* of the meaning of expressive behavior in the text of a shared world, a world whose sharedness is vouchsafed by a 'promise,' a sense of 'advent,' a 'faith.' This faith is the deeper meaning of the perceptual faith that we spoke of in chapter 4. It is a faith that is supported by the meaning of language, or rather, by the constitutive limits of expression to which every actual expression bears an attestation: there remains more to be said, other meanings, meanings *of* the other. Thus, it is in expression that we find the grounds of that other teleology that we spoke of at the end of chapter 3. Or, rather, since there would be no telos apart from the event of expression itself, we could say that the *non*-self-coincidence of the instituting subject, which is the demand for expression, is also, to use Derrida's phrase, 'the threatened chance' of a telos. But, just as the *sense* of the gesture always remains partly outstanding, so too does the *sense* of the self.

This account of expression is thus also crucial for understanding Merleau-Ponty's account of intersubjectivity: "We find the other the same way we find our body" (*PW*, 138/192). We are able to encounter others thanks to the "brute event" (*S*, 86/140) of expression, which renders living movement intelligible by announcing a system of meaning. It at once interrupts the unity of the body *and* makes the unity possible. This happening subtends the unity of my body as an 'expressive unity,' or a 'unity of style.' The body schema is thus properly understood as involving the inscription of my body within a language. This enables us to understand the passage from "The Philosopher and His Shadow" that we quoted in chapter 4: "The constitution of others does not come after that of the body; others and my body are born together from the original ecstasy" (S, 174/284). This original ecstasy is the event of expression.

## II. DIACRITICAL INTERCORPOREITY

As we have indicated, in his writings during the 1950's Merleau-Ponty incorporates the terms of Saussure's structural linguistics into his thinking about language: "language is made of differences without terms; or more exactly . . . the terms of language are engendered only by the differences which appear among them" (S, 39/63). In his investigation of the problem of language during this period Merleau-Ponty directs his attention to the problems of speech, literature, the algorithms of mathematical-scientific language, and the language of philosophy itself. But he does not abandon his earlier claim that language is deeply connected to the motility of the perceiving body—he continues to understand perception and self-consciousness on the basis of expressive movement. We thus still have to ask how it is that the bodily movement by which we, as living organisms, explore and inhabit our world can, *at the same time*, be understood as a kind of institution within the arena of a diacritical system of conventional signs, "a system of expression" (PW, 37/53). It is a question of knowing how the spontaneous and habitual actions of our bodies are at the same time functions within a *system* which binds our own expressivity to that of all the others, past, present, and future (PW, 24/36). It is a question of seeing how, in our expressive gestures, our very life "ceases to be in possession of itself and becomes a universal means of understanding and of making something understood, of seeing and of presenting something to see—and is thus not shut up in the depths of the mute individual but diffused throughout all he sees" (S, 53/85). In short, it is "the problem of knowing how we are grafted to the universal by that which is most our own" (S, 52/84).

In *Phenomenology of Perception*, Merleau-Ponty offers this description of the way in which our gestures involve us in a kind of proto-communication with others:

> The communication or comprehension of gestures comes about through the reciprocity of my intentions and the gestures of others, of my gestures and the intentions discernable in the conduct of other people. It is as if the other person's intention inhabited my body and mine his. (PhP, 185/216)

The movements of the other's body convey their sense directly to my own. George Herbert Mead, like Merleau-Ponty, claims that language is essentially gestural, and he offers an account of gestural communication that is in many ways quite similar to the latter's.[15] Like Merleau-Ponty, Mead is particularly concerned to show how living movement transforms *itself* into *conventional* signification and, in doing so, enables *explicit* self-consciousness to emerge. In order to understand how the gesture becomes a sign, Mead argues, we must view it in the context of what he calls a social "matrix."[16] The gesture becomes a sign when it enables the "mutual adjustment" of behaviors in the context of a "social act." I will here quote a somewhat lengthy footnote from Mead's book *Mind, Self and Society* in which he develops this point:

> Conscious communication—conscious conversation of gestures— arises when gestures become signs, that is, when they come to carry for the individuals making them and the individuals responding to them, definite meanings or significations in terms of subsequent behavior of the individuals making them; so that, by serving as prior indications, to the individuals responding to them, of the subsequent behavior of the individuals making them, they make possible the mutual adjustment of the various components of the social act to one another, and also, by calling forth in the individuals making them the same responses implicitly that they call forth explicitly in the individuals to whom they are made, they render possible the rise of self-consciousness in connection with this mutual adjustment.[17]

In this passage, Mead wants to understand how it is that a gesture first *becomes* a sign—that is to say, how a gesture can be understood as a kind of speech-act that institutes a durable means of conventional ('second-order') expression. What enables a gesture (or, more correctly, a phase of a gesture) to become such a sign is that it comes to actually function, for the individuals involved in the conversation of gestures, as a reliable indicator of subsequent movements.[18] For this to happen, according to Mead, it is crucial that the one making the gesture be able to recognize *another's* movement as a sequel to an earlier phase of her own gesture. And this can happen only because the earlier phase of her movement also motivates *her own* body's continuation of the action.[19] For example, if she begins motioning in a certain direction, she is able to grasp the *significance* of this motion, to grasp that it is significant, because her own subsequent behavior is, as it were, *duplicated* in the body of another. Her gesture ceases to be a continuous movement, rather, a certain phase of her movement comes to differentiate itself and becomes, for her, a reliable means of provoking another behavior. The more clearly differentiated and stylized the movement is, the more effectively will it function in this way.[20] In repeating, and perhaps refining, the initial behavior, her body is in fact responding to another's response to her own movement; that is to say, she is responding to *her own* behavior indirectly, as a certain *sense*. She is able to recognize a significance in her own movement to the extent that, *as* a certain *sense*, it outlives itself in the subsequent motions of her body *and* another's.

The intercorporeal ensemble of living movements must, as it were, come apart, it must break up into a discontinuous series of acts, in order to come together, for the participants, in relations of signifier to signified, of past movement to future movement, of self and other—and this is what then permits the 'mutual adjustment of the various components of the social act.' The movements of the living body thus respond to a new imperative: beyond the demand to make space, we now have the demand to make space by making (linguistic) sense. Mead says that the ensemble of movements making up the social act begins as an "unconscious conversation of gestures."[21] And it is precisely to the extent that the first phase of the gesture is not already the outward expression of a subject's signifying *intention* that it is able to give expression to a *new* meaning; the inaugurating gesture *becomes a sign* not because it was intended as such, but because it effectively *calls for its sequel*. It is only in the moment that the first phase of the gesture comes to differentiate itself as a discrete unit of sense that it also comes to carry the meaning of a repeatable signifying act. But this means that the gesture appears as a sign only insofar as the contextual circumstances of the initial act are effaced, or sublimated, allowing the gesture to function as a *signifier* of some other behavior (the subsequent behavior is thus also absorbed in the order of *sense* inaugurated by the first phase; i.e., it becomes a repeatable *signified*). If, with Mead, we say that explicit self-consciousness emerges only in the recognition of my own body's movements as bearers of a certain *intention* to signify, then we must also say that the possibility of this kind of reflective self-consciousness begins in a kind of retrospective reading of the gestures to which our first movements give rise.[22] The possibility of reflection arises by means of an event of expression which is also the sublimation of that event.

What is crucial here is that the significance of the gesture, and thus the self-consciousness that it makes possible, relies on its inscription within a social and temporal horizon in which it can come to be recognized as a conventional sign. It effaces itself as a certain piece of behavior in order, precisely, to *signify*; it is, to be sure, a certain pattern of bodily movement with a specific morphology and kinetic configuration, but it *means* some other possible behavior and thus these features can come to appear as arbitrary bearers of meaning. Notice that this power of signification does not presuppose anything outside of the internal articulation of the intercorporeal conversation of gestures; it presupposes neither a synthesizing consciousness, nor any reference to a ready-made world. Neither Mead's nor Merleau-Ponty's accounts of the gestural character of language is intended to explain how gestures might come to signify bits and pieces of the world; rather, their accounts are intended to explain how a body might come to function for itself, and for others, as a bearer of significations. The social act described by Mead is an intercorporeal whole of living movement that articulates itself; it is an event of expression, and what is expressed by means of its articulations, a certain *sense*, is thus different from the expression itself. But neither does it respond to an imperative, a principle of intelligibility, ideality, or a ready-made reality that would have existed outside of, or prior to, the event of expression itself. The social act is thus, to borrow a term from Merleau-Ponty, a "ferment of transformation" (VI, 202/252); it can only be one social matrix insofar as it is an ensemble that also breaks up, thus articulating a plurality of movements in which one type of movement can come to function as a signifier of other possible movements.

Expressive movement thus must be the identity of an identity *and* a difference. In Mead's analysis of the way in which a gesture transforms itself into a sign, we see that the beginning phase of the gesture must at once establish its identity with, and difference from, all of the other movements making up the totality of the social act. But, as we just saw, this can only happen, so to speak, retroactively. The *whole* movement must unfold itself before a beginning phase of the movement can come to *differentiate* itself as a relatively discrete bearer of significance. Recall, in this connection, David Morris' observation that "to become a beginning, the beginning of a movement has to wait for the whole movement."[23] This, as we have seen, is also the logic of institution. An institution is an event which endows an experience 'with durable dimensions.' Its sense thus lies not in its determination according to an idea, concept, or essence, but in its demonstrable fecundity. Institutions take time to reveal themselves.

This fecundity of the institution also enriches the notion of style that we discussed in chapter 3. The style inaugurated by an expression is only 'intelligible' to me insofar as I take it up into a new behavior and insofar as it thereby discloses a certain manner of comporting myself toward the world (*PhP*, 327/378). Style is thus a kind of "preconceptual generality" that does not presuppose a rule or an essence but that marks out an inexhaustible field of possibilities for expressive behavior (*PW*, 44n./63n.). As we saw in chapter 3, style is the way expressive movement lets a singularity appear only by inscribing it within a horizon of generality. Expressive movement thus stylizes only by, so to speak, letting itself be interrupted. As Merleau-Ponty says, "*transpositions* . . . constitute the *constancy* of style" (*S*, 65/106; my italics).

Consider, for example, a child who attempts to grasp a crystal wineglass from the coffee-table during a dinner party and is prevented from doing so by the adults around her. For the child, this simple action involves a wealth of meanings that she has perhaps only dimly discerned. The gestures of the adults around the child are *stylized*—undoubtedly they are reflective of the proper *manners* that we have all at some point learned and incorporated into our behaviour at adult dinner parties. It is in virtue of the expressive style of these gestures that the child has come to 'understand' that there is something at stake in the situation, something that concerns her own involvement in (or exclusion from) the social milieu. The gestures of the adults around the child have, as it were, interrupted the child's world, her sensorimotor situation, in order to insert a new sense of the situation, a new way for the child to be situated. These gestures have awakened, in her sensorimotor body, the possibility of access to a sophisticated adult world that has come to be vested in the wineglass on the table like an occult power. In other words, the adults' actions of grasping the wineglasses awakens a motor possibility in the child who perceives them, but this very awakening is also the intimation of a way into the adults' 'world.' Again, what I am aiming to illustrate with this example is not the way in which a gesture might come to signify a wineglass—I am not suggesting, nor does Merleau-Ponty suggest, that language emerges on the basis of the way in which gestures point to or depict objects—rather, I want to describe the way in which behavior makes itself available for signification, how the body accomplishes its own dynamic identity as a tissue of instituted meanings. The gestures of the adults around the child manifest relatively invariant patterns, or structures, of possible expressive behaviour, kernels of significance, which are discernable to the child only in the sense that her own actions are sequels to these gestures. The style manifested in this 'conversation of gestures' is constitutive of a world in which the child is already moved to assert her place—it constitutes a horizon of significance in which she dimly glimpses her own possibilities for expressive action. It is in precisely this way that, according to Merleau-Ponty, a child acquires language—as a style of expression that "snaps him up like a whirlwind" (S, 41/65).

Notwithstanding our earlier hesitations, we can see how it is that ordinary gestures, insofar as they are stylized, might come to function as signifiers within a language if we consider the way in which gestures do in fact come spontaneously to function within the languages of communities of deaf people. Adam Kendon has remarked on the way in which certain ordinary expressive or functional gestures come to be incorporated into the lexicons of primary or alternate sign languages.[24] As this happens, he notes, the function and morphology of the gesture undergoes significant alterations, a process that is termed 'lexicalization.' What is notable is that, through this process, the iconic features of signs (the ways in which certain gestures might be said to 'depict' objects or actions) diminishes and gives way to increased arbitrariness. Kendon writes:

> [The gesture] turns into an arbitrary form as it comes to be shaped by the requirement that it be a distinctive form within a system of other forms. Further, however, as it undergoes this process, it is freed of any requirement that it be a 'picture' of something. However, it is this that frees it, also, to take on a general meaning. It thus becomes available for recombination with other forms and so may come to participate in compound signs or sentences.[25]

This is of course exactly what we would expect to see in the development of a language insofar as languages function as diacritical *systems* of signs. As Merleau-Ponty observes, "[language] is far less a table of statements which satisfy well-formed thoughts than a swarm of gestures all occupied with differentiating themselves from one another and blending again" (*PW*, 115/161). In this connection, I would argue that the very idea of an 'iconic' sign is misleading insofar as it relies on the presupposition of a ready-made world to which the actions of the expressive body are presumed to refer. In fact the so-called iconic gesture is intelligible to the extent that it already makes some use of available *meanings* within the expressive system of a culture. The expressive gesture is no more reliant on a ready-made world than on the prior signifying intention of a thinking subject. Rather than understanding this process as involving the transformation of iconic signs into linguistic signs, we should think of lexicalization as a process which simply makes use of a conventional intelligibility that is always already evident in the movements of our bodies insofar as they are inscribed in a culture and a history. A conventional sign language is an elaboration of possibilities opened up by what Merleau-Ponty calls "this primordial institution of the body" (*PW*, 45n./63n.).

Recent research into gesture has supported this claim. David McNeill and Susan Duncan, in a recent study on language and gesture, have proposed the concept of "growth points," which they define as "an analytic unit combining imagery and categorical content."[26] What they aim to demonstrate through the deployment of this notion is that the gestural forms used, say, in the narration of events, are structurally correlated to the semantic properties of (spoken or written) languages. Their use of the term 'growth point' is meant to express the idea that the meanings of speech and gesture are differentiated only on the basis of a common structure—thus the term 'growth point' might be roughly what Merleau-Ponty has in mind when he speaks of 'significant cores.' More generally, McNeill and Duncan hypothesize that language is not an expression of a prior thought (which is of course also what Merleau-Ponty says); they argue that the study of the relation between gesture and speech, as these are deployed by speakers of different languages, can show that bodily behaviour is already a way of making sense of events according to the structural demands of particular languages. The mutual influence of imagery and speech "enables language to influence imagery, and imagery to influence language as the utterance unfolds in real time. Speech is not a translation of one medium, image, into another, language."[27] In their study, they had speakers of Chinese, Spanish, and English, narrate a simple sequence of events. The subject's speech, as well as their use of gesture, was in each case recorded and analyzed. They observed that speakers of different languages deploy correspondingly different ensembles of gestures, and in quite different ways. Here is an example of some of their reported findings:

> Describing the same motion events, languages encourage different forms of thinking. English and Spanish (as well as Georgian) are predicative in their focus, but thinking differs in how motion-event semantics are focused. Chinese induces thinking in which the focus is a frame for other information. Observations thus show an effect of linguistic organization on thinking on two levels—predicative and discourse—and different patterns of both.[28]

Results from such research lend support to the idea that the movements of our bodies respond to the demands of language in responding to the demands of situations. And, insofar as perception is accomplished as stylized movement, this suggests a fundamental involvement of language in the way in which we perceive the world. As Merleau-Ponty observes in a note: "perception [is] a diacritical, relative, oppositional system" (VI, 213/263). This is because the Sinngenesis of perceptual meanings is enacted in bodies that are already claimed by the demands of languages. This is not to say that there is no difference between language and perception, but rather that this difference is articulated out of a common ground.[29] This common ground, the significant core, is precisely what does not show itself in our experience other than as a fecund silence, a demand for more saying, and saying otherwise (and we could include here all of the concepts that we have deployed previously: phantom, spectral depth, constitutive emptiness, a call).

## III. EXPRESSION AND SUBJECTIVITY

It is because our living bodies are always already organized according to the structured possibilities constitutive of language that Merleau-Ponty, in the working notes, echoes the Heideggerian insight that "language has us . . . it is not we who have language." But to this remark he immediately appends the question: "But then how understand the subjectivity?" (VI, 194/244–5) It is to this question that we now turn.

Expression announces and responds to a paradoxical two-fold demand: "It is the achievement of the word not only to be the expression of *this here* but also to surrender itself entirely as a fragment of universal discourse, to announce a system of interpretation" (PW, 144/201). Expression answers to these two demands simultaneously precisely by also *failing* to answer to either of them adequately. As we have seen in our analysis of the paradox of expression (as well as in our analyses of sensation and motility), the gesture only becomes significant, only acquires its power to be the expression of a *this here*, retroactively. And, in considering expressive movement as language, we have learned that it must have inscribed itself within a system of expression. Expressive movement can never quite live up to the demand of expressing a *this here* since it can never be at once a *singular* eveı.t of contact between a sentient body and the world *and* significant; expression is always the enactment of a decision about the sense of sensible being and for this reason, as we have seen, perception always involves a certain violence. Our consideration of the gesture thus exhibits the peculiar logic of institution according to which sense depends on the historico-cultural fecundity of an event. This logic entails that every movement of my body begins, so to speak, as non-sense. Or, better, we could say that there is no beginning of the movement of expression except as a certain *absence* borne (paradoxically) in the system of *sense* inaugurated by the gesture.[30]

That which inheres in the expressive gesture (insofar as it is inscribed within an order of signification whose resources can never be adequate to that which demands to be expressed), as a certain absence, is what permits the gesture to be the expression of a *this here*. In *The Visible and the Invisible* Merleau-Ponty writes,

> We are interrogating our experience precisely in order to know how it opens us to what is not ourselves. This does not even exclude the possibility that we find in our experience a movement toward what could not in any event be present to us in the original and whose irremediable absence would thus count among our originating experiences. (VI, 159/209)

This 'irremediable absence' is what allows our experience to open us 'to what is not ourselves.' This is possible because experience happens as expression. What is expressed in the expression is a sense, a signified, but this signified never completely exhausts the fecundity of the 'brute event' of expression, of a certain originary encounter between an intercorporeal, sentient body and its world. Expression is "called forth from its first movement by perceptual evidence which it continues without being reducible to perceptual evidence" (PW, 125/175). In fact, what renders possible the very durability of the instituted sense, that which allows for a "surpassing of the signifying by the signified" (S, 90/146), is precisely this impossibility of its ever coinciding with its origin. There is always more to be said. The irremediable absence carried in the heart of expression is a fecund singularity, or, with respect to any existing system of expression, a 'fecund negative,' which escapes every saying and every said, which resists its own absorption into an idea or a concept, but which nonetheless ceaselessly calls for its expression. As Merleau-Ponty writes, "Being is what requires creation of us for us to experience it" (VI, 197/248).

This would mean that language, every system of expression, also carries within itself a silence. Rather than a silence of consciousness from which the subject would have to break forth by means of its spontaneous act of expression, silence is a constitutive feature of the diacritical system of language—as Merleau-Ponty writes, "the system of synchrony must at every moment allow fissures where brute events can insert themselves" (S 86/140). These fissures in the system of language are not voids but silences calling for something more to be said. Language is thus a "structure [that] propels itself toward its own transformations" (PW, 128/179).

The 'I can' of the expressive body is itself structured according to the system of language. Its sensorimotor possibilities are thus always already possibilities for making itself intelligible. In the lecture course on nature, Merleau-Ponty writes, "An organ of the mobile senses (the eye, the hand) is already language because it is an interrogation (movement) and a response (perception as erfühlung of a project), speaking and understanding. It is a tacit language" (N, 211/273). As we learn in the "Cogito" chapter of Phenomenology of Perception, the self must be the enactment of its own reality. And the expressive self-enactment called for here is one which is also a response in the face of a silence that already indicates its own pathways, according to an order of meaning that has already organized our expressive bodies.[31] Merleau-Ponty offers what is perhaps his most succinct formulation of this notion of silence in a working note: "Silence = absence of the word due" (VI, 263/311). This silence is thus not a mute self-coincidence from which the subject would have to break forth, but a certain tension within the field of expressive possibilities. It is a singular demand, a not-yet-said, to which a belated subjectivity must respond by means of a new act of expression. The enactment that is called for can only ever be a "coherent deformation" of that order of meaning which will have already structured the possibilities for responding. We could say that the silence with which Merleau-Ponty is concerned is thus always a pregnant silence. And we might think of this pregnancy in terms of a remark made by Merleau-Ponty in the working notes: "My body *obeys* the pregnancy, it 'responds' to it, it is what is suspended on it, flesh responding to flesh" (VI, 209/259).[32]

But every response to this silence, every attempt to utter 'the word due,' will always end in a renewal of the demand. For this silence is also "that openness ever to be reopened between the sign and the sign" (VI, 153/199). Merleau-Ponty writes that "language is the system of differentiation through which an individual articulates his relation to the world" (PPOE, 91/37). But, as we have seen, every expressive movement of my body begins as a certain non-sense that cannot be exhaustively translated into any system of sense. If I discover what I meant to express with my 'authentic' expressive gesture only retroactively, by deciphering its sense, then I must admit that I cannot be sure of what I meant, or who that 'I' is who stands behind the signifying intention. And yet this very residue of non-sense is the silence from which language lives, and thus from which I live, for "Language is a life, is our life, and the life of the things" (VI, 125/165). The idea that every attempt to utter the word due will always be a 'coherent deformation' of available meanings in some ways captures the sense of the paradox of subjectivity in Merleau-Ponty's philosophy. The relation of a subject to his world is articulated through the transformations of a system of language precisely insofar as the subject is at once included and excluded from that system which translates his gestures into meanings. Merleau-Ponty says, of the painter, that his work "changes him into himself" (S, 57/93). He becomes *himself* in responding to a call for *coherent* expression—he is thus a responsible agent who can live up to the demands of sense. But he also *becomes* himself in not being himself, because his expression is also a response to the call for a *deformation*—a word that has not yet been said *must* be said, and it is only in the terms of the order of sense inaugurated by this word that he will be able to learn of the self who utters it. And thus, "with a single gesture he links the tradition that he recaptures and the tradition that he founds" (S, 63/101). Being, at once, incarnate logos and irreducible singularity, the subject exists as a respondent to the demand for expression:

> It is well that some people try to set up obstacles to the intrusion of this spontaneous power [of language] and oppose it with their rigor and ill will. But their silence ends in further words, and rightly so. . . . In the end, what should we call this power to which we are vowed, and which, however we feel, pulls significations from us? Certainly it is not a god, since its operation depends upon us. It is

not an evil genius, since it bears the truth. It is not the "human condition"—or, if it is "human," it is so in the sense that man destroys the generality of the species and brings himself to admit others into his deepest singularity. (*PW*, 146/203)

# CONCLUSION

In the Introduction, I referred to Merleau-Ponty's call for an "ontological rehabilitation of the sensible" (S, 166–7/271) and I suggested both that this task, in a certain sense, defines Merleau-Ponty's philosophical project and that it is in the context of this project that we must understand what he says about subjectivity. In these concluding remarks, I want to suggest that this project also involves a rehabilitation of an ethical meaning of the sensible and, thus, of subjectivity.

At the heart of our interpretation of Merleau-Ponty's notion of subjectivity are the concepts of 'expressive movement,' 'consciousness,' and 'sensation.' Consciousness, in Merleau-Ponty's sense, emerges on the basis of a kind of auto-legibility of living movement, movement that is always already responding to the 'call' of sensible being. In responding to this call, which is that of a certain singularity, movement *stylizes*, generating a meaning (*sens*) out of that which has no meaning. In fact, it is not quite right to speak here of '*that* which has no meaning,' as though the sensible were originally a thing-in-itself, or a content of consciousness, an immanent sense-datum, awaiting a meaning that would be bestowed upon it. Rather, *that* which calls only appears, *après coup*, in the response that it elicits. In this sense, living movement is creative. It is only possible to speak of movement as 'responding' to a 'call' of sensible being insofar as movement has already begun to stylize, already begun to creatively articulate the contours and boundaries of a meaningful context in whose terms a sentient subject can oppose itself to, or involve itself with, something *other* than *itself*. "Being," as Merleau-Ponty says, "is *what requires creation of us* to experience it" (VI, 197/248). The subject and its others are thus, as Merleau-Ponty writes, born out of the same "original ecstasy" (S, 174/284). This original ecstasy is, we have argued in the preceding chapters, living movement, movement that generates meaning (*sens*) out of non-meaning (*non-sens*). If there is a call only, so to speak, retroactively, as a referent for the movement that has already begun to respond to it, then movement lets there be a meaning by also letting there be a non-meaning. The sensible is that which, separating itself, retroactively, from the perceptual act that it elicits, would have no meaning of its own and would put every order of meaning into question. As we have said, sensible being appears as a kind of 'original past' of experience;

193

it haunts the present while resisting its own inscription into the order of meaning (*sens*) that is the 'field of presence.'

It is, I believe, this original past that Merleau-Ponty has in mind when he says that "there may well be, either in each sensory experience or in each consciousness, 'phantoms' which no rational approach can account for" (*PhP*, 220/254). These phantoms are a problem for any 'rational approach' because they are, first of all, a problem for any consciousness. What is here named 'phantom' is that within our experience that cannot be exhaustively determined as subject or object, I or not-I. The phantom is, as we have suggested throughout the preceding chapters, precisely the ambiguous presence, in experience, of the non-presence (non-meaning) of the sensation. On the one hand, sensation is the event of a *contact* with sensible being; and the sense of the unassailable presence of a *reality* in my experience is vouchsafed by the reference of each perception back to this unanticipated event of contact. But, on the other hand, as we have said, the subject of sensation is only distinguished from the sensible by means of a movement that is also a departure, so to speak, from the site of the original contact. And this anteriority of the sensation thus also subtends the sense of reality because it lets something other than the 'I' appear precisely *to* an 'I.' As a self-conscious, sentient body, this problem is my own heritage: reality, *my* reality, as well as that of the *world*, presupposes this impossible presence of the non-presence of the sensation. I am only in contact with the sensible insofar as I have broken from it, stylized it, and translated it into an order of meaning. But the 'phantoms' of the sensible persist in contesting this meaning, this determinacy, and, thus, they contest the identity of the subject and the object. I am, therefore, a question for myself; the sentience of my body both supports and undermines my sense of my own subjectivity. As Henri Maldiney writes,

> Until it first appeared, what was unknown to us and was nothing for us, and that suddenly approached us—at each moment of the world and of us—perhaps in the unpredictable emergence of the most humble sensation, possesses an authority of presence that to us is all the more foreign as it carries with it the experience of our own otherness. But this otherness is precisely proper to us only because, as foreign, it is at the same time that which is to us the most intimate and the most originary: it belongs to the order of the encounter and of the contact whose event is each time that of our origin.[1]

My self-consciousness emerges with the enactment of decisions (beginning in living movement) concerning the meaning of an event in which the 'I,' and what is 'foreign' to it, are mutually implicated and intertwined. My sense of reality (which, as we have seen, is subtended by an irreducible tension between the determinacy, and the resistance to determination, of sensible being) is also a sense precisely of the contingency of those decisions.

This sense of contingency, which concerns the haunting of conscious-ness by an 'original past,' also has a corresponding futural orientation. It is implied in Merleau-Ponty's notion of the "order of *advent*" (S, 68/109). Advent, as we noted in chapter 5, is defined by Merleau-Ponty as "the promise of events" (S, 70/112). There is, of course, an ambiguity in the idea of an *order* of a *promise* of *events*. On the one hand, a *promise* implies an awakened expectation, something toward which one looks in advance, with hope, with desire, or, perhaps, with dread. But, on the other hand, the ordinary sense of *event* implies a brute happening, something literally *extra*-ordinary, something that, in terms of its *what, when,* or *where,* pre-cisely cannot be anticipated. And this is the paradox that is at the heart of Merleau-Ponty's notion of the sentient body: it attests simultaneously to an order of meaning and to the impossibility of an order. The paradox is also expressed in Merleau-Ponty's claim, in "Cézanne's Doubt," that the artist summons us to "a reason which contains its own origins" (SNS, 19/32). As Merleau-Ponty also says, in the same essay, that "the meaning of what the artist is going to say *does not exist* anywhere" (SNS, 19/32), we must therefore conclude that 'a reason which contains its own origins' is to be understood as an order of meaning that attests to its own contingent emergence out of non-meaning, an order that resists its own final determination *as* an order. This is also what we had in mind when, at the end of chapter 3, we spoke of a 'teleology *of* the other,' a teleology emerging from events—events, such as the gestures of our own bodies, that institute a direction, an order of meaning, the provisional unity of a project—but a teleology whose meaning includes the sense of a resistance to any final determination of a destination, normativity, or final cause. It is this ambiguous notion of teleology that, I am suggesting, Merleau-Ponty's phenomenology responds to and affirms. And in this, I would like to say, we grasp its ethical implications. In order to illustrate this, it may be helpful to contrast the interpretation that I am proposing with another interpretation of the implications of Merleau-Ponty's philosophy.

Alphonso Lingis claims that, according to the Merleau-Ponty of *Phe-nomenology of Perception,* perception is first of all a sensorimotor know-how that responds to the demand of its situation. Perception always answers to the "imperative" of a kind of practical mastery. This imperative is not imposed on a subject from outside, but arises in the very experience of perceptual life; we encounter things not as simple givens, but as "tasks to which perception finds itself devoted."[2] Lingis illustrates the nature of this imperative by contrasting it with the imperative that Kant's philosophy affirms. We could say that, for the philosophical tradition that Merleau-Ponty names "intellectualist," philosophy's task primarily consists in a self-conscious reflection on the subjective grounds of its own knowing. As Lingis points out, this is a task that intellectualist philosophy claims is imposed upon a subject by the experience of thinking itself. It is the imperative of the kind of self-consistency, or self-responsibility, that *thinking* intrinsically demands: "thought is commanded to be in command."[3] According to Lingis, this "imperative for rational autonomy" requires the thinker to "disengage the activating will in our composite sensible nature from the lures of objects given as sensuous."[4] But Lingis finds a different imperative at work in Merleau-Ponty's philosophy, one that, again, directly arises from the world of perception:

> For Merleau-Ponty, the world-imperative is received not in our understanding in conflict with our sensuality, but in our postural schema that integrates our sensibility and mobilizes our efficacity. The world-imperative commands our sensibility first to realize itself, as a praktognosis oriented to things. It commands our sensitive-sensible body to inhabit a world of things with the most centred, integral, and efficacious hold, from which every subsequent kind of comprehension will be derived. It orders competence. . . . For perception is praktognosis. Perceived things are objectives. To perceive one has to look, one has to mobilize oneself and manipulate one's surrounding.[5]

Thus, according to Lingis, the imperative that Merleau-Ponty finds already at work in perception is an imperative of mastery; its aim is, to use a term employed by Hubert Dreyfus, "maximal grip."[6] Lingis thus argues that Merleau-Ponty overlooks another imperative that is announced in our experience as sentient bodies. He asks:

> And what of the imperative not to hold onto things and maintain the world, but to release every hold and to lose the world, an imperative which everyone who has to die, himself or herself, knows? There is none of this in Merleau-Ponty's *Phenomenology of Perception*, no word of this, only the imperative figure of an agent that holds onto things that are objectives and that maintains himself in the world.[7]

Thus, according to Lingis's interpretation, Merleau-Ponty does not recognize an imperative 'not to hold onto things' because he understands perception as a practical know-how whose constant aim is precisely always to get a grip on things, to determine the world as a field of 'objectives.'

Lingis finds, in this other imperative, the imperative 'not to hold onto things,' a kind of ethical meaning. It is a call to *care* for things:

> The care for things, the perception devoted to the sensible patterns that pass, is not only a presumptive apprehension of their integrated, intersensorially consistent, graspable and manipulatable, real structures. It is also a movement that lets the patterns pass, the reliefs merge into levels, the configurations dissolve into light and resonance and terrestrial density. It follows them as they pass, passes with them.[8]

What is missing from the notion of perception as praktognosis is, according to Lingis, a demand for a certain "incompetence."[9] This imperative of incompetence is in tension with the imperative of self-maintenance and skillful mastery, but in *Phenomenology of Perception*, Lingis claims, we find only this imperative of competence. It seems to me, however, that Lingis's interpretation overlooks the ambiguity that we have found in the analyses of *Phenomenology of Perception*.

The problem is evident in the way in which Lingis understands the emergence of a norm of objectivity in human experience. He writes: "Merleau-Ponty argues that the theoretical objective, to represent the things we observe as objects and the field opened by our perception as an objective universe, is itself motivated by the structure of things that command our perception."[10] In other words, the norm of scientific objectivity is, according to Lingis's interpretation, understood by Merleau-Ponty simply as a further implication of the imperative to determine things as objectives, to achieve practical mastery of our situation. But what I believe Lingis' interpretation overlooks, in Merleau-Ponty's philosophy, is the manner in which the norm of objectivity also responds to the imposition, within our praktognosic engagement with the world, of another imperative, an imperative that is announced in the experience of another living body. Merleau-Ponty writes, "No sooner has my gaze fallen upon a living body in process of acting than the objects surrounding it immediately take on a fresh layer of significance: they are no longer simply what I myself could make of them, they are what this other pattern of behaviour is about to make of them" (*PhP*, 353/406). The norm of objectivity is not *merely* a further implication of the imperative of practical mastery, but rather presupposes this interjection, or imposition, within my surrounding world of another manner of making sense of the world—the imperative imposed upon me by the perception of another living body is the imperative to be open to other imperatives. It is only insofar as I am always already responding to *this* imperative, that I can recognize other self-conscious subjects. As Merleau-Ponty writes, "Round about the perceived body a vortex forms, towards which my world is drawn and, so to speak, sucked in: to this extent, it is no longer merely mine, and no longer merely present" (*PhP*, 353/406). This is what it is to perceive another self: it is to undergo a kind of dispossession that puts me into relation with a non-presence right in my field of presence. And it is only insofar as this experience, this original rupture in the fabric of my world, issues in a new imperative, the imperative precisely to self-consciously recognize the limits of my own perspective, that a norm of objectivity emerges. We could say that this experience of the other merely awakens me to new practical demands and possibilities for realizing them, but it could only do so insofar as it first of all announces a world in depth and thereby reveals to me the relativity of my own praktognosic interpretation of the world.

We must attend to those passages (to which we have often referred in the previous chapters) in which Merleau-Ponty links the experience of the presence/non-presence of the sensible (exemplified in monocular images, 'ghost-things' and 'dark spaces') to the sense of one's own birth and death, and then links these to the sense of intersubjectivity. Both are linked, for Merleau-Ponty, to a sense, emergent within my experience, of my own contingency and the contingency of the determinacies constituting my surrounding world. Thus, for example, Merleau-Ponty writes: "my life has a social atmosphere just as it has a flavour of mortality" (*PhP*, 364/418). This contingency does not merely imply something lacking in my present knowledge: it is what accounts for my sense of reality, a reality apart from my passing experience of it. For Merleau-Ponty, the resistance of sensible being to the meanings that it initially has *for me*, with respect to *my projects*, is a function of the haunting of my field of presence by other presences, those of other sentient bodies. Thus my very sense of reality, of the commanding presence of things, and my sense of myself as a subject of meaning, is subtended by the imposition, within my experience, of another imperative, beyond *merely* practical know-how: that of responding to the other's meanings, of acknowledging the openness of my surrounding world to an infinity of other possible determinations. As an intercorporeal body, my sentient body also enacts a certain *resistance* to determination, both of my self and of my world.

This then is the core of Merleau-Ponty's notion of subjectivity. Subjectivity is, as we have argued, enacted in living movement, movement that generates sense. But this means that, in a certain sense, subjectivity is always older than itself. As Husserl says, the 'I move' precedes the 'I can.' This means that my selfhood—the complex of habits, dispositions, ideas, commitments, and values characterizing my own unique manner of being in the world—is enacted as a kind of response, a self-conscious taking up of that historical situation of which my body is already the incarnation. To be a self-conscious, intercorporeal body, is to find myself answerable for the ways in which things in my environment come to be determined according to the sense of my own moving body's 'objectives.' To be concerned with *real* beings, with beings whose sense constitutively includes the sense of being for others, is precisely to loosen *my* grip on things, and, in a certain sense, to self-consciously resist the grip that the praktognosic imperative has on me and on my world. This resistance is something I can consciously perform, as, for example, when I make myself answerable to a norm of detached objectivity in scientific research, but it is important to remember that this stance is possible because, as an intercorporeal body, I am already implicitly open to this imperative to loosen my grip on things, to make space for otherness, at the level of perceptual experience. I experience this resistance of reality to my determinations (whether as a totality of objects, or as a field of practical objectives) because, as a sentient body, a body open to the sensible, I am also open to the demands of language.

In an essay entitled "A Responsive Voice: Language Without the Modern Subject," David Michael Levin writes, concerning Merleau-Ponty's account of perception and language:

> Since perception is already communication, we grow into a language that, like the atmosphere we breathe, is already our environment, the origin of the subject's voice posited by metaphysics is not really an origin at all: beyond memory, beyond retrieval, a mere phantom, it will always already have been a response, a gathering into itself the voices breaking through the silence of its world.[11]

Because language is not the outward expression of a subject's interior monologue but, 'like the atmosphere we breathe,' it already makes its claim in my sentient body, my sensible reality always already includes within itself the sense of being destined toward others. This, rather than a discrete thinking subject, is what accounts for the emergence, within sensible being, of ideality, of objectivity. But the sense of objectivity and ideality here will be quite different than the one generally presupposed by modern science. Reason is responsive to the extent that it 'contains its own origins.'

In a certain sense, Merleau-Ponty's philosophy, not unlike the intellectualist philosophies of the enlightenment, responds to a norm of self-responsibility, and takes up a reflective orientation concerned with the grounds of objectivity and meaning. But we must also qualify this by noting that, as an 'ontological rehabilitation of the sensible,' Merleau-Ponty's philosophy locates these grounds in a certain non-ground, in the very non-presence of the sensible and, in a certain sense, in the non-self-presence of the sentient body itself. It is because my body is always already determining itself in responding to the two-fold demand of things and communication with others that it is (I am) concerned with truth. Phenomenology explicitly takes up the demand that is already implicit in our bodily engagements with our world. It responds to a demand to be responsible for my own responsive-creative behavior, to acknowledge the constitutive sense of otherness *within* perceptual sense, and to recognize the determination of sense as a creative operation that can never exhaust its 'motivations.' Let me offer a brief example of how this kind of reflection can alter our sense of objectivity.

Molecular biologist and ethicist Christoph Rehmann-Sutter, in an essay entitled "Poiesis and Praxis," writes about the scientific study of the development of organisms. He begins by differentiating his approach from reductionist approaches that attempt to understand development on the basis of what he calls a "genetic program" that would be encoded in an organism's DNA. As he puts it:

> If we think that the dynamic structure and developmental capacities of an organism are essentially stored in the sequence of its DNA, there is little room for speculations about any inherent sense of the developmental steps; they appear to be nothing but the executions of instructions.[12]

This reductionist model in molecular biology is a product of what, from the perspective of Merleau-Ponty's philosophy, must be seen as a fairly naïve understanding of the norm of objectivity. According to this norm, the task of the scientist is to, as it were, remove her own subjectivity from the encounter with her object. In observing developing organisms, she in fact observes changes, dynamic processes, and variety across individuals, but her aim is to explain all of this in terms of what does not change and does not vary. This she can only assure herself of having accomplished insofar as she is able to explain, in this case, developmental processes, in terms of essential 'parts and processes,' basic (molecular) elements and unchanging laws.

There is now a wide body of scientific research findings that put this model of development into question.[13] One obvious problem, upon which many molecular biologists now agree, is that there is simply not enough DNA to account for all of the complexities, both in terms of morphology and what we could call ontogenetic timing (*when* a plant begins to flower, *when* a bird develops its breeding plumage, etc.), involved in the actual developmental processes taking organisms from, for example, fertilized egg to sexual maturity. Further, in connection with this, it is now widely recognized that there are many things going on in developmental processes that involve contingent responses to environmental conditions, both at the cellular level and at the level of the whole organism, and that therefore cannot be accounted for by simply appealing to a developmental program. But Rehmann-Sutter is not so much concerned with these debates over the implications of research findings in molecular biology as with the way in which developmental biologists understand themselves, their practice, in relation to the organisms they study, and how this self-understanding determines what they are looking for and what they find. That is to say, he is concerned with the way in which the reductionist model (which is precisely a *model*, a particular way in which one set of living organisms, humans, as scientific observers, interprets another set of living organisms) unconsciously structures what scientists see. He argues that it is imperative for scientists to recognize that they are active interpreters:

> There may be a basic insecurity about whether to apply hermeneutic terms like *describing* or *interpreting* to biology. The most convincing answer to this insecurity is the fact that we are living organisms ourselves: we do biology essentially from the perspective of participant observers. This causes some epistemological troubles but also gives us an advantage; at the same time it makes a critical hermeneutic reflection indispensable. Otherwise we would be in danger of being unaware of "what we make of ourselves" when adopting a particular scientific regime. . . . Describing (and thereby necessarily interpreting) development means positioning ourselves in a morally relevant way with regard to the living entities we describe.[14]

These remarks, it seems to me, reflect, in contrast to the naïve objectivist stance of the dogmatic reductionist, a self-conscious stance toward the norm of scientific objectivity itself, one that, recognizing the nature of the inter-corporeal, and intersubjective, practices out of which this norm emerges, thus discovers, in that very norm, a further imperative precisely to reflect on the nature of these practices. In other words, the very endeavor to know the truth about organisms and developmental processes is seen to imply a kind of ethical requirement to reflect on our own subjectivity and, thus, on our own explicit, or implicit, objectives, norms, and methods. From the point of view of biology, Rehmann-Sutter suggests that the criterion for the evaluation of scientific models or practices be this: "Is the practice capable of coming into the presence of other living beings?"[15] Here the norm of objectivity, of a certain self-conscious, self-critical, rigor in the pursuit of truth, coincides with a kind of ethical imperative to be mindful of the relational character of the practices out of which this norm emerges.

As we have suggested, this understanding of the ethical character of the norm of objectivity arises from reflection on the very emergence of that norm. This reflection is neither a question of uncovering a normativity wholly intrinsic to pure thought, nor is it simply a matter of uncovering the roots of this norm in a praktognosic agency that would grasp the world as the field of its own projects. Rather, more fundamentally, the ideal of objectivity has its roots in the experience of other selves and in the corresponding experience of a certain constitutive non-presence within the present of my experience. As Merleau-Ponty writes, "just as the instant of my death is a future to which I have not access, so I am necessarily destined never to live through the presence of another to himself" (*PhP*, 364/418). This *other* presence, a presence that will never be a present for me, polarizes the world along new axes, giving it an orientation toward another future. The presence/non-presence of the other awakens an order of meaning answering to the demands of truth, even as it withholds from me the grounds or the objective of this order of meaning.

The enquiry into the nature of objectivity turns out to reveal an ethical character of the sentient body: it is an intercorporeal, and expressive, body. As such the body is constitutively responsive to the demands of otherness, and my own reflectively self-conscious life is the enactment of a certain kind of response to that demand. It is of course possible for reflective self-consciousness to enact a form of resistance to the demands of otherness—as when, for example, the ideal of objective knowledge is taken to require of us a certain dispassionate detachment with respect to the presence of living things. But this attitude is itself a kind of response to the demands of otherness, even if it has failed to understand itself as such. Insofar as it does understand itself, it sees that there is no evading responsibility for all that we do in the name of objective 'Truth,' for there is no objectivity apart from our doing and thus nothing absolves us of responsibility for our choices. The very meaning of what we do is subtended, paradoxically, by the presence/non-presence of the other in our experience. The sentient body is at once the grounds of the ideal of truth and normativity, and the attestation of the questionable character of the norms, or imperatives, that determine our senses of ourselves and our world. And it is this dependence of thought on the very thing that also contests its presumptions and its most cherished certainties that draws objectivating thought into a ceaseless reflection on its own conditions and thus leads it to the threshold of phenomenology.

# NOTES

## INTRODUCTION

1. Derrida, *Speech and Phenomena*, 82.
2. Dennett, *Consciousness Explained*, 418.
3. See esp. Barbaras, *The Being of the Phenomenon*, 5–18. In a 2001 essay entitled "Merleau-Ponty and Nature," Barbaras continues this line of criticism: "The phenomenology of perception reveals the descriptive specificity of the perceptive layer but does not go so far as to enquire about the relationship of this perceptive layer to reality in itself: the sense of being of nature does not necessarily seem to be questioned by the discovery of the perceived world" (23).

## CHAPTER ONE

1. For an example of the use of this term see Dreyfus, "Intelligence Without Representation."
2. For example, a 2002 article by Erik Myin and Kevin O'Regan ("Perceptual Consciousness") is subtitled: "A Way to Naturalize Phenomenology?"
3. Olkowski, "Introduction," 1–2.
4. See, for example, Dennett and Hofstadter, *The Mind's I*, 11.
5. Chalmers, *The Conscious Mind*, xi.
6. I will not be highlighting the important distinctions between contemporary physicalist accounts of cognition and the empiricist epistemologies targeted in Merleau-Ponty's critique of representationalism. Lawrence Hass raises the question of whether or not Merleau-Ponty's critique of empiricist 'sensationalism' (which we will consider shortly) foresees the claims made by contemporary physicalists who, to some extent, share his critique of sense-data empiricism. For a discussion of contemporary physicalism in relation to Merleau-Ponty, see Hass, *Merleau-Ponty's Philosophy*, 41–52.
7. Newen and Vogeley, "Self-representation," 530, 541.
8. It is because of what we have called the spatial and temporal thickness of the subjectivity of the first-person perspective that Husserl (in the *Analyses Concerning Passive and Active Synthesis*) describes the field of experience as a "living present" (206), of which he says that it combines a "temporal form and the form of a local field" (208).
9. Zahavi, *Subjectivity and Selfhood*, 21.
10. As Merleau-Ponty writes in his later essay "Eye and Mind": "Science is and always has been that admirably active, ingenious, and bold way of thinking whose

fundamental bias is to treat everything as though it were an object-in-general—as though it meant nothing to us and yet was predestined for our own use" (EM, 159/9).

11. For phenomenology the problem will not be how subjectivity emerged in a world of parts and processes; rather, it is generally inclined to ask how a world of discrete objects and fundamental laws could have emerged on the basis of the phenomenal world of first-personal experience. We will consider Merleau-Ponty's approach to this problem more directly in chapter 5.

12. This is of course also the fundamental concern of Husserl's critique of the "naïve objectivism" of modern science, a critique that remains a persistent theme for the phenomenological tradition. We have suggested that the first-person perspective is, for phenomenology, not a 'what' but the 'how' of appearance. Modern science, in Husserl's view, does not recognize the irreducibility of "the 'how' of the subjective manner of givenness of the life-world and life-world objects" (Crisis, 143).

13. From Merleau-Ponty's 1957–8 lecture course on nature: "The Umwelt marks the difference between the world such as it exists in itself, and the world as the world of a living being. It is an intermediary reality between the world such as it exists for an absolute observer and a purely subjective domain" (N, 167).

14. Shaun Gallagher expresses the implications of this position: "The concepts 'stimulus' and 'response' are only abstractions from the situation that is defined by the relation existing between the organism and the environment. Yet the 'situation' is not composed of two well-defined and distinguished poles that interact. Rather, the situation is precisely what Dewey terms the 'organism-environment.' This means that the organism does not exist without the environment, and that there is no environment without an organism" ("Lived Body and Environment," 162).

15. As many commentators have been careful to note, the translation of the French word sens into the English word "meaning" risks occluding some ambiguities. On the one hand, "meaning" can also translate signification, which, according to Dillon, is the term Merleau-Ponty more often employs when he is speaking of linguistic meaning, whereas "sens typically refers to the meaningfulness of the perceptual world" (Merleau-Ponty's Ontology, 215); on the other hand, sens itself has multiple meanings—it can refer to the senses, to meaning/significance, or to direction, as in a sign indicating a one-way street: "sens unique" (see Morris, The Sense of Space, 24). Merleau-Ponty himself notes the ambiguity between 'meaning' and 'direction' in the French word sens in Phenomenology of Perception (253) and often seems to play upon this ambiguity.

16. This is, of course, not to say that all organisms are reflectively self-conscious. But this account of the 'self' does imply that self-consciousness is perhaps more likely to manifest itself (at least initially) as a certain way of being aware of one's environment rather than of one's own inner mental states. It also implies that it may be fruitful to think of explicit self-consciousness as a particularly developed form of a logical structure of selfhood already evident in organic life. See Russon, "Embodiment and Responsibility," esp. sec. II, pp. 296–9.

17. Merleau-Ponty offers this definition of 'dialectic' in Phenomenology of Perception: "The dialectic is not a relationship between contradictory and inseparable thoughts; it is the tending of an existence towards another existence which denies

it, and yet without which it is not sustained" (167–8/195). We might think of Merleau-Ponty's 'embodied dialectic' as a dynamic structure of bodily life in which forms of behavior and cognition develop by way of a process of making-explicit a meaning already implicitly at work in the previous level. The development reveals what the previous level was trying to realize. We will explore this logic further in chapter 2.

18. I am suggesting here that the idea of life implies a self. Renaud Barbaras writes of the ambiguity of the French verb "to live" (*vivre*) which can imply both living in the sense of lived-experience (as in the German, *Erleben*, or what we have called 'living through' something) and living in the sense of being alive (*Leben*). This ambiguity "is not an accident of language but the mark of a primary sense of life, the mark of an original unity of living, which stops short of the cleavage between living being and lived experience" ("Life, Movement, and Desire," 4). He argues that a phenomenological inquiry into the category of 'life' must reckon with this ambiguity—"the action to which the verb refers affects its subject, and the subject's doing is passively received in the form of a feeling" (4). In our terms, the task of such a phenomenology would not be to reduce the third-personal objects of biology to the first-personal dimension of experience (which would simply be to reverse the standpoint of biological science) but to look into what 'stops short of' this distinction. When I say that for Merleau-Ponty the objects of biology are in some sense 'selves,' I am not asserting the priority of the first-person perspective but simply its irreducibility (in the context of the study of living things) to the third-personal terms of the biological sciences.

19. The radicality of this claim is intensified when we take seriously its implications concerning not only the objects of biology and psychology but with regard to the scientific observers themselves. Again, as Barbaras writes, "In order to work on his object, the biologist must first recognize it, that is, distinguish it, within reality; he must distinguish what is living and what is not. This discrimination is the province of an intuition or an experience that escapes objectification because an intuition or experience is the condition of its possibility" ("Life, Movement, and Desire," 4). As we shall see, Merleau-Ponty is concerned about the possibility that scientists can falsify their insights into the essential situatedness of organisms when they attempt to place it back within a network of objective relations that the scientist takes for granted as defining the norms of scientific truth.

20. The terms "enactive" and "embodied" are from Varela *et al.*, *The Embodied Mind*; the term "situated" is from Clark, *Being There*; the "sensorimotor" approach is proposed by O'Regan and Noë, "A Sensorimotor Account"; "existential" is used by McClamrock, *Existential Cognition*; "ecological" is, of course, the term introduced by J.J. Gibson, *The Ecological Approach to Visual Perception*, but recently employed by a number of thinkers with particular reference to the sense of self (e.g., Butterworth, "An Ecological Perspective on the Origins of the Self").

21. One of the things they do not all share, however, is a wholesale rejection of (internal) representationalism. Andy Clark, for example, argues that representationalism must simply be broadened to include a fuller account of "action-oriented representations" (Clark, *Being There*). Thus, the challenge is not always to rep-

resentationalism per se but to the view that the behavior of organisms must be explained by first accounting for the ways that organisms internally 'map' their external environment. This more attenuated challenge seeks to grasp how motor actions—themselves executed on the basis of motor programs or 'representations of actions'—helps to structure and organize other representational content. With regard to "representations of actions," Marc Jeannerod distinguishes different versions of representationalism: "Indeed, the term representation of an action can be used in its strong sense, to designate a mental state in relation to goals and desires, as well as in its weak sense, to indicate the ensemble of mechanisms that precede execution of a movement" (Jeannerod, "Consciousness of Action and Self-Consciousness," 128). We shall be arguing that the concept of representation is simply not adequate to the sense of living movement and the immanent intelligibility of behavior that is expounded by Merleau-Ponty.

22. I use the term 'phenomenal environment' here because the challenge of situated cognition does not always involve any explicit ontological claim about the status of environments. I am thus using 'phenomenal' here in the sense of *merely* phenomenal—i.e., without any intended implication concerning the ontological status of environments.

23. Thompson, "Sensorimotor Subjectivity," 408.

24. See, for example, Lakoff and Johnston's analysis of the grounding of cognition and language in metaphors that are rooted in embodied life (*Philosophy in the Flesh*).

25. See Dorothée Legrand's critical rejoinder to the above-cited article by Newen and Vogeley (Legrand, "How not to find the neural signature of self-consciousness").

26. Husserl links the egoic 'I can' to embodiment and self-movement in *Ideas II*, 159–60.

27. Related to both of these positions is a third, which we do not directly discuss. It is the view that self-awareness is somehow related to what are called *qualia*. On this view, associated with such cognitive processes as perception or imagination there are specific qualitative dimensions. This is often expressed in the following terms: in addition to the cognitive processes involved in the perception of a tomato, there is also 'something it is like' to perceive a tomato, and this dimension calls for an explanation of its own. This qualitative dimension (which, after all, concerns something particularly subjective about our experience) is thought, by some, to be related to the problem of self-awareness. Zahavi and Parnas ("Phenomenal Consciousness and Self-awareness") argue that this approach does not in fact address the question of the first-personal dimension of experience as it is understood by phenomenologists.

28. Strawson, "The Self and the SESMET," 488–9.

29. In fact, many of them do offer accounts of how the sense of self as 'mental something' arises in developed forms of experience, but they do not treat this 'mental something' as a 'fundamental' feature of self-awareness.

30. Varela et al., *The Embodied Mind*, 79.

31. Ibid., 80.

32. Clark, *Being There*, 216.

33. Ibid., 218.

34. Merleau-Ponty's interpretations of the results of such experiments often rely on his attentiveness to the *meaning* of the experimental situation for the subjects involved. Normal subjects may well experience the significance of the situation quite differently than subjects with neural pathologies. It follows that only by admitting the notion of existential significance into our interpretations can the phenomenological value of such results be properly evaluated. Gallagher and Marcel ("The Self in Contextualized Action") discuss the importance of understanding "intentional attitudes" and the difference between "contextualized" and "decontextualized" action for designing experimental research and interpreting results.

35. O'Regan and Noë, "A Sensorimotor Account," 940.

36. Ibid., 942.

37. Ibid., 944.

38. Ibid., 939.

39. This problem concerns the 'explanatory gap' to which we referred above. Though O'Regan and Noë do not employ this vocabulary, we can safely say that their problem stems from the recognition that claims about cortical maps (third-personal facts) do not obviously provide answers to questions about (first-personal) visual experience.

40. O'Regan and Noë, "A Sensorimotor Account," 941.

41. Ibid.

42. For a general discussion of empirical research into the study of such eye-movements and their effect on perception, see Ditchburn, *Eye-movements and Visual Perception*, esp. chapter 4 on 'small eye-movements.'

43. Ditchburn, *Eye-movements and Visual Perception*, 131. See also O'Regan and Noë, "A Sensorimotor Account," 947–950, for a survey of empirical research in this area.

44. O'Regan and Noë, "A Sensorimotor Account," 951.

45. See Rogers, "Perceiving Pictorial Space," for a survey of recent research on depth-perception and representational images which supports this hypothesis. Rogers is particularly interested in the historical development of representational techniques employed by artists in the construction of various kinds of pictorial space.

46. For a discussion of the limitations of such accounts in connection with Merleau-Ponty's approach to problem of depth see Ed Casey, "The Element of Voluminousness."

47. Morris, *The Sense of Space*, 7–9.

48. Ibid., 9.

49. The following list, which is not exhaustive, is derived from Gillam, "The Perception of Spatial Layout." See also Gibson, *The Ecological Approach*: "The theory of depth perception assumes that the third dimension of space is lost in the two-dimensional retinal image. Perception must begin with the form perception, the flat patchwork of colors in the visual field. But there are supposedly *cues* for depth, which, if they are utilized, will add a third dimension to the flat visual field" (148).

50. Cutting and Vishton, "Information Potency and Spatial Layout," 77 (my italics).

51. Ibid., 97.

52. Similarly, McClamrock's reflections on the way in which the perception of environments tends to be underdetermined in traditional models leads him to posit the necessity for what he calls "situated cues" (McClamrock, *Existential Cognition*, 96–7).

53. The concept of *motivation*, which is a fundamental concept in Merleau-Ponty, is derived from Husserl (see *PhP*, 49n.1/61n.1). Merleau-Ponty writes, "The phenomenological notion of *motivation* is one of those 'fluid' ["flieszende": Husserl] concepts which have to be formed if we want to get back to phenomena. One phenomenon releases another, not by means of some objective efficient cause, like those which link together natural events, but by the meaning which it holds out—there is a *raison d'être* for a thing which guides the flow of phenomena without being explicitly laid down in any one of them, a sort of operative reason" (*PhP*, 49–50/61). Later, he again undertakes to explain this notion: "What do we understand by a motive, and what do we mean when we say, for example, that a journey is motivated? We mean thereby that it has its origin in certain given facts, not in so far as these facts by themselves have the physical power to bring it about, but in that they provide the reasons for undertaking it. The motive is an antecedent which acts only through its significance" (*PhP*, 258–9/299). It is significant that, in the chapter on space, Merleau-Ponty contrasts the relation of cause and effect with that of motivation and *decision*.

54. Gibson's 'affordance' is similar to Merleau-Ponty's '*manipulandum*' in this passage: "I can therefore take my place, through the medium of my body as the potential source of a certain number of familiar actions, in my environment conceived as a set of *manipulanda* and without, moreover, envisaging my body or my surrounding as objects in the Kantian sense, that is, as systems of qualities linked by some intelligible law, as transparent entities, free from any attachment to a specific place or time, and ready to be named or at least pointed out" (*PhP*, 105/122).

55. Gibson, *The Ecological Approach*, 127.

56. Lewontin, *Biology as Ideology*, 83–4. Lewontin's use of the terminology of outsideness—as in the 'the world outside these organisms'—is, we shall see, somewhat problematic when considered from the point of view of a phenomenological ontology of the self. In fact his whole description of the relation of the organism and its environment implies that the 'self' of the organism is precisely constituted in its relations to these bits and pieces of its world. This means that the self is not originally an 'inside' at all.

57. Gibson, *The Ecological Approach*, 205.

58. Ibid., 168.

59. Ibid., 65.

60. There are, as we shall see later in this chapter, important differences concealed in this apparent analogy. Merleau-Ponty's use of the term 'situation' will turn out to demand a different ontology then the one that is implicit in Gibson's notion of 'ecology.'

61. See Casey, "The Element of Voluminousness," for a discussion of Gibson's approach to the problem of depth and for an account of depth in relation to 'place.'

62. Gibson, *The Ecological Approach*, 150.

63. Ibid., 123.

64. Ibid., 148.

65. This claim also reflects the views of a number of recent figures in the phenomenological tradition. Maxine Sheets-Johnstone, for example, has written: "We *literally discover ourselves in movement*. We grow kinetically into our bodies. . . . We make sense of ourselves in moving. We discover ourselves as animate organisms" (*The Primacy of Movement*, 136). For Sheets-Johnstone, then, movement is prior to, and founds, the sense of one's own subjectivity, and is, thus, prior to the sense of one's *power* to move ("I can"). For this claim, she takes inspiration from Husserl's claim (in *Ideas II*, 273) that the 'I move' precedes the 'I can' (134). Renaud Barbaras has also claimed that the subjectivity of perception is fundamentally living movement. He writes: "In truth, it is *movement itself* that perceives in the sense that the object exists *for* it, in which movement has its meaning, as its oriented nature attests, inspired and clairvoyant with regard to the living movement that often demonstrates an intimacy with its objective, an intimacy that runs deeper than that which knowledge exhibits. . . . We are confronted by a strictly motor perception that unfolds exclusively in exteriority and rejoins rather than represents its object" (*Desire and Distance*, 91–2). Sheets-Johnstone's claim concerning the primacy of movement differs from Barbaras's, however, in that she ultimately is interested in the "kinesthetic consciousness" of movement as the transcendental ground of appearance (*The Primacy of Movement*, 149), whereas Barbaras's claim is more radical: movement *is* itself subjectivity. In the coming chapters I will argue that it is only by grasping the meaning of subjectivity *as* expressive movement, that we fully overcome the epistemology of representation.

66. Thus, I am deliberately using the term *subjectivity* here instead of *the subject*. This is to suggest that, before being the term designating an entity, subjectivity is a feature of the *dynamics* of living movement.

## CHAPTER TWO

1. Steinbock, "Merleau-Ponty's Concept of Depth," 350n.1 (my italics). Steinbock claims that the phenomenological investigation of depth in Merleau-Ponty's early work, which is particularly concerned, he says, with the "body-world matrix," develops directly into the ontology of "flesh" in his later work: "The relationship of depth which expresses the interplay of perceiver and perceived was already a theme for Merleau-Ponty's early phenomenological investigations. With the notion of flesh, he interpreted this peculiar commerce between seer and seen more explicitly" (346).

2. Morris, "What is Living and What is Non-Living," 230.

3. Barbaras writes: "Living movement is automovement not only because it proceeds from the self but above all because it is its own source, because it nourishes itself, and because the impulse is not exhausted but restored by its realization" (*Desire and Distance*, 93). The impulse is restored by its realization because the sense of movement never absorbs the facticity of its own beginning—it has the character of a response to a motive that is not exhausted in the response.

4. Another way of expressing this is in terms of the logic of possibility and actuality deployed by John Russon in "The Self as Resolution." Offering an

interpretation of the de(con)struction of the metaphysics of presence in Heidegger and Derrida, he shows that the sense of possibility belongs to the sense of being, but that the sense of possibility is never exhausted in any actuality: "Actuality actualizes the possible, but the possible is a 'remainder' in the equation, which is not assimilable within the actual, i.e., there is no actuality that can 'be' it" (97). In these terms, we could say that movement is a decision that, as it were, intends a determinacy—it establishes an actuality. But in doing so it also announces, or, as Merleau-Ponty says, 'marks round itself,' a field of possibility, a horizon of possible meanings in terms of which it makes sense. It retroactively determines its beginning as a motive in relation to which it makes sense. But the actuality never exhausts the field of possibilities that it marks round itself.

5. Merleau-Ponty writes, concerning the meaning of 'horizon': "The horizon . . . is what guarantees the identity of the object throughout the exploration; it is the correlative of the *impending power* which my gaze retains over the objects which it has just surveyed, and which it already has over the fresh details which it is about to discover" (*PhP*, 68/82; my italics).

6. Husserl, *Cartesian Meditations*, 45.

7. Steinbock, "Merleau-Ponty's Concept of Depth," 340. Rather than emphasizing the Husserlian logic of horizonality, which seems to subordinate indeterminacy to the determinacy of a structure, Steinbock sees, in the phenomenon of depth, an indeterminacy which destabilizes structure: "It is through depth that things stagger out as near or far, present and absent, rearranging themselves in diverse contexts in a struggle for recognition such that they can come to be for us. . . . Depth— "*dimensionality itself*"—makes something seen or heard to coexist with other sights or sounds by allowing some to be concealed as background, while this background as a certain absence sustains the very prominence of the other: in other words, indeterminacy in determinacy" (340).

8. David Morris writes: "When I say that lived depth is labile, I mean that it is open to alterations that propagate from within our experience of it, where the kinds of alterations are themselves open to alteration. In this usage a piece of clay is malleable but not labile (since it does not alter itself from within), and the caterpillar's metamorphosis into a butterfly is not a case of lability, since the change is biologically fixed, it cannot alter its way of altering; our sexual being, on the other hand, is labile, since it alters itself and develops new ways of self-altering (this is the sense in which we find the term in psycho-analytic literature)" (Morris, *The Sense of Space*, 19).

9. Alphonso Lingis has argued that, for Merleau-Ponty, "perception is praktognosis" ("Imperatives," 99). That is to say, perception is animated by practical objectives, and the perceiver responds to practical "imperatives" that she/he encounters in the "exteriority of the world" (98); the perceiving subject is characterized by her competence (what we have been calling the 'sensorimotor know-how' of the 'I can'). What Merleau-Ponty does not entertain, according to Lingis, is the possibility of an "imperative of incompetence" (113). This would be the imperative of precisely *not* subtending the determinacy of 'objects' and of the world as a unified totality, but rather of letting one's gaze adhere to "those phantoms, caricatures, and doubles that even in the high noon of the world float and scintillate over the contours of

things and the planes of the world" (114). The subject would be responsive to this imperative in being a not-being-able. I want to suggest here that Merleau-Ponty is attentive to such an imperative even if only because one's ability to perceive transcendent things presupposes an openness to new forms of space. This imperative is brought out most clearly when Merleau-Ponty reflects upon the imperatives guiding the activity of the painter (and we shall consider this in chapter 3). There is, in Merleau-Ponty's phenomenology, the sense of an imperative to remain responsive to imperatives that one cannot foresee.

10. In the context of his analysis of 'attention,' Merleau-Ponty writes: "Empiricism cannot see that we need to know what we are looking for, otherwise we would not be looking for it, and intellectualism fails to see that we need to be ignorant of what we are looking for, or equally again we should not be searching. They are in agreement in that neither can grasp consciousness *in the act of learning*, and that neither attaches due importance to that circumscribed ignorance, that still 'empty' but already determinate intention which *is* attention itself" (*PhP*, 28/36). I am arguing here that, to truly grasp the significance of learning, we must see how, beyond the 'circumscribed ignorance' of an 'already determinate intention,' subjectivity must run up against an alterity, a provocation to reconfigure its 'determinate intention.' But this alterity cannot be totally unanticipated or it would never be able to appear—the intentionality that intends this otherness must be a certain powerlessness of the 'I can.'

11. Maria Talero offers an interpretation of the experiment that nicely captures the full implications with respect to the ontology of situation: "What the experiment as a whole brings out is that the visible spectacle or the spatial surroundings actually visible to the subject—for we must remember, he cannot see the room around him except by looking in the slanted mirror—do not function as objective *causes* of spatial orientation. If they did, there would be no reason for the initial 'failure' in reorientation. Rather, they function through the mediation of the spatial level as motivations for a transformation and reorganization of the subject's spatial 'compact' with the world" ("Perception, Normativity, and Selfhood," 447). Talero draws the conclusion, from her analysis of this discussion in Merleau-Ponty, that "the spatial level is the perceptual correlate of selfhood" (448).

12. Talero describes this sense of given space with the idea of home: "Being in a space, then, is a two-sided phenomenon that involves a cooperation or complicity between body and world: on the one side is my body with its power of agency and, on the other, vitally linked to it, are certain worldly 'anchoring points,' into which it is 'geared.' This 'gearing in,' according to Merleau-Ponty, is what affords me the possibility of being spatially 'at home' in the room, able to move in it in an oriented manner" (444).

13. Russon, "The Spatiality of Self-Consciousness," 213. Russon's analysis is based upon Merleau-Ponty's account of the spatiality of one's own body (*le corps propre*), which we will discuss more directly in chapter 4. But the same sense of an originary passivity is entailed by the analysis of spatial 'levels' in the chapter on space in *Phenomenology of Perception*.

14. The ambiguities and difficulties in Merleau-Ponty's notion of a teleology of consciousness are examined in Barbaras's book *The Being of the Phenomenon*: "On

the one hand [in *Phenomenology of Perception*], Merleau-Ponty unveils a universe of originary experience such that objectivity can have there only a teleological status, that is, objectivity can constitute only a genuinely derived dimension. But, on the other hand, we get to this experience by means of categories that have not been criticized—in particular, that of consciousness. The result is that in order to avoid empiricism and therefore to remain on the phenomenological level, Merleau-Ponty is led to subordinate the world to nature, to conceive the subject of experience as transcendental consciousness and teleology as something already accomplished. . . . Consciousness, which is presupposed instead of being reconceived on the basis of the teleology, determines a precession of the *telos* at the heart of the world, which is then thrust back onto nature" (12). The problem, for Barbaras, is that, by presupposing consciousness, Merleau-Ponty conceives the telos of this teleology as objectivity, as the in-itself of 'one single natural world.' However, the whole analysis of perception has taught us that objectivity is not only derivative, but that the determination of being as objectivity involves an occlusion of the phenomena of perception.

    15. This is the understanding of the prereflective that is proposed by M.C. Dillon (see his *Merleau-Ponty's Ontology*, esp. chapter 6). He argues that the notion of a tacit cogito is awkward and that it is the livedness of the lived body that Merleau-Ponty really has in mind when he speaks of the prereflective. He writes: "The body can touch things, but it can touch things only to the extent that it is touched *by* things: to touch something is necessarily to feel the touch of the thing on oneself—an anaesthetized finger does not properly touch, it only bumps up against things, precisely because it cannot feel. Here, then, is the genuine tacit cogito, in the reflexivity intrinsic to bodily perception, but it is misnamed tacit cogito, for it is not a thought; it is, rather, our primordial contact with things" (105). Thus, for Dillon, the past that has never been a present is the past of the body understood as *prereflectively* self-conscious. Notice that this reflexivity of the body presupposes the immediacy of the feeling-oneself-touched. We shall raise some concerns about this in chapters 4 and 5.

    16. See, for example, *PhP*, 62/76: "Reflection is truly reflection only if it is not carried outside itself, only if it knows itself as reflection-on-an-unreflective-experience, and consequently as a change in the structure of our existence."

    17. This is made especially clear in the "Temporality" chapter, which we shall discuss in more detail in chapter 4.

    18. Lawlor, "The End of Phenomenology," 24.

    19. Ibid.

    20. *PhP*, 474n.1/415n.1 (cited in Lawlor, "The End of Phenomenology," 24).

    21. Lawlor, "The End of Phenomenology," 24.

    22. Ibid., 25.

    23. Ibid. The words in quotation marks are cited from an article by M.C. Dillon, who reads the text in the manner of the first of the two alternate readings that I presented above. See Dillon, "The Unconscious: Language and World."

    24. Bernet's interpretation of the concept of nature in *Phenomenology of Perception* seems to me to identify this original past with 'nature': "Nature in Merleau-Ponty's sense is not foreign or opposed to human existence, but has rather an essential relationship with it. Nature is 'something' at the heart of human existence that

does not properly *belong* to the human subject: a ground (*Grund*) of its constituting capacities, that is at the same time a non-ground (*Abgrund*), a capacity that evades constituting reason. . . . Letting nature appear as a dimension of human existence that refers to and calls for constitution without being enclosed in it, requires a new form of phenomenological reduction" (Bernet, "The Subject in Nature," 57). We could say that the original past is precisely that which 'calls for constitution without being enclosed in it.' On the basis of what I will argue in coming chapters, I want to suggest that this identification of the original past with nature also requires an account of nature that relates it closely to the concept of 'expression.'

25. The logic of referring backward here can perhaps be usefully compared to the notion of 'backward reference' (*zurückweisen*) that Jay Lampert elucidates in his dialectical reading of Husserl's *Logical Investigations* (Lampert, *Synthesis and Backward Reference*). Lampert argues (in chapter 3, on parts and wholes) that, for Husserl, perceptual syntheses constituting individuals proceed according to a dialectical logic that necessarily involves references to the contexts in which those individuals can emerge, even though those contexts are not explicitly given. On Lampert's reading this logic of backward reference accounts for the differences between *a priority* and empirical determinacy, subjectivity and objectivity, continuity and discontinuity, individuation and contextualization, presence and absence. Consciousness ceaselessly refers backward in constituting the grounds in which something can appear. The relationship between parts and wholes, for example, is understood in terms of a "drive towards interpretative synthesis, a drive propelled by open-ended parts that continually fix boundaries even as they exceed them" (87). We could say that the sense of movement, in Merleau-Ponty, also exemplifies this logic of retroactive sense-bestowal characteristic of the logic of parts and wholes. But precisely insofar as this is not, for Merleau-Ponty, the activity of a synthesizing consciousness but a logic-in-movement, consciousness takes over this sense by referring not only to grounds, but to a certain *Abgrund*, to the contingency of the ground as a spectral non-sense within the order of sense announced in living movement.

26. Merleau-Ponty speaks of sensation as a kind of "communion" (*PhP*, 322/370; 212/246).

27. Here I am relying on Rudolf Bernet's interpretation of Levinas's concept of trauma in connection with the psychoanalytic notion of the peculiar 'retroactive' character of the force of a traumatic event: "It is the shock of an anonymous association and the temporality of a retroaction unforeseeable for the subject that constitutes a subject by confronting it with an experience it can only recognize as its own by misrecognizing it" ("The Traumatized Subject," 163). The trauma has the same temporal structure as what we are calling the presence/non-presence of the sensation. The task of a phenomenology of sensation is thus "to understand how something totally foreign can give itself, or better, impose itself upon a subject and how this subject can relate itself to this impossibility" (164). Bernet, following Levinas, concludes with a discussion of the sensation as trauma that is completely in keeping with what we are arguing here: "What endowment of the subject is attested to by its being traumatized without being annihilated, its giving itself without suppressing itself, its recovering itself in between periods of total self-forgetting? What if not the humble sensation, the incarnate consciousness of the ordeal undergone that

introduces that minimal distance upon which the survival of the subject depends? Without this sensation, delayed slightly from the sensed, there would be no narcissism or self-givenness, no overcoming of trauma or consent to trauma out of love for the other, no appeal or response" (178).

28. We can interpret the doctrines of a 'primordial' space and 'original past' as together reflecting the two-fold necessity that, on the one hand, any actuality must show itself to be a realization of a certain power, or possibility, but, on the other hand, power or possibility as such must be occluded in any actuality. As Russon writes: "The artist who over and over again transforms our perception through her artworks, demonstrates precisely her power thereby, but that power *as power, as possibility*, never appears as such; on the contrary her power always appears *as* an actual work. The works are traces of her power, but the power itself never comes into view as such" ("The Self as Resolution," 96). The sense of 'trace' here is equivalent to the idea of spectrality that we have found in Merleau-Ponty. That which calls for a decision or resolution into a field of presence, into an identity, has no place in that present—the motive force, the power, or possibility with which my *situation* is pregnant, necessarily remains outstanding in any actual decision. The act manifests itself as a trace, haunted by that which it cannot succeed in presenting. Russon writes: "This means that I am (will be) I only with a loss of myself. Every actual identity will thus tacitly be witness to such a loss, will be a trace of a loss, a memorial to that loss. Self-consciousness, no less than being an enactment of self-identity, will therefore always tacitly be an act of mourning" (99n.14).

29. This means that it is accomplished as *expression* (this will be our subject in chapter 5). For an account of the way in which self-consciousness must be understood to be a *result* of the articulation of a spatial situation, see Kirsten Jacobson, "The Experience of Home and the Space of Citizenship," esp. 241–2. From the Merleau-Pontian insight that self-consciousness is the *accomplishment* of a spatial situation, Jacobson develops a powerful critical reflection on a certain naïveté in the modern liberal ideal of the autonomous political subject.

30. For a survey of recent experimental research in this area, see Lewkowicz, "Development of Intersensory Perception."

31. For an account of these two theoretical models, see Bahrick and Pickens, "Amodal Relations," pp. 206–8.

32. We will examine Merleau-Ponty's concept of 'style' in chapter 3.

33. Barbaras writes: "In a certain way, the entire difficulty of a philosophy of perception resides in . . . the requirement that one conceive of an identity that does not depend on a positing, that one account for a *sensory* unity that does not differ from the diversity of which it is the unity" (*Desire and Distance*, 7). We could say that the same demand applies when it is a question of accounting for the unity of the sentient body.

34. Kermoian and Campos, "Locomotor Experience."

35. For a survey of research in this area, see Newcombe and Huttenlocher, *Making Space*, chapter 3.

36. Newcombe and Huttenlocher, *Making Space*, 40.

37. Jacobson, "A Developed Nature," 372.

38. Lingis, "Imperatives," 93.

39. Recall, in this connection, the passage cited above in which Merleau-Ponty says that the dreamer lives in a space 'peopled with phantasms' whereas in waking life we live in a world of 'realities.' But here we can see that 'reality' also *depends* upon the possibility of 'phantasms'—monocular images, intersensory conflict, dream-spaces, illusions, 'dark space,' etc. It is these possibilities that vouchsafe the appearance of a world in depth, a reality.

## CHAPTER THREE

1. Myin and O'Regan, "Perceptual Consciousness," 44.

2. O'Regan and Noë, "A Sensorimotor Account," 941, 942 (my italics, except where otherwise noted).

3. Ibid., 952 (italics in original).

4. Ibid., 941–2.

5. Ibid., 969.

6. Steinbock employs the term "coherent deformation," which Merleau-Ponty adopts from Malraux, and which repeatedly appears in the former's middle and later works (and it is significant that it originally and usually occurs in reference to painting), to account for this aspect of depth: "Depth, then, is the ineluctable process of 'open' structure-formation through coherent deformation" (Steinbock, "Merleau-Ponty's Concept of Depth," 339).

7. My criticism of the 'law' that governs the sensorimotor and ecological approaches relies heavily on David Morris's (Bergson-inspired) claims concerning the incompatibility between phenomenological description and a certain form of scientific naturalism: "the tension can be put in terms of opened and closed systems. Science is theoretically inclined to pursue a closed, completed system, namely, the universe as a totality of laws and entities that would explain everything within it. In practice, science experiments with moving systems that are in some degree open to their surround, and this is emphatically the case in biology. The theoretical and experimental imperatives of science are methodologically at odds with the open, self-organizing movement of a body crossed with the world." (Morris, *The Sense of Space*, 58).

8. In this connection, it has been shown that even saccadic eye movements are responsive to a whole host of contextual factors (Andrews and Coppola, "Idiosyncratic Characteristics of Saccadic Eye Movements"). That is, the frequency and size of the movements vary both according to the nature of visual exploratory tasks—the exploration of a visual scene, or the reading of a passage of text—and according to the repetitiveness or complexity of patterns and structures within a scene that is being viewed. It is not surprising, in terms of O'Regan and Noë's sensorimotor account of perception, that visual exploration would vary according to the features of what is being viewed. But it is significant that these variations are also task specific and idiosyncratic—that is, they rely partly on the significance of a situation as construed by an individual. It has recently been shown that these differences do indeed depend on endogenous factors. Andrews and Coppola find that context and task dependent variations are not the same from one subject to

the next: "The main result from this study is that individuals have idiosyncratic eye movements. The size and frequency of an individual's saccadic eye movements when viewing a complex natural scene covaried significantly with these same parameters in the dark or viewing simple patterns" ("Idiosyncratic Characteristics of Saccadic Eye Movements," 2951). It is thus possible that the formation of motor habits in individuals may make an important contribution to the structures of sensorimotor contingencies even at the level of involuntary eye movements.

9. Thompson, "Sensorimotor Subjectivity," 413. This two-sidedness is reflected in the distinction, made by Husserl, between the 'lived body' (*Leib*) and the 'objective body' (*Körper*). We will discuss this in more detail in subsequent chapters.

10. Ibid.

11. Ibid., 417.

12. Myin and O'Regan, "Perceptual Consciousness," 30 (also cited in Thompson, "Sensorimotor Subjectivity," 416).

13. See O'Regan and Noë, "Authors' Response," 1012.

14. Ibid., my italics.

15. Myin and O'Regan clarify this concept of subjectivity as follows: "Someone is perceptually aware of something because she is interacting with it. It is her putting all the resources she has onto whatever she is conscious of that makes her conscious of it. So, once she is conscious of it, it is 'for her'—it is her subjective project to which she is devoting all her capacities. So, consciousness is, by definition, 'for the subject'" ("Perceptual Consciousness," 39; also cited in Thompson, "Sensorimotor Subjectivity, 417).

16. O'Regan and Noë, "A Sensorimotor Account," 943.

17. Thompson, "Sensorimotor Subjectivity," 417. For an account of *autopoiesis*, self-organization, and autonomous systems, see also Varela, Thompson, and Rosch, *The Embodied Mind*, esp. chapters 5 and 8.

18. Ibid.

19. Thompson offers a helpful example of a bacterium in a food gradient of sugar: "These cells tumble about until they hit an orientation that increases their exposure to sugar, at which point they swim forward, up-gradient, toward the zone of greatest sugar concentration. This behavior happens because the bacteria are able to sense chemically the concentration of sugar in their local environment through molecular receptors in their membranes, and they are able to move forward by rotating their flagella like a propeller. These bacteria are *autopoietic* and embody a sensorimotor loop: the way they move (tumbling or swimming forward) depends on what they sense, and what they sense depends on how they move" (Ibid., 418). The important thing here is that the bacterium's motion is an activity of self-organization, which is, for this very reason, at the same time, an evaluating activity that lets sugar 'appear' to it as a certain motivation. The bacterium's 'perception' is a discriminating moved-movement.

20. Ibid., 419.

21. See, for example, Gibson's list of "ecological laws of surfaces." These are properties of surfaces understood in relation to the properties of observers (Gibson, *The Ecological Approach*, 23–4).

22. Ibid., 22.

23. Turvey, "Affordances and Prospective Control."

24. Dispositional properties are defined in the following passage: "In [prospective control], the organism is the propertied thing functioning as a frame of reference for the surrounding layout of surfaces and immersing nesting of events. Its states [i.e., its dispositional properties] (e.g., width, grip strength, wing frequency, glucogen production) are separable in significant degree from the states of surfaces. Furthermore, its states can be used to quantify the states of surfaces and events" (Ibid., 183).

25. Ibid., 174.

26. Ibid., 180.

27. Ibid., 177.

28. Turvey's ecological ontology thus makes clear that science operates on the basis of a certain notion of 'possibility.' As Morris writes: "Theoretically, science is inclined to turn actuality into possibility, to abstract phenomena from time and install them in an abstract framework of possibility in which time is simply a variable that is yet to be given a value. Empirically, science immerses itself in the movie of life; theoretically, science rolls up the movie into a program, a system of laws, that is already done in advance" (*The Sense of Space*, 69). Morris suggests that science turns actuality into possibility, whereas I have been implying that ecological psychology (like the sensorimotor approach) turns possibility into actuality. I take these to be equivalent: Morris thinks of actuality in terms of unpredictable events that open their own horizons of possibility. He insists that such events do not begin by being possible (where possibility is understood as predictable according to a law). As we shall see, Merleau-Ponty is going to think of futurity in terms of what he calls 'advent' which he will define as 'the promise of events.' This implies a different sense of possibility. For Merleau-Ponty, contra Turvey, real possibility is not identical to lawfulness but to 'advent' understood as 'promise.' I want to suggest that the subject is a relation to possibilities that cannot be anticipated, and thus it is an openness to possibility that cannot be exhausted in any actuality.

29. Gibson, *The Ecological Approach*, 123.

30. Ibid., 76.

31. Ibid., 115.

32. Butterworth, "An Ecological Perspective."

33. Neisser, "Five Kinds of Self-knowledge"

34. Ibid., 36.

35. Ibid.

36. Zahavi, *Subjectivity and Selfhood*.

37. Gallagher, *How the Body Shapes the Mind*.

38. Sheets-Johnstone, *The Primacy of Movement*.

39. Zahavi, *Subjectivity and Selfhood*, 204.

40. Ibid.

41. Gallagher, *How the Body Shapes the Mind*, 137 (my emphasis).

42. Ibid. When Gallagher says that this prereflective bodily awareness is not itself egocentric, he means that the body itself is not arrayed around a center. As we noted above, the first-personal spatial view-point is not really a point. The body has its own spatiality that is to be distinguished from the spatiality of its surround. See *PhP*, Part I, Ch. 3.

43. O'Regan and Noë, "A Sensorimotor Approach," 943.

44. Ibid., 965.

45. Thompson, "Sensorimotor Subjectivity," 421.

46. Ibid.

47. Ibid.

48. Ibid.

49. Linda Singer writes, concerning style: "A personal style is never simply given or simply chosen. It is a response to and founded upon the conditions of existence and embodiment. It constitutes the establishment of a lived coherence which gathers the elements of existence into a life, a project with direction and character. Style ensures my existence of a stability, while allowing for the possibility of growth and change" ("Merleau-Ponty on the Concept of Style," 161). The unity of our bodies is comparable to that of works of art because our bodies, as the grounds of our identities, are unities of style, enactments of ourselves that are neither simply given nor chosen.

50. The idea of an "expressive teleology" is discussed in Barbaras, *The Being of the Phenomenon*, pp. 60–67. Barbaras writes that, unlike a teleology of consciousness, the infinity of a striving toward an objectivity posited in advance, this teleology responds to the infinite as such: "Then, to the infinity of the *telos* brought to light in the expressive act, there *corresponds the infinity of an* archē. Insofar as it is the soil of the expressive movement, the world will have this infinite depth inherent in the fact that sense is never completely fulfilled. Because no expression erases itself in the face of a pure sense, because no expression can claim to be nailed down in a full meaning, the world will be given only as withdrawal, as this presence which, through its obscurity, gives birth to expression without ever being absorbed into the expressed. Considered on the basis of expression, the world can no longer be defined through presence but as that whose being consists in exceeding every presentation. When it becomes the philosophy of expression, the phenomenology of perception is fulfilled as ontology" (60). While I share the view that the phenomenology of perception is only fulfilled in an ontology of expression, I want to show that this ontology is already richly foreshadowed in *Phenomenology of Perception*, especially in the whole thematics of sensation and the being of the sensible. And the sense of this teleology of expression is evident in Merleau-Ponty's repeated appeal to painting when it is a matter of demonstrating the limits of objectivist intellectualism and empirical psychology.

## CHAPTER FOUR

1. Nancy J. Holland recounts an exchange with Jacques Derrida in which he reportedly agrees with her concerning the meaning of this passage, and of the "Temporality" chapter in general: "Several years ago, Jacques Derrida visited a class I was taking on the philosophy of Merleau-Ponty. When the instructor, Bert Dreyfus, asked him if Merleau-Ponty's work would fall within the metaphysics of presence, Derrida said that it would. Pressed for some justification of this claim, Derrida referred to the chapter on time in *The Phenomenology of Perception*" ("Merleau-Ponty

on Presence," 111). According to her report of this encounter, she then cited, in Derrida's presence, the passage quoted above and "this actually turned out to be the passage Derrida had in mind." Later in her paper, in which she seeks to show that the picture of Merleau-Ponty as a metaphysician of presence may not be quite accurate, she offers another interpretation of this passage: "We see here that the present moment, like the perceptual object, has horizons, that it appears as a figure on a background of the past and future moments which surround it. For this reason, the present moment also cannot be fully present because, like the perceptual object, it will always give us the non-posited horizons of its appearance" (116). It seems to me that this interpretation does not answer the charge. First of all, Merleau-Ponty does not speak of the present's having *non-posited* horizons, because the present is generally not itself posited: "the present, in the narrow sense, is not posited" [*PhP*, 416]). The privilege of the present here is not obviously a privilege accorded to the present only of a *reflective* consciousness—although it may turn out to be based on the possibility of reflection, this would have to be shown to be the case. Further, as we have been arguing, any privilege afforded to the present rests upon the claim that the present (as the arena of the 'I can') lays down the 'essential structures' according to which the absent, or non-present (which remains unthematic and indeterminate), can be determined. To say that non-presence is in the background of the present is not to contest the latter's privilege—it is in fact precisely to affirm it. Rather, if we are going to respond to the 'metaphysics of presence' charge, we would have to show that non-presence is *in* the present, and that the present is *dependent* on non-presence, rather than the reverse. This non-presence would have to be shown to have no 'place' in reference to the present. This is what we have been arguing on the basis of Merleau-Ponty's notion of an original past. John F. Bannan also argues that the "Temporality" chapter is an assertion of the primacy of presence—though, writing before 1967, he does not engage with the question of a '*metaphysics* of presence' (*The Philosophy of Merleau-Ponty*; see esp. 125–133). I will argue that we must be careful about the way in which we interpret Merleau-Ponty's claims about the privilege of presence, to grasp the precise nature and limits of this privilege.

    2. Husserl, *Time*, 79.

    3. Derrida, *On Touching*, 180.

    4. See Husserl's *Phenomenology of the Consciousness of Internal Time*, §17: "Perception . . . is the act that places something before our eyes as the thing itself, the act *originally constitutes* the object. Its opposite is *re-presentation* [*Vergegenwärtigung, Re-Präsentation*], understood as the act that does not place an object itself before our eyes but just *re-presents* it; that places it before our eyes in image, as it were, although not exactly in the manner of a genuine image-consciousness" (43). The wider discussion of retentional modifications is carried out over §§10–17.

    5. In fact it is precisely this immediate *self*-manifestation of the appearance that defines the present. The present is thus not defined by any duration of time in the mundane sense, though some have attempted to specify, by combining phenomenology and evidence from neuroscience, the duration of the living present. See Varela, "Present-time Consciousness."

    6. Though Husserl does not carry out this analysis with respect to the anticipation of distantly futural events, the same logic would presumably hold. To

anticipate a future experience (beyond the field of my 'present' experience), I would be experiencing, not the presence of things and events, but a future experience of them. Thus the things or events would only appear to me as re-presentations.

7. Merleau-Ponty's use of *je compte* here suggests a connection to Heidegger's *rechnen mit*, a formula that the latter uses repeatedly in *Being and Time*, in connection with 'use' and 'making use' of something, including time, in terms of a pre-theoretical understanding : "In using time, Dasein reckons with it. Time is first discovered in the concern which reckons circumspectively, and this concern leads to the development of a time-reckoning. Reckoning with time is constitutive for Being-in-the-world. Concernful circumspective reckoning, in reckoning with its time, permits those things which we have discovered, and which are ready-to-hand or present-at-hand, to be encountered in time" (Heidegger, *Being and Time*, 382). Heidegger's notion of reckoning-with here suggests a response to the availability and solicitation of things, a response that would also be a making-present (a time-reckoning). Thus, the present, for Heidegger, is not simply a given *form* of experience, but the function of a responsive activity that does not *begin* from, or is not grounded in, a presence-to-self. I want to suggest that this sense of a 'making-present' (rather than simply 'presence' as such) is retained in Merleau-Ponty's sentence: 'I do not so much perceive objects as reckon with an environment.'

8. It should be noted that Husserl himself subsequently also comes to this position. Thus, for example in the lectures on passive synthesis he says that the "living present" has a "temporal shape," that it combines a "temporal form and the form of a local field" (Husserl, *Active and Passive Synthesis*, 189, 208)

9. See Heidegger *Being and Time*, §65.

10. Ibid., 380.

11. Ibid., 345.

12. Ibid., 167.

13. Merleau-Ponty describes time as a "transition synthesis" (*Übergangssynthesis*), a Husserlian term that he uses repeatedly, in a number of different contexts in *Phenomenology of Perception*. He contrasts it with a synthesis that would add contents together. Like living movement, a transition synthesis establishes a new sense by means of an articulation and transformation from within.

14. Which, in addition to the passages from Husserl's manuscripts on 'absolute consciousness,' is a major source for the discussion of auto-affection in the "Temporality" chapter.

15. Heidegger, *Kant and the Problem of Metaphysics*, 132.

16. Sheets-Johnstone interprets Husserl's account of 'absolute subjectivity' in terms of living movement (*The Primacy of Movement*, 148).

17. See Husserl's discussions of the concept of "intentionality," in *Logical Investigations*, Vol. 1, §§ 9–10, and *Ideas I*, §§ 36, 84. Consciousness, as we have indicated, is not, in Husserl's view, always intentional in the sense of being explicitly directed toward an object, but the possibility of being so directed, belongs to it essentially (see *Ideas I*, 199).

18. See Husserl, *Ideas I*, § 88.

19. As Husserl writes: "The essence of meaning is seen by us, not in the meaning-conferring experience, but in its 'content,' the single, self-identical intentional unity set over against the dispersed multiplicity of actual and possible experiences of speakers and thinkers" (*Logical Investigations*, Vol.1, 228).

20. Husserl, *Ideas I*, 199.

21. Ibid., 9: "Of whatever sort intuition of something individual may be, whether it be adequate or inadequate, it can take the turn into seeing an essence; and this seeing, whether it be correspondingly adequate or correspondingly inadequate, has the character of a *presentive* act."

22. Derrida, *Speech and Phenomena*, 15.

23. Ibid., 6.

24. Derrida is here interpreting chapter 1 ("Essential Distinctions") of the first of Husserl's *Logical Investigations* ("Expression and Meaning").

25. The German captures the relation of meaning and meaning to say: *Bedeuten* names the act of meaning and *Bedeutung* names the meaning content.

26. Derrida, *Speech and Phenomena*, 22.

27. Ibid.

28. Ibid., 10.

29. Let us note, at this point, that this makes a Merleau-Pontyian account of the 'primacy of movement' differ from that of Maxine Sheets-Johnstone. She argues that the sense of self is primarily established on the basis of what she calls an "*internally* structured corporeal consciousness" that relies on kinesthesis and proprioception in movement (*The Primacy of Movement*, 74). That is, the sense of self relies on "a direct sensitivity to movement through internally mediated systems of corporeal awareness" (72). We feel our own movement (56). She defines proprioception, then, as "*surface recognition sensitivity*" (67). Thus, for Sheets-Johnstone, auto-affection is an internal dynamic in an organism who feels its own movement and thus is always aware of itself and its surfaces on the basis of a kind of kinesthetic-proprioceptive integrity of the body. She thus asks: "Is not tactile-kinesthetic introspection—attentive reflections upon our tactile kinesthetic lives—the pivotal and critical ontological and epistemological source of our being no strangers to ourselves?" (297). For Merleau-Ponty, on the other hand, it is precisely by means of exteriority, by means of surfaces, that the body is in contact with itself—which is to say that this contact is not internally structured, but precisely a matter of self-externalizing in movement.

30. Husserl, *Ideas II*, 159 (also cited in Derrida, *On Touching*, 161).

31. Derrida, *On Touching*, 168.

32. Husserl, *Ideas II*, 158–9.

33. Ibid., 171.

34. Ibid., 172.

35. Ibid., 157.

36. Ibid.; also cited in Derrida, *On Touching*, 174.

37. Derrida, *On Touching*, 175–6.

38. Husserl, *Ideas II*, 174 (cited in Derrida, *On Touching*, 178).

39. The italics and notes referring to Husserl's text, which do not appear in Merleau-Ponty's text, are here retained from the translation of Derrida's text. The page references to *Ideas II* are to the English translation.

40. The "it," which appears in the English translation of Merleau-Ponty, and accurately reflects the French original, but which is omitted in the English translation of Derrida, has been inserted here.

41. Cited in Derrida, *On Touching*, 190.

42. Ibid., 191.

43. Ibid., 190.

44. Husserl, *Ideas II*, 175 (cited in Derrida, *On Touching*, 190).

45. Derrida, *On Touching*, 190.

46. Ibid., 191.

47. Ibid.

48. Levinas, "Intersubjectivity," 58–9.

49. This concern is also implicit in Derrida's reading, as is suggested by the words "It is necessary to watch over the other's alterity."

50. Levinas, "Intersubjectivity," 59.

51. This phrase occurs repeatedly in Derrida's writings (e.g. *On Touching*, 195).

52. Also cited in Derrida, *On Touching*, 193.

53. Ibid.: "This 'confusion' would be as originary as the 'primordial thing' and would make possible the substitutions (that we have noted are impossible) between the other and me, between our two bodies, in what Merleau-Ponty unhesitatingly terms 'the absolute presence of origins.'"

54. Ibid.

55. Ibid., 191.

56. Recall, in this connection, the passages we cited earlier from *Phenomenology of Perception*: "I can *identify* the hand touched as the same one which will in a moment be touching," "I can *anticipate* for an instant the integument or incarnation of that other right hand," etc. (*PhP*, 93/109).

57. Dillon, *Merleau-Ponty's Ontology*, 117.

58. Ibid., 122.

59. Ibid., 117.

60. Ibid., 105.

61. Ibid., 111.

62. Ibid., 124 (my italics).

63. The problem is not helped by the fact that Colin Smith translates Merleau-Ponty's "*schéma corporel*" as "body image." See Gallagher, *How the Body Shapes the Mind*, 20.

64. Gallagher, *How the Body Shapes the Mind*, 24. The claim that the body schema works best when perception is directed toward something other than one's own body can be demonstrated phenomenologically by considering the fluidity and competence of the body in the performance of tasks for which one has already acquired a certain mastery, and that generally do not involve explicit self-monitoring (e.g., walking, dancing, playing a musical instrument). This fluidity can be contrasted with the notable lack of fluidity in these performances when carried out while attentively monitoring one's own body in the course of the performance. The point can also be demonstrated by observing pathologies involving the loss of proprioception. In this connection, Gallagher offers an account of the case of Ian Waterman. Waterman suffered neurological damage that destroyed his tactual sensitivity from the neck down. As a result of this damage he lost his capacity for somatic proprioception and for intermodal perceptual integration. Waterman's case affords the opportunity to study movement and bodily awareness in one whose body schema is severely damaged. Waterman's movements require constant visual monitoring because he would otherwise have no idea where his limbs were, nor would he otherwise know of his bodily attitude and posture. For Waterman it is necessary not only to consciously observe

his own movements, but actually to plan his movements, and to consciously re-adjust his planned movements to their intended goals. On the basis of his analyses of the resultant impairments to normal movement, Gallagher argues that our movements are generally "pre-noetic" performances—"Conscious experience is normally, in this regard, out ahead of movement, directed at the environment; it does not have to hang back to make sure my body is moving in the right direction" (64). See Gallagher, *How the Body Shapes the Mind*, chapter 2, "The Case of the Missing Schema."

65. This term is inspired by John Russon's use of the notions of "figure" and "figured contact" in *Human Experience*. The term captures the sense of 'form' (which Merleau-Ponty uses in speaking of the body schema), but I think it also captures the sense of the dynamic and sketchy, or tentative, character of form-in-motion.

66. Gallagher uses the term "absently available" to designate this peculiar mode of appearance of the lived body ("Lived Body and Environment") 153.

67. Rochat, *The Infant's World*, 50–55. The traditional view, advocated by Piaget, was that this activity was random and disorganized in infants until about the age of two months.

68. The development of the body schema, then, likely begins in fetal development. See Gallagher, *How the Body Shapes the Mind*.

69. Rochat, *The Infant's World*, 52.

70. Gallagher, "Lived Body and Environment," 155.

71. Ibid., 154.

72. As Gallagher writes, "The absently available performance of the lived body is prior to any subject-object distinction. In this performance no distinction between the lived body and the environment can be made. The proximity, this lack of distinction can be termed the 'lived body-environment.' This concept signifies that the environment is lived to the same extent, and in so far as, the body is lived. Here there is neither intermediary nor 'distance'" (Ibid., 162). While the idea that the lived body and the environment form one circuit is consistent with Merleau-Ponty's position, the claim that this implies no distance or intermediary seems unwarranted. On the contrary, this claim seems to me to imply that the identities of bodies and environments are precisely mediated by each other.

73. Zahavi, *Self-Awareness and Alterity*, 240n.24.

74. Ibid., 143.

75. Ibid., 143–4.

76. For Zahavi, this position would be unacceptable. He approves of Husserl's position that consciousness must be conscious in each of its phases: "Husserl explicitly insists that the *retentional* modification presupposes an *impressional* (primary, original, and immediate) self-manifestation, not only because consciousness is as such self-given, but also because a retention of an unconscious content is impossible. The retention retains what has just appeared, and if nothing appears, there is nothing to retain" (Ibid., 86). But the position that I have proposed does not involve the claim that consciousness only becomes conscious retroactively. If the subjectivity of perception is to be sought in living movement then its manifestation takes place across its phases, as the manifestation of an immanent *sens*.

The idea that the subjectivity of perception is accomplished in expressive movement also seems to me to be at the heart of Kym Maclaren's challenge to Zahavi in "Embodied Perceptions of Others as a Condition of Selfhood?" Zahavi's claim about the first-personal givenness of experience has led him to reject the thesis of "syncretic sociability" proposed by Jean Piaget and endorsed by Merleau-Ponty. According to this notion, infants pass through a developmental stage in which they lack a clear sense of the difference between self and other. According to Zahavi (as well as Philippe Rochat, Ulric Neisser, Shaun Gallagher, and others) this notion is untenable—self-consciousness, they argue, is subtended by first-personal givenness which is an original structural feature of consciousness. Zahavi also rejects, on the same grounds, the Merleau-Pontyan thesis that sensation represents a stratum of anonymity in our experience. Against Zahavi's view, Maclaren demonstrates that a 'relative indeterminacy' is itself a structural feature of experience and she compellingly demonstrates that this accounts for observed phenomena in infant behavior.

77. Nancy, *Corpus*, 75 (cited in Derrida, *On Touching*, 185).

78. "*C'est cet avénement ou encore cet événement transcendental.*" (*PhP*, 407/466)


CHAPTER FIVE


1. Barbaras, *The Being of the Phenomenon*, 14.

2. Cited in Vallier, "Institution," 284.

3. Ibid., 285. I have modified the format of the reference to Merleau-Ponty's text to accord with our own reference format.

4. Barbaras discusses this problem in *The Being of the Phenomenon*; see esp. chapter 4.

5. Barbaras, The Being of the Phenomenon, 44.

6. Ibid., 43–4.

7. Ibid., 14–5.

8. Waldenfels, "The Paradox of Expression," 89.

9. Ibid., 91.

10. Ibid., 92. This problem is similar to the one highlighted by Lawlor ("The End of Phenomenology"). He poses a two-fold challenge (inspired by Deleuze) to Merleau-Ponty's account of expression—the challenge of immanence and the challenge of difference. If phenomenology is to overcome subjectivism, it must offer an account of expression in which what is expressed is different from the expression, but does not exist outside of the expression. Expression is thus the plane of immanence to which no transcendence would be opposed.

11. Merleau-Ponty is here speaking of 'authentic speech,' a creative speech-act in which something is said for the first time, thus inaugurating a new order of sense. As we noted in chapter 3, in connection with our discussion of the different ways in which movement can be said to 'make sense,' this is to be contrasted with "second-order expression" in which already available meanings are, as it were, re-deployed. Thus second-order expression can be thought of as the set of conventional meanings making up a language (see *PhP*, 178n.1/207n.2).

12. James Edie relates Merleau-Ponty's notion of 'silence,' which emerges in the context of his appropriation of structuralism, to the development of his later ontology. See *Merleau-Ponty's Philosophy of Language*, 49–51.

13. This simultaneous inscription and resistance to enclosure is implied in Jean Luc-Nancy's neologism "exscription." For a discussion of this notion in Nancy,

in connection with Merleau-Ponty's account of expression, see Don Landes, "Expressive Body, Exscriptive Corpus."

14. For a very illuminating discussion of the concept of institution based on Merleau-Ponty's 1954 lecture course on that topic, see Robert Vallier, "Institution."

15. See Rosenthal and Bourgeois (*Mead and Merleau-Ponty*) for a discussion of the similarities between these two thinkers. Most important for our purposes is this claim concerning Mead's account of the emergence of meaning: "Meaning, for Mead, is neither subjective nor psychological. . . . Meaning is an emergent which arises out of a behavioral context and has a relational existence which is dependent upon this context but is not reducible to it" (35).

16. Mead, *Mind, Self, and Society*, 69n.7.

17. Ibid.

18. "Any society, to be a society even on a minimal level, must be made up of biological organisms participating in a social act, using the early stages of each other's actions as guides to the completion of the act" (Rosenthal and Bourgeois, *Mead and Merleau-Ponty*, 87).

19. As we have seen, Merleau-Ponty says that the unity of the body is achieved as the unity of expressive movement. But what Mead's account highlights is the fact that the unity which could subtend a consciousness must be a movement that is, as it were, interrupted by another's movement.

20. Expression thus stylizes movement in a manner that allows it to be detached from immediate contexts. Adam Kendon has called this the "quotable" character of gestures ("Language and Gesture: Unity or Duality"). David McNeill and Susan Duncan ("Growth Points") have described gestures as "material carriers of thinking," and that meaning is embodied in bodies that can detach themselves from contexts—this then would be the meaning of stylization: "The development of an individual child in this view is, in part, a process of establishing semiotic distance between movement and the expressive qualities it can have" (155).

21. Mead, *Mind, Self, and Society*, 69n.7. Thus Mead is concerned with the passage from 'unconscious' to 'conscious' expression. For Merleau-Ponty, all living movement is expressive, and as we have seen, the living body is an expressive unity. The question for Merleau-Ponty is thus how this expressive unity subtends explicit self-consciousness. But, like Mead, he thinks that this development presupposes a conversation of gestures that links bodies into one 'intercorporeity.' For a discussion of the inherent expressivity of living movement, see Maclaren, "Life is Inherently Expressive." For a discussion of the development of explicit self-consciousness on the basis of bodily life and within the context of a broader account of Merleau-Ponty's philosophy of nature, see Russon, "Embodiment and Responsibility."

22. For a description of the way in which others' recognition of the significance of our own behaviors conditions our own self-recognition, see Maclaren, "Embodied Perceptions of Others as a Condition of Selfhood?," esp. 82–3.

23. Morris, "What is Living and What is Non-Living," 229.

24. Kendon, *Gesture*, 309.

25. Ibid.

26. McNeill and Duncan, "Growth Points," 144.

27. Ibid., 146.

28. Ibid., 154.

29. As Sue Rechter says, concerning Merleau-Ponty's theory of language: "Strictly speaking, while there are differentiations and degrees of articulation, there is no hierarchy among structures of pre-signification and signification, no 'passage' to higher significations, only a symbolics which is simultaneous with perception. In this sense, all modes of articulation of the world are co-original" ("The Originating Breaks Up," 38).

30. Thus, among what Waldenfels terms the "operative concepts" in Merleau-Ponty's account of expression is "après coup," or "delayed effect." See Waldenfels, "The Paradox of Expression," 96.

31. Having said this, I also do not want to succumb to the temptation to overstate the difference between this later thinking and the account of subjectivity that we find in *Phenomenology of Perception*. Rudolf Bernet, in the conclusion to his insightful study of subjectivity in that work says: "Arising out of things within a common world and affirming its identity through its difference from things, the human subject is at once itself and another, one and manifold, present and absent, visible and invisible. Within the universal intersubjectivity or 'intercorporeity' of the world, the subject is that singularity by which the world is articulated as an open system of diacritical differences. This advent of difference is as an earthquake, the shock of which propagates itself through the totality of the world; every thing is shaken by it, even the subject that has brought forward the wave of universal vibration that traverses the symbolic system of the flesh of the world" ("The Subject in Nature," 67).

32. For discussions of responsibility in connection with Merleau-Ponty's notion of expression, see Waldenfels, "The Paradox of Expression," esp. 97–100, and Russon, "Embodiment and responsibility," esp. 299–304. For a discussion of the ethical implications of Merleau-Ponty's philosophy of expression and the singularity of the expressive body, see Alia Al-Saji, "Vision, Mirror and Expression."

## CONCLUSION

1. Maldiney, "Flesh and Verb," 53.
2. Lingis, "Imperatives," 95.
3. Ibid., 97.
4. Ibid., 98–9.
5. Ibid., 99.
6. Dreyfus, "Intelligence Without Representation."
7. Lingis, "Imperatives," 114.
8. Ibid., 115.
9. Ibid., 113–5.
10. Ibid., 103.
11. Levin, "A Responsive Voice," 70.
12. Rehmann-Sutter, "Poiesis and Praxis, 314.
13. For a survey of some of these findings, see Keller, *The Century of the Gene.*
14. Rehmann-Sutter, "Poiesis and Praxis," 314.
15. Ibid., 331.

# BIBLIOGRAPHY

Al-Saji, Alia. "Vision, Mirror and Expression: The Genesis of the Ethical Body in Merleau-Ponty's Later Works." In *Interrogating Ethics: Embodying the Good in Merleau-Ponty*, edited by James Hatley, Janice McLane, and Christian Diehm. Pittsburgh: Duquesne University Press, 2006.

Augustine. *Confessions*. Translated by F.J. Sheed. Indianapolis: Hackett Publishing, 1993.

Andrews, Timothy J., and David M. Coppola. "Idiosyncratic characteristics of saccadic eye movements when viewing different visual environments." *Vision Research* 39 (1999): 2947–2953.

Armstrong, David F., William C. Stokoe, and Sherman E. Wilcox. *Gesture and the Nature of Language*. Cambridge, UK: Cambridge University Press, 1995.

Bahrick, Lorraine, and Jeffrey N. Pickens. "Amodal Relations: The Basis for Intermodal Perception and Learning in Infancy." In *The Development of Intersensory Perception: Comparative Perspectives*, edited by David J. Lewkowicz and Robert Lickliter. Hillsdale, NJ: Lawrence Erlbaum Associates, 1994.

Bannan, John F. *The Philosophy of Merleau-Ponty*. New York: Harcourt, Brace and World, 1967.

Barbaras, Renaud. *The Being of the Phenomenon: Merleau-Ponty's Ontology*. Translated by Ted Toadvine and Leonard Lawlor. Bloomington: Indiana University Press, 2004.

———. *Desire and Distance: Introduction to a Phenomenology of Perception*. Translated by Paul B. Milan. Stanford: Stanford University Press, 2006.

———. "Life, Movement, and Desire." *Research in Phenomenology* 38 (2008): 3–17.

———. "Merleau-Ponty and Nature." *Research in Phenomenology* 31 (2001): 22–38.

Bernet, Rudolf. "The Subject in Nature: Reflections on Merleau-Ponty's *Phenomenology of Perception*." In *Merleau-Ponty in Contemporary Perspective*, edited by P. Burke and J Van der Veken. Dordrecht: Kluwer Academic Publishers, 1993.

———. "The Traumatized Subject." *Research in Phenomenology* 30 (2000): 160–179.

Birdwhistell, Ray L. *Kinesics and Context: Essays on Body Motion Communication*. Philadelphia: University of Philadelphia Press, 1970.

Butterworth, George. "An Ecological Perspective on the Origins of the Self." In *The Body and the Self*, edited by José Luis Bermudez, Anthony Marcel, and Naomi Eilan. Cambridge, MA: MIT Press, 1995.

Carbone, Mauro. *The Thinking of the Sensible: Merleau-Ponty's A-Philosophy*. Evanston: Northwestern University Press, 2004.

Casey, Edward S. " 'The Element of Voluminousness': Depth and Place Reexamined." In *Merleau-Ponty Vivant*, edited by M.C. Dillon. Albany: SUNY Press, 1991.

————. *The Fate of Place: A Philosophical History.* Berkeley: University of California Press, 1997.

Calbris, Genevieve. *The Semiotics of French Gestures.* Translated by Owen Doyle. Bloomington: Indiana University Press, 1990.

Chalmers, David. *The Conscious Mind: In Search of a Fundamental Theory.* Oxford: Oxford University Press, 1996.

Clark, Andy. *Being There: Putting Brain, Body, and World Together Again.* Cambridge, MA: MIT Press, 1987.

Costello, Peter. *Layers in Husserl's Phenomenology: On Meaning and Intersubjectivity.* Toronto: University of Toronto Press (forthcoming).

Cutting, James E., and Peter M. Vishton. "Perceiving Layout and Knowing Distances: The Integration, Relative Potency, and Contextual Use of Different Information about Depth." In *Perception of Space and Motion* (2nd ed.), edited by Edward C. Carterette and Morton P. Friedman. San Diego: Academic Press, 1995.

Damasio, Antonio R. *The Feeling of What Happens: Body and Emotion in the Making of Consciousness.* New York: Harcourt Brace and Co., 1999.

Darwin, Charles. *The Expression of the Emotions in Man and Animals.* Oxford: Oxford University Press, 1998 (1872).

Dastur, Francoise. "World, Flesh, Vision." In *Chiasms: Merleau-Ponty's Notion of Flesh,* edited by Fred Evans and Leonard Lawlor. Albany: SUNY Press, 2000.

De Jorio, Andrea. *Gesture in Naples and Gesture in Classical Antiquity.* Translated by Adam Kendon. Bloomington: Indiana University Press, 2000 (1832).

Dennett, Daniel C. *Consciousness Explained.* Boston: Little, Brown, 1991.

Dennett, Daniel C., and Douglas R. Hofstadter, eds. *The Mind's I: Fantasies and Reflections on Self and Soul.* New York: Basic Books, 1981.

Derrida, Jacques. *On Touching—Jean-Luc Nancy.* Translated by Christine Irizarry. Stanford: Stanford University Press, 2005.

————. *Speech and Phenomena and Other Essays on Husserl's Theory of Signs.* Translated by David B. Allison. Evanston: Northwestern University Press, 1973.

Descartes, Rene. *Discourse on Method and the Meditations.* Translated by F.E. Sutcliffe. London, UK: Penguin Books, 1968.

Dillon, M.C. *Merleau-Ponty's Ontology.* Bloomington: Indiana University Press, 1988.

————. "The Unconscious: Language and World." In *Merleau-Ponty in Contemporary Perspective,* edited by P. Burke and J. Van der Veken. The Hague: Kluwer, 1993.

Ditchburn, R.W. *Eye-Movements and Visual Perception.* Oxford: Clarendon Press, 1973.

Dreyfus, Hubert L. "Intelligence Without Representation: Merleau-Ponty's Critique of Mental Representation." *Phenomenology and Cognitive Science* 1 (2002): 367–383.

Edie, James M. *Merleau-Ponty's Philosophy of Language: Structuralism and Dialectics.* Lanham, MD: The Center for Advanced Research in Phenomenology and University Press of America, 1987.

Efron, David. *Gesture, Race and Culture.* The Hague: Mouton, 1972.

Gallagher, Shaun. *How the Body Shapes the Mind.* Oxford: Clarendon Press, 2005.

————. "Lived Body and Environment." *Research in Phenomenology* 16 (1986): 139–170.

Gallagher, Shaun, and Anthony Marcel. "The Self in Contextualized Action." *Journal of Consciousness Studies* 6 (1999): 4–30.

Gibson, J. J. *The Ecological Approach to Visual Perception*. Boston: Houghton Mifflin Co., 1979.

Gillam, Barbara. "The Perception of Spatial Layout from Static Optical Information." In *Perception of Space and Motion* (2nd ed.), edited by Edward C. Carterette and Morton P. Friedman. San Diego: Academic Press, 1995.

Gurwitsch, Aron. *Studies in Phenomenology and Psychology*. Evanston: Northwestern University Press, 1966.

Hass, Lawrence. *Merleau-Ponty's Philosophy*. Bloomington: Indiana University Press, 2008.

Head, Henry. *Aphasia and Kindred Disorders of Speech*. Vol. 1. Cambridge, UK: Cambridge University Press, 1926.

Heidegger, Martin. *Being and Time*. Translated by John Macquarrie and Edward Robinson. New York: Harper Collins, 1962.

———. *The Basic Problems of Phenomenology*. Translated by Alfred Hofstadter. Bloomington: Indiana University Press, 1982.

———. *Kant and the Problem of Metaphysics*. Translated by Richard Taft. Bloomington: Indiana University Press, 1997.

Holland, Nancy J. "Merleau-Ponty on Presence: A Derridian Reading." *Research in Phenomenology* 16 (1986): 111–120.

Husserl, Edmund. *The Crisis of European Sciences and Transcendental Phenomenology*. Translated by David Carr. Evanston: Northwestern University Press, 1970.

———. *Analyses Concerning Passive and Active Syntheses: Lectures on Transcendental Logic*. Translated by Anthony Steinbock. Dordrecht: Kluwer Academic Publishers, 2001.

———. *Ideas Pertaining to a Pure Phenomenology and to a Phenomenological Philosophy, First Book*. Translated by F. Kersten. The Hague: Kluwer Academic Publishers, 1982.

———. *Ideas Pertaining to a Pure Phenomenology and to a Phenomenological Philosophy, Second Book*. Translated by R. Rojcewicz and A. Schuwer. Dordrecht: Kluwer Academic Publishers, 1989.

———. *Logical Investigations*. Vol. 1. Translated by J.N. Findlay. New York: Routledge, 2001.

———. *On the Phenomenology of the Consciousness of Internal Time 1893–1917*. Translated by J. Brough. Dordrecht: Kluwer Academic Publishers, 1991.

Jacobson, Kirsten. "Embodied Domestics, Embodied Politics: Women, Home, and Agoraphobia." *Human Studies* 34 (2011): 1–21.

———. "The Experience of Home and the Space of Citizenship." *The Southern Journal of Philosophy* 48 (2010): 219–245.

———. "A Developed Nature: A Phenomenological Account of the Experience of Home." *Continental Philosophy Review* 42 (2009): 355–373.

———. "Agoraphobia and Hypochondria as Disorders of Dwelling." *International Studies in Philosophy* 36 (2004): 31–44.

Jeannerod, Marc. "Consciousness of Action and Self-Consciousness: A Cognitive Neuroscience Approach." In *Agency and Self Awareness: Issues in Philosophy and Psychology*, edited by Johannes Roessler and Naomi Eilan. Oxford: Clarendon Press, 2003.

Keller, Evelyn Fox. *The Century of the Gene*. Cambridge, MA: Harvard University Press, 2000.

Kermoian, Rosanne, and Joseph J. Campos. "Locomotor Experience: A Facilitator of Spatial Cognitive Development." *Child Development* 59 (1988): 908–917.

Kendon, Adam. *Gesture: Visible Action as Utterance*. Cambridge, UK: Cambridge University Press, 2004.

———. "Language and gesture: unity or duality?" In *Language and Gesture*, edited by David McNeill. Cambridge, UK: Cambridge University Press, 2000.

Kristeva, Julia. *Language the Unknown: An Initiation into Linguistics*. Translated by Anne M. Menke. New York: Columbia University Press, 1989.

Lakoff, George, and Mark Johnson. *Philosophy in the Flesh: The Embodied Mind and Its Challenge to Western Thought*. New York: Basic Books, 1999.

Lampert, Jay. *Synthesis and Backward Reference in Husserl's Logical Investigations*. Dordrecht: Kluwer Academic Publishers, 1995.

Landes, Donald A. "Expressive Body, Exscriptive Corpus: The Tracing of the Body from Maurice Merleau-Ponty to Jean-Luc Nancy." *Chiasmi International* 9 (2008): 237–257.

Lawlor, Leonard. *Derrida and Husserl: The Basic Problem of Phenomenology*. Bloomington: Indiana University Press, 2002.

Lawlor, Leonard. "The end of phenomenology: expressionism in Deleuze and Merleau-Ponty." *Continental Philosophy Review* 31 (1998): 15–34.

Legrand, Dorothée. "How not to find the neural signature of self-consciousness." *Consciousness and Cognition* 12 (2003): 544–546.

Lefort, Claude. "Flesh and Otherness." In *Ontology and Alterity in Merleau-Ponty*, edited by Galen Johnson and Michael B. Smith. Evanston: Northwestern University Press, 1990.

Levin, David Michael. "A Responsive Voice: Language Without the Modern Subject." *Chiasmi International* 1 (1999): 65–103.

Levinas, Emmanuel. "Intersubjectivity: Notes on Merleau-Ponty" and "Sensibility." Translated by Michael B. Smith. In *Ontology and Alterity in Merleau-Ponty*, edited by Galen A. Johnson and Michael B. Smith. Evanston: Northwestern University Press, 1990.

Lewkowicz, David J. "Development of Intersensory Perception in Human Infants." In *The Development of Intersensory Perception: Comparative Perspectives*, edited by David J. Lewkowicz and Robert Lickliter. Hillsdale, NJ: Lawrence Erlbaum Associates, 1994.

Lewontin, Richard C. *Biology as Ideology: The Doctrine of DNA*. Toronto: House of Anansi Press, 1991.

Lingis, Alphonso. "Imperatives." In *Merleau-Ponty Vivant*, edited by M.C. Dillon. Albany, NY: State University of New York Press, 1991.

Maclaren, Kym. "Embodied Perceptions of Others as a Condition of Selfhood? Empirical and Phenomenological Considerations." *Journal of Consciousness Studies* 15 (2008): 63–93.

———. "Emotional Disorder and the Mind-Body Problem: A Case Study of Alexithymia." *Chiasmi International* 8 (2006): 139–155.

————. "Life is Inherently Expressive. A Merleau-Pontian Response to Darwin's *The Expression of the Emotions in Man and Animals.*" *Chiasmi International* 7 (2005): 241–62.

Madison, Gary Brent. "Flesh as Otherness." In *Ontology and Alterity in Merleau-Ponty,* edited by Galen A. Johnson and Michael B. Smith. Evanston: Northwestern University Press, 1990.

Maldiney, Henri. "Flesh and Verb in the Philosophy of Merleau-Ponty." In *Chiasms: Merleau-Ponty's Notion of Flesh,* edited by Fred Evans and Leonard Lawlor. Albany, NY: State University of New York Press, 2000.

Marcel, Antony. "The Sense of Agency: Awareness and Ownership of Action." In *Agency and Self-Awareness: Issues in Philosophy and Psychology,* edited by Johannes Roessler and Naomi Eilan. Oxford: Clarendon Press, 2003.

Mauss, Marcel. *Sociology and Psychology Essays.* Translated by Ben Brewster. London: Routledge and Kegan Paul, 1979.

McClamrock, Ron. *Existential Cognition: Computational Minds in the World.* Chicago: University of Chicago Press, 1995.

McNeill, David. *Hand and Mind: What Gestures Reveal About Thought.* Chicago: University of Chicago Press, 1992.

McNeill, David, and Susan Duncan. "Growth points in thinking-for-speaking." In *Language and Gesture,* edited by David McNeill. Cambridge, UK: Cambridge University Press, 2000.

Mead, George Herbert. *Mind, Self and Society.* Chicago: University of Chicago Press, 1934.

Merleau-Ponty, Maurice. *Nature: Course Notes from the Collége de France.* Translated by Robert Vallier. Evanston, IL: Northwestern University Press, 2003. (*La nature: notes, cours du Collége de France.* Établi et annoté par Dominique Séglard. Paris: Seuil, 1995.)

————. "Eye and Mind." Translated by Carleton Dallery. In *PrP.* (*L'Oeil et l'Esprit.* Paris: Gallimard, 1964.)

————. *Phenomenology of Perception.* Translated by Colin Smith. London: Routledge and Kegan Paul, 1962. (*Phénoménologie de la perception.* Paris: Gallimard, 1964.)

————. *In Praise of Philosophy and Other Essays.* Translated by John Wild and James M. Edie. Evanston, 1970. (*Éloge de la philosophie.* Paris: Gallimard, 1953; and *Résumés de cours, Collège de France 1952–1960.* Paris: Gallimard, 1968.)

————. *The Primacy of Perception and Other Essays on Phenomenological Psychology, the Philosophy of Art, History and Politics,* edited by J.M. Edie. Evanston, IL: Northwestern University Press, 1964.

————. *The Prose of the World.* Translated by John O'Neill. Evanston, IL: Northwestern University Press, 1973. (*Le prose du monde.* Paris: Gallimard, 1969.)

————. *Signs.* Translated by Richard C. McCleary. Evanston, IL: Northwestern University Press, 1964. (*Signes.* Paris: Gallimard, 1960.)

————. *The Structure of Behavior.* Translated by Alden L. Fisher. Boston: Beacon Press, 1963. (*La structure du comportement.* Paris: Quadrige / Presses Universitaires de France, 1942.)

232 BIBLIOGRAPHY

——. *Sense and Non-sense*. Translated by Hubert L. Dreyfus and Patricia Allen Dreyfus. Evanston, IL: Northwestern University Press, 1964. (*Sens et non-sens*, Paris: Nagel, 1948.)

——. *The Visible and the Invisible*. Translated by Alphonso Lingis. Evanston, IL: Northwestern University Press, 1968. (*Le visible et l'invisible*. Paris: Gallimard, 1964.)

Morris, David. *The Sense of Space*. Albany: State University of New York Press, 2004.

——. "What is Living and What is Non-living in Merleau-Ponty's Philosophy of Expression." *Chiasmi International* 7 (2005): 225–239.

Morris, Desmond. *Manwatching: A Field Guide to Human Behaviour*. New York: Henry Abrams, 1977.

Morrison, Alexandra. "Nicholson: Through Self-loathing to Philosophy." In *Philosophical Apprenticeships: Contemporary Continental Philosophy in Canada*, edited by Jay Lampert and Jason Robinson. Ottawa: University of Ottawa Press, 2009.

Myin, Erik and Kevin O'Regan. "Perceptual Consciousness: Access to Modality and Skill Theories." *Journal of Consciousness Studies* 9 (2002): 27–45.

Nancy, Jean-Luc. *Corpus*. Translated by Richard A. Rand. New York: Fordham University Press, 2008.

Neisser, Ulric. "Five Kinds of Self-knowledge." *Philosophical Psychology* 1 (1988): 35–59.

Newcombe, Nora S., and Janellen Huttenlocher. *Making Space: The Development of Spatial Representation and Reasoning*. Cambridge, MA: MIT Press, 2000.

Newen, Albert, and Kai Vogeley. "Self-representation: Searching for a neural signature of self consciousness." *Consciousness and Cognition* 12 (2003): 529–543.

Olkowski, Dorothea. "Introduction." In *Merleau-Ponty, Interiority and Exteriority, Psychic Life and the World*, edited by Dorothea Olkowski and James Morley. Albany: State University of New York Press, 1999.

O'Regan, J. Kevin, and Alva Noë, "Authors' Response." *Behavioural and Brain Sciences* 24 (2001): 1011–1031.

——. "A Sensorimotor Account of Vision and Visual Consciousness." *Behavioural and Brain Sciences* 24 (2001): 939–973.

Parnas, Josef. "The Self and Intentionality in the Pre-psychotic Stages of Schizophrenia: A Phenomenological Study." In *Exploring the Self: Philosophical and Psychopathological Perspectives on Self-Experience*, edited by Dan Zahavi. Amsterdam: John Benjamins Publishing Company, 2000.

Rechter, Sue. "The Originating Breaks Up: Merleau-Ponty, Ontology, Culture." In *Thesis Eleven*, 90 (2007): 27–43.

Rehmann-Sutter, Christoph, "Poiesis and Praxis: Two Modes of Understanding Development." In *Genes in Development: Re-reading the Molecular Paradigm*, edited by Eva M. Neumann-Held and Christoph Rehmann-Sutter. Durham: Duke University Press, 2006.

Rochat, Philippe. *The Infant's World*. Cambridge, MA: Harvard University Press, 2001.

Rogers, Sheena. "Perceiving Pictorial Space." In *Perception of Space and Motion* (2nd ed.), edited by Edward C. Carterette and Morton P. Friedman. San Diego: Academic Press, 1995.

Rosenthal, Sandra B., and Patrick L. Bourgeois. *Mead and Merleau-Ponty: Toward a Common Vision*. Albany, NY: State University of New York Press, 1991.

Russon, John. *Bearing Witness to Epiphany: Persons, Things, and the Nature of Erotic Life*. Albany: State University of New York Press, 2009.

———. "Embodiment and Responsibility: Merleau-Ponty and the Ontology of Nature." *Man and World* 27 (1994): 291–308.

———. *Human Experience: Philosophy, Neurosis, and the Elements of Everyday Life*. Albany: State University of New York Press, 2003.

———. "The Self as Resolution: Heidegger, Derrida and the Intimacy of the Question of the Meaning of Being." *Research in Phenomenology* 38 (2008): 139–155.

———. "The Spatiality of Self-Consciousness: Originary Passivity in Kant, Merleau-Ponty and Derrida." *Chiasmi International* 9 (2008): 209–220.

Sartre, Jean-Paul. *The Transcendence of the Ego*. Translated by R. Kirkpatrick and F. Williams. New York: Farrar, Straus and Giroux, 1956.

Sass, Louis. "Schizophrenia, Self-experience and the So-called 'Negative Symptoms.'" In *Exploring the Self: Philosophical and Psychopathological Perspectives on Self-experience*, edited by Dan Zahavi. Amsterdam: John Benjamins Publishing Company, 2000.

Saussure, Ferdinand de. *Course in General Linguistics*. Translated by Roy Harris. LaSalle, IL: Open Court, 1986.

Sheets-Johnstone, Maxine. "Phenomenology and Agency: Methodological and Theoretical Issues in Strawson's 'The Self.'" In *Models of the Self*, edited by Shaun Gallagher and Jonathan Shear. Thorverton, UK: Academic Imprint, 1999.

———. *The Primacy of Movement*. Amsterdam: John Benjamins Publishing Company, 1999.

Singer, Linda. "Merleau-Ponty on the Concept of Style." *Man and World* 14 (1981): 153–163.

Steinbock, Anthony J. "Merleau-Ponty's Concept of Depth." *Philosophy Today* [Winter] (1987): 336–351.

Stern, Daniel N. *The Interpersonal World of the Infant*. New York: Basic Books, 1985.

Strawson, Galen. "The Self." In *Models of the Self*, edited by Shaun Gallagher and Jonathan Shear. Thorverton, UK: Academic Imprint, 1999.

———. "The Self and the SESMET." In *Models of the Self*, edited by Shaun Gallagher and Jonathan Shear. Thorverton, UK: Academic Imprint, 1999.

Talero, Maria L. "Joint Attention and Expressivity: A Heideggerian Guide to the Limits of Empirical Investigation." In *Heidegger and Cognitive Science*, edited by Julian Kiverstein and Michael Wheeler. New York: Palgrave-Macmillan, 2011.

———. "The Experiential Workplace and the Limits of Empirical Investigation." *International Journal of Philosophical Studies* 16 (2008): 453–472.

———. "Perception, Normativity, and Selfhood in Merleau-Ponty: The Spatial 'Level' and Existential Space." *Southern Journal of Philosophy* 43 (2005): 443–461.

Tallis, Raymond. *The Hand: A Philosophical Inquiry into Human Being*. Edinburgh: Edinburgh University Press, 2003.

Thompson, Evan. "Sensorimotor subjectivity and the enactive approach to experience." *Phenomenology and Cognitive Sciences* 4 (2005): 407–427.

Turvey, M.T. "Affordances and Prospective Control: An Outline of the Ontology." *Ecological Psychology* 4 (1992): 173–187.

Vallier, Robert. "Institution: The Significance of Merleau-Ponty's 1954 Course at the Collège de France." *Chiasmi International* 7 (2005): 281–303.

Varela, Francisco. "Present-Time Consciousness." *Journal of Consciousness Studies* 6 (1999): 111–140.

Varela, Francisco J., Evan Thompson, and Eleanor Rosch. *The Embodied Mind: Cognitive Science and Human Experience.* Cambridge, MA: The MIT Press.

Waldenfels, Bernard. "The Paradox of Expression." Translated by Chris Nagel. In *Chiasms: Merleau-Ponty's Notion of Flesh*, edited by Fred Evans and Leonard Lawlor. Albany, NY: State University of New York Press, 2000.

Watson, J. S., and C. T. Ramey. "Reactions to Response-Contingent Stimulation in Early Infancy." In *Cognitive Development in Early Infancy*, edited by J. Oates and S. Sheldon. Hillsdale, NJ: Erlbaum, 1987.

Zahavi, Dan. "The Embodied Self-Awareness of the Infant: A Challenge to the Theory-theory of mind." *The Structure and Development of Self-Consciousness*, edited by Dan Zahavi. Amsterdam: John Benjamins Publishing Company, 2004.

———. "Self and Consciousness." In *Exploring the Self: Philosophical and Psychopathological Perspectives on Self-Experience*, edited by Dan Zahavi. Amsterdam: John Benjamins Publishing Company, 2000.

———. *Subjectivity and Selfhood.* Cambridge, MA: MIT Press, 2005.

Zahavi, Dan and Josef Parnas. "Phenomenal Consciousness and Self-Awareness: A Phenomenological Critique of Representational Theory." *Journal of Consciousness Studies* 5 (1998): 687–705.

# INDEX